ACCENTS ON SHAKESPEARE

General Editor: TERENCE HAWKES

Spiritual Shakespeares

There are more things in heaven and earth, Horatio, than are dreamt of in secular materialism, theology, or contemporary theory. That at least is what the present collection sets out so suggestively to show.

John D. Caputo (from the Foreword)

Readers will find here an engagement with both Shakespeare and spirituality which is intelligent, original, and challengingly optimistic, one which surely succeeds in its wish to 'reinvigorate and strengthen politically progressive materialist criticism'.

Jonathan Dollimore (from the Afterword)

Spiritual Shakespeares is the first book to explore the scope for reading Shakespeare spiritually in the light of contemporary theory and current world events. Ewan Fernie has brought together an exciting cast of critics in order to respond to the 'religious turn' in recent thought and to the spiritualised politics of terrorism and the 'War on Terror'.

Opening a genuinely new perspective within Shakespeare Studies, this volume suggests that experiencing the spiritual intensities of the plays could lead us back to dramatic intensity as such. It tests spirituality from a political perspective, as well as subjecting politics to an unusual spiritual critique. Among its controversial and provocative arguments is the idea that a consideration of spirituality might point the way forward for materialist criticism.

Spiritual Shakespeares reaches across and beyond literary studies with challenging, powerful contributions from Philippa Berry, John D. Caputo, Jonathan Dollimore, Ewan Fernie, Lisa Freinkel, Lowell Gallagher, John J. Joughin, Richard Kearney, David Ruiter and Kiernan Ryan.

Ewan Fernie is Senior Lecturer in English at Royal Holloway, University of London, and the author of *Shame in Shakespeare* (Routledge, 2002).

ACCENTS ON SHAKESPEARE
General Editor: TERENCE HAWKES

It is more than twenty years since the New Accents series helped to establish 'theory' as a fundamental and continuing feature of the study of literature at the undergraduate level. Since then, the need for short, powerful 'cutting edge' accounts of and comments on new developments has increased sharply. In the case of Shakespeare, books with this sort of focus have not been readily available. **Accents on Shakespeare** aims to supply them.

Accents on Shakespeare volumes will either 'apply' theory, or broaden and adapt it in order to connect with concrete teaching concerns. In the process, they will also reflect and engage with the major developments in Shakespeare studies of the last ten years.

The series will lead as well as follow. In pursuit of this goal it will be a two-tiered series. In addition to affordable, 'adoptable' titles aimed at modular undergraduate courses, it will include a number of research-based books. Spirited and committed, these second-tier volumes advocate radical change rather than stolidly reinforcing the status quo.

IN THE SAME SERIES

Spiritual
Shakespeares

Edited by EWAN FERNIE

Routledge
Taylor & Francis Group

LONDON AND NEW YORK

First published 2005
by Routledge
2 Park Square, Milton Park,
Abingdon, Oxon OX14 4RN

Simultaneously published in
the USA and Canada
by Routledge
270 Madison Avenue,
New York, NY 10016

Routledge is an imprint of the
Taylor & Francis Group

Editorial matter and selection
© 2005 Ewan Fernie
Individual chapters © the
contributors

Typeset in Baskerville by
Florence Production Ltd,
Stoodleigh, Devon
Printed and bound in Great Britain
by TJ International Ltd,
Padstow, Cornwall

British Library Cataloguing in
Publication Data

A catalogue record for this book is
available from the British Library

Library of Congress Cataloging in
Publication Data

Spiritual Shakespeares / edited by
Ewan Fernie.
    p. cm. – (Accents on Shakespeare)
Includes bibliographical references and
index.
Contents: Introduction: Shakespeare,
spirituality, and contemporary criticism /
Ewan Fernie – 'Where hope is coldest':
All's well that ends well / Kiernan
Ryan – Harry's (in)human
face / David Ruiter – Waiting for
Gobbo / Lowell Gallagher – 'Salving
the mail': perjury, grace, and the
disorder of things in Love's labour's lost
/ Philippa Berry – The Shakespearean
fetish / Lisa Freinkel – Bottom's secret /
John J. Joughin – Spectres of
Hamlet / Richard Kearney – The last
act: presentism, spirituality, and the
politics of Hamlet / Ewan Fernie.
1. Shakespeare, William, 1564–1616
– Religion.   2. Spiritual life in
literature.   3. Spirituality in literature.
I. Fernie, Ewan, 1971–.   II. Series.

PR3011.S65 2005
822.3'3–dc22   2005004410

ISBN 0–415–31966–8 (hbk)
ISBN 0–415–31967–6 (pbk)

And what impossibility would slay
In common sense, sense saves another way.
                    (All's Well That Ends Well)

No settled senses of the world can match
The pleasures of that madness.
                          (The Winter's Tale)

Contents

Contributors

Philippa Berry was Fellow and Director of Studies at King's College, Cambridge until 2004. She is Visiting Fellow in the Department of English at the University of Bristol. She is author of *Of Chastity and Power: Elizabethan Literature and the Unmarried Queen* and *Shakespeare's Feminine Endings: Disfiguring Death in the Tragedies*. She is co-editor of *Shadow of Spirit: Postmodernism and Religion* and *Textures of Renaissance Knowledge*.

John D. Caputo is the Thomas J. Watson Professor of Religion and Humanities at Syracuse University. His most recent books include *Augustine and Postmodernism: Confessions and Circumfession*, *On Religion* and *More Radical Hermeneutics*. He is also the author of *The Prayers and Tears of Jacques Derrida* and editor of the Fordham University Press book series 'Perspectives in Continental Philosophy'.

Jonathan Dollimore recently left the academy to concentrate on writing. His books include (with Alan Sinfield), *Political Shakespeare: Essays in Cultural Materialism* (2nd edn, 1994); *Sexual Dissidence*; *Death, Desire and Loss in Western Culture*; *Sex, Literature and Censorship* and *Radical Tragedy: Religion, Ideology and Power in the Drama of Shakespeare and His Contemporaries* (3rd edn, 2003).

Ewan Fernie is Senior Lecturer in English at Royal Holloway, University of London. He is the author of *Shame in Shakespeare* and the leading editor of *Reconceiving the Renaissance: A Critical Reader*. His latest essay, 'Shakespeare and the Prospect of Presentism', appears in *Shakespeare Survey* 58. He is a founding editor (with Simon Palfrey) of a new series of 'minigraphs' called 'Shakespeare Now!'

Lisa Freinkel is Associate Professor of English and Director of the Program in Comparative Literature at the University of Oregon. Her publications include *Reading Shakespeare's Will: The Theology of Figure from Augustine to the Sonnets* and articles on subjects ranging from Reformation iconoclasm, to Dante's *Inferno*, to formalism in Kant's *Critique of Judgment*. Her current project, *The Use of Shakespeare*, examines the intersection of economic and linguistic theory in Shakespeare's work.

Lowell Gallagher is Associate Professor of English at the University of California, Los Angeles. He is author of *Medusa's Gaze: Casuistry and Conscience in the Renaissance* and numerous articles examining the relation between religion, ethics and literary figuration in Shakespeare and in early modern English Catholic cultures. He is currently completing a book on the ethical provocation mounted by the biblical figure of Lot's wife in patristic and early modern texts, twentieth-century visual arts and postmodern philosophy.

John J. Joughin is Head of Humanities at the University of Central Lancashire and Chair of the British Shakespeare Association. He is editor of *Shakespeare and National Culture* and of *Philosophical Shakespeares*. His monograph on *Shakespeare and the Aesthetic* is forthcoming.

Richard Kearney holds the Charles B. Seelig Chair at Boston College and is a Visiting Professor at University College Dublin. He has authored over 20 books, including two novels and a volume of poetry, and edited 14 more. His most recent trilogy, 'Philosophy at the Limit', comprises the following volumes: *On Stories*; *Strangers, Gods and Monsters*; and *The God Who May Be*.

David Ruiter is an Associate Professor of English and the Director of the Literature Program at the University of Texas at El Paso. He is the author of *Shakespeare's Festive History: Feasting, Festivity, Fasting, and Lent in the Second Henriad*.

Kiernan Ryan is Professor of English at Royal Holloway, University of London and a Fellow of New Hall, University of Cambridge. His most recent books include *Shakespeare* (3rd edn, 2002); *King Lear: Contemporary Critical Essays*; *New*

Historicism and Cultural Materialism: A Reader, *Shakespeare: The Last Plays*, and *Shakespeare: Texts and Contexts*. He wrote the Introduction for the New Penguin edition of *King Lear* (2005), and is currently completing a study of Shakespearean comedy.

General editor's preface

In our time, the field of literary studies has rarely been a settled, tranquil place. Indeed, for over two decades, the clash of opposed theories, prejudices and points of view has made it more of a battlefield. Echoing across its most beleaguered terrain, the student's weary complaint 'Why can't I just pick up Shakespeare's plays and read them?' seems to demand a sympathetic response.

Nevertheless, we know that modern spectacles will always impose their own particular characteristics on the vision of those who unthinkingly don them. This must mean, at the very least, that an apparently simple confrontation with, or pious contemplation of, the text of a 400-year-old play can scarcely supply the grounding for an adequate response to its complex demands. For this reason, a transfer of emphasis from 'text' towards 'context' has increasingly been the concern of critics and scholars since the Second World War: a tendency that has perhaps reached its climax in more recent movements such as 'New Historicism' or 'Cultural Materialism'.

A consideration of the conditions (social, political or economic) within which the play came to exist, from which it derives, and to which it speaks, will certainly make legitimate demands on the attention of any well-prepared student nowadays. Of course, the serious pursuit of those interests will also inevitably start to undermine ancient and inherited prejudices, such as the supposed distinction between 'foreground' and 'background' in literary studies. And even the slightest awareness of the pressures of gender or of race, or the most cursory glance at the role played by that strange creature 'Shakespeare' in our cultural politics, will reinforce a similar turn towards questions that sometimes appear scandalously 'non-literary'. It seems clear that very different and unsettling notions of the ways in which literature might be addressed can hardly be avoided. The worrying truth is that nobody can just pick up Shakespeare's plays and read them. Perhaps (even more worrying) they never could.

The aim of *Accents on Shakespeare* is to encourage students and teachers to explore the implications of this situation by means of an engagement with the major developments in Shakespeare studies over recent years. It will offer a continuing and challenging reflection on those ideas through a series of multi- and single-author books that will also supply the basis for adapting or augmenting them in the light of changing concerns.

Accents on Shakespeare also intends to lead as well as follow. In pursuit of this goal, the series will operate on more than one level. In addition to titles aimed at modular undergraduate courses, it will include a number of books embodying polemical, strongly argued cases aimed at expanding the horizons of a specific aspect of the subject and at challenging the preconceptions on which it is based. These volumes will not be learned 'monographs' in any traditional sense. They will, it is hoped, offer a platform for the work of the liveliest younger scholars and teachers at their most outspoken and provocative. Committed and contentious, they will be reporting from the forefront of current critical activity and will have something new to say. The fact that each book in the series promises a Shakespeare inflected in terms of a specific urgency should ensure that, in the present as in the recent past, the accent will be on change.

Terence Hawkes

Acknowledgements

I'm (once again) grateful to Terence Hawkes for help, warmth, efficiency and wit. I'm also happily indebted to Liz Thompson and everyone at Routledge and at Florence Production – and, of course, to all the contributors. Eleni Pilla supplied an admirable index. Many have kept the campfire burning. Foremost among them are Philippa Berry, Mark Thornton Burnett, Patrick Cheney, John Caputo, Katharine Craik, Jonathan Dollimore, Deanna Fernie, Lisa Freinkel, Hugh Grady, Colin Graham, John Joughin, James Knapp, Simon Palfrey, David Ruiter and Kiernan Ryan. I have to single out Eric Mallin, whose extraordinary generosity helped kindle the thing. Ken Jackson's recent suggestions kept it blazing till the end.

Note

Unless otherwise indicated, all quotations from Shakespeare are from *The Norton Shakespeare*, General Editor Stephen Greenblatt (New York: Norton, 1997); all biblical quotations are from the Authorized Version/King James Bible.

Foreword
Of hyper-reality
John D. Caputo

The essays that follow are meant to open up links between the world of Shakespeare and that surprising twist in postmodernism sometimes called its "religious turn." They proceed from the premise that literature does not illustrate pre-established philosophical principles but can instruct philosophy about matters too concrete and singular for philosophy's purview. So if, as Peter Brook says, theater is "life in a more concentrate form," condensing a lifetime into a few hours on the stage (cited in Janik 2003), then who better than Shakespeare can instruct philosophy about the meaning and texture of concrete experience? Who better than Hamlet, to take a famous example, can teach us about the dynamics of decisions made in the midst of life's uncertainties? To this exciting venture I wish to add my modest oar. I suggest that these essays should be read as operating within a uniquely postmodern horizon that I will call "hyper-reality" (Caputo 2001).

The nineteenth-century prophets assure us God is dead. According to Marx and Feuerbach, the absolute has renounced its transcendent foothold in the sky and come down to earth, annulling the alienation of its absolute alterity for a life of immanence in the sublunary world. The positivists propose that mysteries that once were the province of myth and philosophy have found a demystified resting place in modern science. But in 1967 Jacques Derrida remarked, "what is dead wields a very specific power" (Derrida 1972: 6). There are signs of advanced secularization, like the decline in regular church attendance among the larger confessions or the virtual collapse of vocations to the Catholic priesthood in Western countries. But non-traditional forms of spirituality flourish. Above all, the entire world, west and east, north and south, has been swept by surging tides of Christian evangelicalism and Islamic fundamentalism. These are contemporary realities with which academic skepticism is totally out of touch.

"Modernity" is more complicated than previously imagined. The very idea of the death of God in Nietzsche constituted a denial of Overarching Truth, be it scientific or theological. There are only as many little pragmatic truths (Nietzsche called them "fictions") as are required for the complexities of life. Secularism's monopoly is as dead as God's, allowing many flowers to bloom. If God is dead, a funny thing happened on the way to the funeral. A profusion of new gods was born.

The ancients invested a considerable effort trying to convince us that the supersensible sphere is "really real," while the nineteenth century proclaimed that realm to be an "un-real" fantasy and asked us to content ourselves with the sensible reality below. But in this postmodern age it is the "hyper-real" that holds sway. In a world of interplanetary space probes the very pre-Copernican distinction between an upper world and a lower one has lost all sense, even as totalizing omni-explanations have lost their cachet. Our world is what James Joyce called a "chaosmos" (see Eco 1989), neither *simple* cosmos nor *simple* chaos, but a complex loosely joined and supple configuration given to chance and the unexpected, open-ended and reconfigurable. We no longer live by the simple distinction between presence and absence. Our lives are suffused and haunted by shades and spectres, quasi and virtual realities. Within the ultra-horizon of the "hyper-real" diverse patterns of what this book calls "spirituality" unfold.

In speaking of the "hyper-real," I am first of all commending to the reader Jean Baudrillard's analysis of an electronic replication of reality in a "virtual" world so uncanny as to blur the distinction between the real and the unreal (to what extent was the "Gulf War" real and to what extent was it a media event? (see Baudrillard 1995)). Baudrillard's point, whose importance cannot be overestimated, goes to the heart of one of the senses of postmodernism that has been artfully explored in the works of Mark C. Taylor (see Taylor 2003 and 2004). In such a world, the insubstantiality of what the materialists call matter is visited upon us with a fury. We lead lives in which the lines between nature and *techne*, bodily organs and artificial transplants are so complex that the very meanings of "mother," "birth" and "nature" have been made to tremble. In such a world, materialistic reductionism or "naturalism" is an anachronism, while Elizabethan ghosts and angels have become interestingly timely.

But I use "hyper-real" in a second and distinctly ethico-religious sense that bears quite directly on the present volume. For if it is true that contemporary theorists are critics of realism and essentialism, as they certainly are, still it brushes against the grain to call them (simply) "anti-realists," if that is taken to connote any kind of vicious subjectivism. For the truth is that by and large contemporary theory is turned toward the affirmation of the "Other." This is the very opposite of self-ishness or fantasy. Derrida's discontent with realism arises not from *anti*-realist motives but from *hyper*-realist ones, from a love and a desire for the real beyond what today passes for real, which springs from a desire for a justice or a democracy to come!

And yet the point here, let us recall, is not to fit Shakespeare into any pre-established theory but to shush the philosophers and make them listen to the play because the play's the thing, *die Sache selbst*, in which the whole of life has been concentrated.

Shakespeare knows that our lives are haunted by shades and shadows of the dead who remind us of what they expect, that they are uplifted by the voice of a "divinity" who "shapes our ends", and that they are disturbed by the demonic distortions of evil. He knows that we are called to respond in the present even as we are solicited by the promise of things to come.

There are more things in heaven and earth, Horatio, than are dreamt of in secular materialism, theology or contemporary theory. That at least is what the present collection sets out so suggestively to show.

Introduction
Shakespeare, spirituality and contemporary criticism
Ewan Fernie

I

Before he is 'environed' by 'a legion of foul fiends' in a dream of 'the kingdom of perpetual night', Clarence is assailed by his angry father-in-law.

> Then came wandering by
> A shadow like an angel, with bright hair,
> Dabbled in blood, and he shrieked out aloud,
> 'Clarence is come: false, fleeting, perjured Clarence,
> That stabbed me in the field by Tewkesbury.'
> *(Richard III*, 1.4.52–6)

Ass-headed Bottom, in a very different dream, enjoys unfathomable ecstasies in a fairy bower. His is a comic, synaesthetic experience that deforms (reforms?) Pauline pieties in the expression: 'The eye of man hath not heard, the ear of man hath not seen, man's hand is not able to taste, his tongue to conceive, nor his heart to report what my dream was' (*A Midsummer Night's Dream*, 4.1.204–7). Uncomfortably hard on the heels of Shylock's humiliation, Lorenzo apprehends a musical sympathy between all things, a 'sweet harmony' that 'creeps' into the ears of men and women, tames savage horses and wields a charming power over 'trees, stones and floods', but also reverberates at a superhuman pitch in the heights:

> There's not the smallest orb which thou behold'st
> But in his motion like an angel sings,
> Still choiring to the young-eyed cherubins.
> Such harmony is in immortal souls,
> But while this muddy vesture of decay
> Doth grossly close us in, we cannot hear it.
>
> (*The Merchant of Venice*, 5.1.53–90)

Cordelia is a 'soul in bliss' to the unhappy father who gazes up at her while he turns on a wheel of fire that his tears (mysteriously) 'scald like molten lead' (*King Lear* (conflated text), 4.4.46–8). Othello cries for devils to whip him from the 'heavenly sight' of Desdemona's innocent corpse; to blow him about in winds, roast him in sulphur, wash him in 'steep-down gulfs of liquid fire' (*Othello*, 52.285–7). Cleopatra elegises a cosmic Antony whose 'reared arm crested the world' and who dropped 'realms and islands' like loose change from his pockets (*Antony and Cleopatra*, 5.281–91). Hermione is seemingly resurrected.

To a greater or lesser degree, such moments have embarrassed the predominantly materialist criticism of the last twenty years, and they have typically been passed over in silence or treated as an historical curiosity.[1] But, as the current volume demonstrates, this significantly misrepresents and curtails Shakespearean drama. *Spiritual Shakespeares* treats Shakespearean spirituality as a distinctive, inalienable and challenging dimension of the plays, one that may be illuminated by, but remains irreducible to, any established theory or theology. Although it draws liberally from history, the volume offers a primarily 'presentist' engagement with its topic.[2] It is a book that treats Shakespeare as a 'living thinker', one whose dramatic explorations of spirituality can make a real contribution to contemporary debates and life. Much recent work on Shakespeare and early modern literature has filtered spirituality through the variegated light of religious difference.[3] Distinctions between Catholicism and Protestantism, Christianity and

Islam, and so on, will play their part in what follows, but the collection also has critical and theoretical claims to make about spirituality as such. Perhaps most controversially, *Spiritual Shakespeares* argues that a fresh consideration of spirituality might reinvigorate and strengthen politically progressive materialist criticism.

All the instances I began with are charged to an extraordinary, even astonishing degree with 'otherness', which (in different forms) has been the defining preoccupation of contemporary critics. From the more orthodoxly Christian imaginings of Clarence, Lear and Othello, to Cleopatra's exceptional humanism and the heterodox experiences of Bottom and Hermione, each example conjures *another life* – in the theatre of divine judgement, on a cosmically larger scale, as transcendent sex, as a voice in harmony with the universal choir, as simply renewed mortality. That the most powerful Shakespearean instances of being otherwise are explicitly spiritual has largely escaped attention. In *1 Henry VI*, when the Countess Auvergne scorns the hero she has trapped in her house, he answers:

> You are deceived; my substance is not here.
> For what you see is but the smallest part
> And least proportion of humanity.
> I tell you, madam, were the whole frame here,
> It is of such a spacious lofty pitch
> Your roof were not sufficient to contain't.
> $(2.3.51-6)^4$

Talbot's assertion of a colossally elevated spiritual subjectivity begs attention in the context of more predictable discussions of alternative identity in terms of the social varieties of difference. In spite of the long-standing critical prejudice against 'essentialism', specifically spiritual alterity is aesthetically and theoretically interesting because it is configured not just as totally different from ordinary life but also as ultimately significant and real. Spirituality affords a credible alternative, or rather a range of such alternatives. It has a special power to break the illusion of what all-too-often is taken to be 'this world's eternity' (*2 Henry VI*, 2.4.91). The conviction that an alternative world is more desirable as well as somehow more profoundly real than this one can motivate a hermit-like withdrawal from the world as it is, but it can also inspire positive revolutionary change. As Gerard Winstanley said, 'Why may not we have our heaven here?' (quoted in Hill 1968: 60).[5]

Shakespeare at least once conceived of his art as having the broadly 'spiritual' function of materialising another world. Theseus famously describes the 'poet's eye in a fine frenzy rolling' between heaven and earth as he (or she) brings forth 'the forms of things unknown' (A Midsummer Night's Dream, 5.1.12ff.). Poetry and spirituality are kin in that both traffic beyond the known world; they are alike, too, in their disputed relation to what is real. If both are sometimes thought to reach through the world of mere appearances into the heart of reality, they are equally often regarded as empty-headed distractions from what really is. It depends on whether 'the forms of things unknown' are revelations or illusions. Shakespeare conveys the epistemological insecurity of poetry and spirituality via Theseus's association of poetry's spiritual reach with the doubtful states of mind of the lover and lunatic, and by filtering some of the most profound spiritual experiences in his plays through the rich but unstable medium of dreams. Poetry and spirituality both promise no less than another world. But this promise may be hollow, which only makes them the more sensationally interesting.[6] Shakespeare deliberately mixes the promise and unlikelihood of poetry and spirituality into something rich and strange in the last scene of The Winter's Tale. Even if Hermione's revival is a simple trick, it is infused with the aura of resurrection.

Theseus speaks of poetry, not plays, and some of the examples I started with could be said to exert only a secondary, purely verbal pressure within an art-form that at its most convincing fuses verbal with physical form. But the dreamy union of Bottom and Titania is acted out in full view of the audience and the staging of Hermione's 'resurrection' is the great *coup de théâtre* of The Winter's Tale and perhaps of all the late plays. Hermione's reanimation is also a 'recognition scene' for the process of incarnation whereby Shakespearean drama generally brings its characters to life: everyone on stage watching the 'miracle' is witnessing the strange secret of their own creation as well, for they as much as Hermione have sprung into life by the magical grace of the playwright and the theatre company. And if humanity can be recreated on stage, perhaps it can be renovated off stage as well?

Theseus and *The Winter's Tale* encourage us to consider the plays as a real or fantasised advent of the beyond within reality. But it is clear from the speeches and experiences of Talbot, Clarence, Bottom, Cleopatra etc. that Shakespearean drama is also sufficiently 'real' to be haunted by spiritual alterity from within. Sometimes this fourth dimension seems only obscurely to inhabit quotidian character or action, but such 'sightless substances' as Lady Macbeth speaks of can exert powerful spiritual pressure (*Macbeth*, 1.5.47). Richmond is too obviously the vehicle of Tudor providence to be convincingly himself, but when Othello looks down for Iago's cloven feet, the absolute isn't so easily identified or 'earthed'; the infernal energies that course through the tragedy are frighteningly, uncontrollably obscure, as is intimated in the 'hell' that gapes in the centre of Othello's name and the 'demon' snugly smiling in Desdemona's.[7] In such cases, we are tempted to feel that we could scratch the play's surface to reveal another, perhaps more terrible drama going on beneath but are doomed to discover we can't. As a result, we as much as the protagonists themselves are stranded between the particular and ultimate, between an accidental world of misplaced hankies and a terrible threat of absolute judgement. The sense of simultaneous spiritual urgency and disorientation is crystallised by *Othello*'s trope of the wilderness – 'antres vast and deserts idle, rough quarries, rocks and hills' (1.3.139–40) – where meaninglessness and the fullness of revelation traditionally contend for human souls, as in Christ's temptation in the wilderness or the careers of the so-called Desert Fathers.[8]

If the spirituality of the plays has scandalised the materialism of contemporary thought, it has also often been depreciated or ignored because the truth-claims it involves are presumed to be at odds with Shakespeare's theatrical polyphony. It is certainly the case that spiritual utterances or experiences are often ironised by the plays. Thus Lorenzo's rhapsody on harmony is partly wrecked by the sullen resistance, then edgy silence it elicits from Jessica, reminding us of her relinquished Jewish faith and father, and highlighting the coercive power of a metaphysics that tames all but the most reprobate and wild creatures. But the ironic power of spiritual truth itself has been underestimated in recent criticism. Although it retains a glittering Venetian materialism in its heavenly vision of 'patens of bright gold', Lorenzo's verse of universal concord soars beyond the divisive theologies of the play to expose him, exclusive Belmont and his complacently corrupt 'Christian' community far more than Jessica's sullen resistance does. Lorenzo, who can't even manage a real conversation with his bride-to-be, has insufficient harmony in *his* soul. He is damned out of his own mouth: 'Let no such man be trusted.' Nor is it any wonder that celestial harmonies are inaudible in 'a naughty world' where a fraudulent peace and unity have been secured by a forced conversion. And yet, the merest echo of them indicates how bitterly far from heaven the happiness of Belmont is. The touch of spirituality threatens the cruelly provisional 'realities' of the plays. In his more tragic idiom, Lear expects the 'great gods' he feels bestirring themselves in the storm on the heath to break the moulds and forms of things as they are (*King Lear*, 3.2.48).

Shakespeare's protagonists are often ruined by spiritual crisis. Stephen Greenblatt's explanations of Clarence's dream, Richard III's supernatural forebodings before Bosworth Field, the apparition of Ceasar's ghost to the doomed Brutus and the posthumous appearance of 'blood-baltered Banquo' to Macbeth are a touch too mundane (Greenblatt 2001: 180ff.). Conducted in terms of 'deep psychic disturbance', 'history's nightmare', 'the poetic or tragic structure of history' and 'good theatre', they acknowledge but step quickly around the fact that the revenant murder-victims who appear to Clarence, Richard, Brutus and Macbeth are accusing figures of guilt disclosing (to the audience as well as the murderers themselves) what Greenblatt calls 'an ineradicable, embodied objective power' so far pathetically evaded and ignored (Greenblatt 2001: 180). The alternative reality of ethics invades the fantasy-lives of megalomaniac dreamers, thus partly prophesying, partly effecting the ruination of their tyrannical plans to shape reality to their own desire. They are left, to paraphrase Richard II, self-affrighted, trembling at their sin (*Richard II*, 3.2.49).

But, in order to do justice to Shakespeare's heterodoxy, it must quickly be said that Richard III and Macbeth are simultaneously cloaked in a countervailing devilish charisma and resolve. As the range of contributions to this volume suggests, Shakespearean spirituality cuts both ways, and more. Unlike Dante or Milton, Shakespeare isn't an orthodox or systematic religious thinker. It is necessary to think in terms not so much of spiritual truth as *truths*. For a drama cut loose of its medieval moorings in an epoch of religious fission and the emergence of scepticism, spirituality is not a secure given, so much as a questionable and open structure of being and experience. Shakespeare's is the drama of the *possibility* of spirituality. Shakespearean pluralism involves competition between possible absolutes, and resistance to the absolute as well. This leads us into territory as existentially and ethically treacherous and exciting as experience itself.[9]

For example, a sensation of the ultimate seems to release Hamlet's trigger-hand, but what is the status of this 'divine' transaction? Is it an experience of the opaque, compelling efficiency of ideology at its purest? Or does it access a higher sphere beyond ideology that motivates or compels action in the world? Is Hamlet's subjectivity lost in his last, eschatological act, or is it there exactly that he finds himself at last? Macbeth seems to make a selfish choice through which radical evil operates. Or is his mundane choice of 'mine own good' already demonic (*Macbeth*, 3.4.134)? What does it mean to 'jump the life to come' (1.7.7)? Is the master-narrative of 'The Scottish Play' simply commitment politics imbued with and refigured as spirituality? In *Measure for Measure*, Isabella confronts Angelo's secular absolutism with her own religious commitment; or perhaps two forms of egotism meet under cover of this conflict. In any case, both are subverted by the Duke's providential ideology, while cynics such as Lucio and Barnardine reject all transcendence. There are puzzling spiritual tensions between individual plays as well. What is the relationship between Hamlet's 'divinity' of 'rashness' and the 'supernatural soliciting' that starts Macbeth on his career of violence (*Hamlet*, 5.2.11, 7; *Macbeth*, 1.3.129)? How does any of this relate to the spirituality of specifically brutish sexual congress in Bottom's dream? Or to the spirituality of female generativity that emerges when a mother is 'resurrected' by a female Paul and reunited with her resplendent daughter in *The Winter's Tale*?

By playing up the ludic qualities of Shakespeare's plays, recent criticism has obscured their agonistic intensity. Tragedies and comedies alike are struggles between more or less 'mighty opposites' (*Hamlet*, 5.2.63). They take up fundamental questions of human ontology and ethics and offer competing answers. Liberal relativism is only one of the possibilities that stands a fighting chance in Shakespeare. The plays are more liberal than liberalism, which cannot allow for the kind of overriding commitment that threatens liberal freedoms. They are also more compellingly involving. Agonistic drama makes liberal tolerance look more like indifference. Shakespeare's is not postmodern shadow play *avant la lettre* but serious, sometimes bloody play for real stakes that has more in common with dialectical politics. Dramatic tension and interest depends crucially on two factors: that one or more characters (Shylock, Falstaff, Cleopatra, Timon, etc.) might be *right*; and that out of the struggle new values and social formations might evolve. This, as much as delight in disorder, keeps us reading or watching the plays. Re-experiencing their spiritual intensities may lead us back to dramatic intensity itself.

II

Time for a definition: spirituality is (or purports to be) the experience or knowledge of what is other and is ultimate, and the sense of identity and 'mission' that may arise from or be vested in that experience.[10] Recent Shakespeare studies have tended to miss spirituality's investment in otherness and have, therefore, typically dismissed it as a form of essentialism that operates, at best, as a distraction from history and, at worst, as justification for pernicious hierarchies of race, gender and class. But, as I have suggested already, such scepticism has resulted in serious neglect not only of important metaphysical dimensions of Shakespeare's text, but also of ideas of emancipation and an alternative world that have real political potential.[11]

Precisely because it isn't just ideology by a prettier name, spirituality can function as an effective cover for ideology. Henry V uses religion as wartime propaganda. But the excessive otherness of spirituality subverts such ideological uses, and spirituality comes back to haunt King Henry in the speech Williams casts in his face:

[I]f the cause be not good, the King himself hath a heavy reckoning to make, when all those legs and arms and heads chopped off in a battle shall join together at the latter day and cry all 'We died at such a place' – some swearing, some crying for a surgeon, some upon their wives left poor behind them, some upon the debts they owe, some upon their children rawly left. I am afeard there are few die well that die in a battle, for how can they charitably dispose of anything when blood is their argument? Now, if these men do not die well, it will be a black matter for the King, that led them to it – who to disobey were against all proportion of subjection.

(Henry V, 4.1.128–38)

This powerfully material evocation of spiritual judgement is a useful reminder that spirituality and materialism should not be simply opposed. It hardly needs saying that after the Iraq war and the tragic farce of 'Weapons of Mass Destruction', the values of the speech have been powerfully renewed.

Because it is committed to an extraordinary world of value beyond particular political interests, spirituality never coincides perfectly with ideology. As Queen Katherine says to her royal husband's spin-doctors, 'Heaven is above all yet – there sits a judge/That no king can corrupt' *(Henry VIII, 3.1.99–100)*. Where there's no tension between ideology and the spirituality through which it operates – as, for example, with the descent of Jupiter in *Cymbeline* – only the form or mechanism of spirituality is involved. This is frustratingly the case in *Measure for Measure*, where the Duke goes undercover as a friar and brings Angelo to judgement. The spiritualised exposure of power, and Angelo's painful liberation from it, are immediately absorbed into the consolidation of Vincentio's original regime. Had the Duke submitted to the spirituality he wields, it would have made an opening for real change.

Nor is spirituality just the same as religion. Though it is religion's heart and inspiration, spirituality precedes religion and may well take place outside it. Spirituality is an experience of truth, and of living in accordance with truth, but it is concerned with the truth not of this world but of a world that has not yet and perhaps never will come to be. Spirituality is a mode of opposition to what is. Sometimes it is especially opposed to the body and the material world – and what could be more oppositional than that? But there are forms of spiritual materialism (for example, in 'new-age religion') where physical life is seen as ultimately valuable and real by comparison with the conventions of social life.[12]

Indeed, as a structure of thought and possibility, spirituality may be a necessary supplement for radical materialism, which, after all, has its roots in Hegelian spiritual 'dialectic'. A salient terminological shift in recent criticism begs attention here: as a result of admittedly complex intellectual upheavals, 'dialectical materialism' became 'cultural materialism', which has recently become the study of 'material culture', implying a degenerative tendency whereby the world-transforming ambition of Marxist materialism is progressively lost.[13] After new historicism and cultural materialism, history is now the far horizon and sole explanatory hypothesis in contemporary criticism to the extent that conceiving of and accounting for resistance to history has become a familiar problem. Subversion is notoriously always contained for the Greenblatt of *Shakespearean Negotiations* (1988). Cultural materialists have managed to evade this hopeless position by emphasising that history is always fractured and divided. Alan Sinfield, for instance, finds a way of combining a commitment to historical determinism with the possibility of resistance to the dominant culture in the notion of 'subcultures' (see Sinfield 1992: 35–48). But while the efforts of radical critics to find counter-histories within the history that prevailed are instructive, they are not very inspirational. Spirituality holds out the hope of a more positive leap into a revolutionary alternative.

This book asks whether radical materialism might not be regenerated by rethinking spirituality, if not by returning to its own spiritual source in Hegel? According to Jürgen Habermas, spirituality remains 'indispensable' in enabling 'discourse with the extraordinary' (Habermas 1992: 51, 145). One premise of *Spiritual Shakespeares* is that the speculative freedom and phenomenological appeal of imaginative literature offer special opportunities for the study of spirituality before it has hardened into institutional religious forms.

Two things in particular opened the way for *Spiritual Shakespeares*. First, the celebrated Shakespeare critic, Stephen Greenblatt, and the most important contemporary philosopher, the late Jacques Derrida, broke ranks with materialism narrowly conceived to publish surprising accounts of the spirituality of *Hamlet*. Both thinkers were captivated by the powerful alterity of Shakespeare's ghost. At the beginning of *Hamlet in Purgatory*, Greenblatt remarks:

> The ghost in *Hamlet* is like none other. . . . It does not have very many lines – it appears in three scenes and speaks only in two – but it is amazingly disturbing and vivid. I wanted to let the feeling of this vividness wash over me . . .
>
> (Greenblatt 2001: 4)

None of Greenblatt's subsequent rationalisation explains away the origins of *Hamlet in Purgatory* in what seems to be something like a spiritual encounter.[14] Before Greenblatt, Derrida derived a novel form of spirituality from his own, similarly intense encounter with the ghost in *Specters of Marx*. This made Shakespeare a surprisingly pivotal figure in the spiritual or religious 'turn' in contemporary thought (Derrida 1994). *Spiritual Shakespeares* is the first book to ask what the Bard really has to say in this context.

Derrida presents the spirituality he finds in *Hamlet* as nothing less than 'another concept of the political' (Derrida 1994: 44). The second opening for *Spiritual Shakespeares* within contemporary culture is the increasing association of religion and politics. 'The end of history' and the triumph of the Western liberal democratic system were proclaimed by Francis Fukuyama in 1992 and, in the same year, Zygmunt Bauman lamented 'living without an alternative' in a global situation where, with communism vanquished, the West seemed free to do as it liked (Fukuyama 1992; Bauman 1992: 175). But, by 2002, Tariq Ali was in no doubt that what he calls American 'imperialist fundamentalism' had inspired the insurgency of an opposing Islamic fundamentalism. That a central component of American 'imperialist fundamentalism' is Christian fundamentalism is clear after the re-election of President Bush in 2004. In *The Clash of Fundamentalisms*, Ali recommends 'an Islamic Reformation' as the way beyond the 'fundamentalist' double-bind (Ali 2002).[15] In their groundbreaking post-Marxist manifesto, *Hegemony and Socialist Strategy* (1985), Ernesto Laclau and Chantal Mouffe urged Marxists to align themselves with the new protest movements that were emerging around the globe, even though they didn't conform to classical Marxist ideas of what revolutionary movements should be. Partly in response to *Specters of Marx* but also as a way of adapting to a new political world, other prominent post-Marxist thinkers have extended this strategy to embrace religious dissidence. Slavoj Žižek endorses Hegel's dictum, 'It is a modern folly to alter a corrupt ethical system, its constitution and legislation, without changing the religion, to have a revolution without a reformation' (Hegel 1959: 436; quoted in Žižek 2003: 5). Žižek also startlingly proclaims that 'to become a true dialectical materialist, one must go through the Christian experience' (Žižek 2003: 6). This is because, as Alain Badiou says, 'Christ's death *sets up an immanentization of the spirit*' (Badiou 2003: 69), empowering what Žižek calls 'a fighting collective' to make an absolute difference to the material status quo (Žižek 2003: 130).

We live in a world much changed from that of Jean-François Lyotard's 'postmodern condition' (Lyotard 1984). For Žižek, the return to religion has renewed political commitment within the post-ideological world of a capitalist monoculture. The Christian Right has essentially brokered a deal with culturally aggressive capitalism in the United States. But it is also true that, after the collapse of Soviet communism and the terrible events of 9/11, Afghanistan, Iraq, Bali and Madrid, the dominant and representative form of political resistance to Western capitalism is religious. For Bush and Blair and Al Qaeda, a transcendent cause matters more than ethics and the lives of innocent people. 'It is the cause, it is the cause, my soul' (*Othello*, 5.2.1ff.): Shakespeare conveys the seduction of such thinking through the driving rhythm and grand vocabulary; but he suggests its potential for insane idiocy through the bitter irony that Othello is on his way to kill his innocent wife.

At this historical juncture, any intellectual engagement with militant spirituality risks being misinterpreted as an endorsement of terrorism. But it's a danger that Žižek, for one, is prepared to risk:

> The proper politically correct attitude is to emphasise, with symptomatic insistence, how the terrorist attacks have nothing to do with the real Islam, that great and sublime religion – would it not be more appropriate to recognise

Islam's resistance to modernization? And, rather than bemoaning the fact that Islam, of all the great religions, is the most resistant to modernization, we should, rather, conceive of this resistance as an open chance, as 'undecidable': this resistance does not necessarily lead to 'Islamo-Facism', it could also be articulated into a socialist project. Precisely because Islam harbours the 'worst' potentials of the Facist answer to our present predicament, it could also turn out to be the site for the 'best'.

(Žižek 2002: 133–4)

In spite of the Christian Right, Žižek celebrates the political potential of Christian advent. In spite of Islamist terrorism, he insists on the positive possibilities of Islamic resistance.

In the context of such religious, political and intellectual ructions, the Shakespearean spirituality that is one of Derrida's most surprising legacies is a genuinely hot topic. According to some, spirituality should be reformed; according to others, it should be stamped out. But it can no longer be dismissed as irrelevant.

III

In *Specters of Marx* (first published in French in 1993), Derrida presents Shakespearean spirituality as powerfully threatening to the material status quo. For Derrida, Shakespeare's ghost is an uncanny revelation of Karl Marx and his arresting demand that we meet our historical responsibilities. It is also a manifestation of the figure of 'the Other', who has long haunted Derrida's thought. Derrida regards Hamlet as ethically exemplary because he recognises (he cannot but recognise) the otherness of the ghost. In light of this, Derrida recasts all ethics as essentially spiritual, because in any ethical encounter the Other must remain other – respected, not conquered, possessed or known; spectrally out of reach. Following the Prince of Denmark's example, Derrida extends political responsibility to 'spirits' – not just of the deceased, but also of those who are not yet born. The spirituality he derives from Shakespeare involves conversion from a narrow investment in the self and what is, to an infinite openness: what his great forebear

Emmanuel Levinas called 'the spirituality of the soul, ceaselessly aroused from its state of soul' (Levinas 1989: 170). Derrida describes this as a 'messianic' expectation of what is always 'to come' and, elsewhere, as 'the experience of what we are unable to experience' (Derrida 2002: 244). Thus, Žižek points out, 'Derrida can indulge in all kinds of paradoxes, claiming, among other things, that it is only atheists who truly pray – precisely by refusing to address God as a positive entity, they silently address the pure Messianic Otherness' (Žižek 2003: 139). According to Derrida, democracy falls within this messianic, spiritual 'structure of experience' (Derrida 1994: 168). For democracy is still 'to come'. It can never be perfectly realised. Instead, it exercises a magnetic force from beyond to keep us striving towards it.

Shakespeare's Ghost has played John the Baptist to Derrida's hooded Messiah. It's a remarkable development that exemplifies the theoretical potency and richness of literature itself. But is Shakespearean spirituality really Derridean? Lowell Gallagher, Julia Reinhard Lupton and Ken Jackson have improvised a fruitful spiritual conversation between the late great philosopher and Shakespeare.[16] Many of the chapters that follow are cued by or resonate with Derrida's work. And there is scope for more Derridean interpretation of Shakespearean spirituality. For instance, the spirituality of deconstruction is anticipated in the famous 'Our revels now are ended' speech (*The Tempest*, 4.1.146–58). Dissolution is given a specifically spiritual twist when Prospero says, 'These our actors,/As I foretold you, were all spirits and/Are melted into air, into thin air'. Presumably Prospero tells Ferdinand to be 'cheerful', not downcast, because the comparable evanescence of the material world will make way for something else to occur. As Howard Felperin proposes:

> Before identifying overhastily that 'something else', let us consider its characteristics. All that is clear is that it will not be more of the same, history as usual and as we have come to know it, the recurrent nightmare. Prospero's invocation of last things, of an ultimate collective destiny, effectively brackets human history within a containing structure of radical indeterminacy and a containing discourse of radical unknowing.
>
> (Felperin 1995: 58)

This suggests that what Derrida calls 'the messianic' may be working as a positive political force through the apparent nihilism of Shakespeare's plays, just as it operates through the seeming pessimism of deconstruction itself. An approach informed by *Specters of Marx* could also delineate Shakespearean fantasies of the afterlife (Claudio's, Hamlet's) as intense experiences of the foreignness of the self: of its simultaneously thrilling and frightening non-coincidence with itself. It has become a cliché of modern criticism to interpret the happy endings of the comedies as bitterly ironic, but Derrida could help us to recognise that they also raise the hope of a 'messianic' *promesse de bonheur*.[17] Which begs the question: is spirituality an unrealisable 'divine comedy' dialectically related to the tragedies of life?

After *Specters of Marx*, poststructuralist spirituality seemed for a while to be the only theoretically credible option. But Badiou and Žižek have now challenged Derrida in a series of books that has given spirituality a sharper political edge in an epoch of 'terror'.[18] Contra Derrida's spirituality of deferral, these thinkers declare, after Jacques Lacan, that 'the impossible happens': that is, it really is possible to bring the beyond absolutely into the world *now*.[19] As part of the 'widespread search for a new militant figure' after communism, Badiou scandalously prefers St Paul (Badiou 2003: 17). Žižek glosses his choice as follows:

> [A]lthough St Paul's particular message is no longer operative for us, the very terms in which he formulates the operative mode of the Christian religion do possess a universal scope as relevant for every Truth-Event; every Truth-Event leads to a kind of 'Resurrection', through fidelity to it and a labour of Love on its behalf, one enters another dimension.
>
> (Žižek 2000a: 143)

A new self is secured here in a new relation to the absolute. One of the most Pauline moments in Shakespeare is in *As You Like It* when Oliver repents his jealous attempt on his brother Orlando's life. Looking back on his earlier, unregenerate self, Oliver comments:

'Twas I, but 'tis not I. I do not shame
To tell you what I was, since my conversion
So sweetly tastes, being the thing I am.
                                    (4.3.134–6)

His old self is completely alien to him. He has been reborn.
For Badiou, real subjectivity as opposed to 'mere being' is
attained when the human agent becomes the militant bearer
of a truth (see Badiou 2001). But whereas poststructuralism
displaces spiritual realisation into an impossible future, Badiou
and Žižek advocate the spirituality of a real advent: a flash of
lightning that may, at any point, strike and transfigure the
world of history. In the midst of terrorist attacks and what
Søren Kierkegaard calls 'the teleological suspension of the
ethical' (Kierkegaard 1983), the controversial and provocative
nature of this will be readily apparent. Badiou and Žižek also
compare Paul with Lenin.[20]

For these thinkers as for Derrida, spirituality is a structure
of experience and possibility, rather than a revelation of the
one true dogma. But Badiou and Žižek are opposed to the
ultimately undetermined spirituality of otherness that Derrida
advocates. As we have seen, Žižek's revolutionary desire to
bring the beyond into the world expresses itself as enthusiasm
for *both* Islamic resistance and Christian advent. This more
committed and manifest spirituality is relevant to Shakespeare.
Drama happens: only exceptionally is the action of a play
deferred, and the power of withholding the action, as in *Love's
Labour's Lost* and *Hamlet*, derives from the seemingly unstoppable
imminence of the dramatic event or advent. The impossible
assumes specific form and invades the reality of the poems and
plays time and again. Oliver's spirituality is not deferred but
achieved absolutely. For Theseus, poetry brings 'the forms of
things unknown' into the world from a specifically metaphysical region, and T. G. Bishop calls Shakespeare's 'a poetics
of incarnation' (Bishop 1996: 15). Of all Shakespeare's works,
potentially most scandalous to Derrideans is 'The Phoenix
and Turtle', which celebrates an actual (if admittedly short-
lived) dissolution of difference in a flamingly intense spiritual
union.

The impossible happens, too, when France throws his lot in
with the discarded and disgraced Cordelia:

Fairest Cordelia, that art most rich, being poor;
Most choice, forsaken; and most loved, despised:
Thee and thy virtues here I seize upon.
Be it lawful, I take up what's cast away.

(King Lear, 1.1.251–4)

Of course, it would be touchingly romantic if France had fallen
in love with his bride in spite of her disgrace, but he actually
falls for her because of it – *her disgrace makes her beautiful to him.*
And clearly this isn't a perverse sentiment that cynically respects
the values it transgresses. As Žižek asserts, the 'true intervention of Eternity in Time' occurs when such moments don't
'stand just for a passing carnivalesque suspension of Order . . .
but start to function as a founding figure of a New Order'
(Žižek 2003: 91). Cordelia's disgrace is a revelation to France.
His plunge into love for his abject bride discovers different
values. That this new model of love is required by the 'cold'st
neglect' of the 'gods' (1.1.242) underlines that it specifically
offers a spirituality beyond conventional religion.[21]

Lear later says to his daughter, 'You are a spirit, I know'
(4.7.49), and spirituality is linked with worldly shame and
dispossession in this extraordinary exchange when a frightened
fool runs out of a hovel:

Fool: Come not in here, nuncle, here's a spirit.
        Help me, help me!
Kent: Give me thy hand. Who's there?
Fool: A spirit, a spirit! He says his name's poor Tom.

(King Lear, 3.4.40–4)

Poor Tom is the spirit of utter poverty but as Edgar he will
ascend the throne. If there's a spiritual injunction in this, it's a
political lesson as well. In the words of Terry Eagleton, 'cling
to your faith that the deathly emptiness of the dispossessed is
the only source from which a more jubilant, self-delighting
existence can ultimately spring' (Eagleton 2003: 296).[22] As we
shall see by the end of this volume, spirituality gleams with a
worrying political edge when Hamlet's mystical experience per-
suades him that 'The readiness is all' (*Hamlet*, 5.2.169).[23]

Of course much of the above chimes with Derrida's interpretation of Shakespeare, but to the extent that it discloses

something like heaven on earth – something to see in a theatre! – it contravenes the French thinker's fastidious deferral of the absolute into a region beyond the real world of history. Shakespeare resonates with Derrida's esoteric political spirituality of hope *and* with Badiou's and Žižek's more 'adventist' political spirituality. Even though each spiritual moment in Shakespeare involves a specific determination of the ultimate, Shakespearean spirituality should not be reified as any one thing. In this it accords with what Derrida calls 'religion without religion': an openness to spiritual possibility that stops short of exclusive dogma. But insofar as the plays involve spiritual *struggle* they equally accord with Badiou's and Žižek's emphasis on ultimate commitment. A postmodern reading of Shakespeare frees up the Badiou and Žižek vs. Derrida debate, restaging it more creatively by putting opposed positions into play.

IV

From the perspective of this volume, Shakespearean spirituality promiscuously, irresistibly breeds with the spiritual possibilities of our own time. Of course the spiritual range of the plays is broader than the controversies surrounding Derrida's 'religious turn'. For instance, the kind of stance which '[f]inds tongues in trees, books in the running brooks,/Sermons in stones, and good in every thing' (*As You Like It*, 2.1.16–17) corresponds more closely with 'new-age' approaches to religion than to the 'religious turn' in theory. The simultaneously fey and full-blooded spirituality of sex and nature in *A Midsummer Night's Dream* is begging for a full-scale new-age treatment.[24] And there is no single contemporary reference point for much of what Shakespeare does: that's why he has *something else* to bring to contemporary debates. In their effort to lay hold of Shakespearean spirituality in the present, the chapters that follow avail themselves of a full complement of critical equipment and techniques. In retrieving some of the spiritual possibilities of the plays, they simultaneously discover much that is of theoretical interest and bring back some of the force of experience that Shakespearean drama conveys. Kiernan Ryan dives directly into *All's Well That Ends Well* and confronts head-on the promise and the violence of spirituality that *Spiritual Shakespeares* explores. In Ryan's reading, the dream of salvation trumps cynical materialism. But *All's Well* is a '*materialist* miracle play' (my emphasis), where hope disrobes at the dead-end of despair as utopian political vision. And yet, as Ryan acknowledges, 'a miracle is also a form of terrorism, an arbitrary manifestation of omnipotence, before which mere mortals are helpless'. Ryan contends that the play nonetheless reserves and calls for an as-yet-unrealised spirituality of hope, which resonates with a larger critical project that significantly anticipated *Specters of Marx*.[25]

In 'Harry's (in)human face', David Ruiter sets his compass by Martin Buber and Emmanuel Levinas. Patiently tracking Hal through the second Henriad, Ruiter discovers that the future Henry V's heroic destiny is simultaneously a process of abject spiritual shrivelling. 'The strange truth of spirituality', Ruiter discovers, 'is that when we look in the mirror we should see *someone else*.' Thus 'Hal is in the end all-too-human and, as a result, not really human at all, because bereft of that extra, precious, spiritual element which defines humanity and yet is engendered in a vital response to ordinary life.' Ordinary life is an insistent theme of this volume. Ryan calls that 'poor fellow' Lavatch the '*spiritus rector*' of *All's Well That Ends Well*; and it is a casual conversation in a bar that particularly illuminates the spirituality of the second Henriad for Ruiter.

In 'Waiting for Gobbo', Lowell Gallagher demonstrates how the comical double-act of *The Merchant of Venice* manage haplessly to anticipate, and magically act out, the vexed twenty-first-century debates on the scope of spiritual possibility. In Gallagher's reading, Shakespeare's clowns – Gobbo *père et fils* – beckon in an incarnate spirituality that would transcend the exclusionary religious politics of the early modern period and our own.

The incarnational, paradoxically materialist temper of *Spiritual Shakespeares* is further intensified by Philippa Berry's chapter. Berry discerns in the baroque language-games of *Love's Labour's Lost* a 'heterodox meditation upon the grace and salvation that may – or may not – follow man's mortal end'. The distinctly feminine version of salvation she teases out of the play has Marian elements but is best epitomised by 'greasy

Joan' in the play's final song of Hiems. Its medium is palpably erotic, its effect to expose the men of the play to the awful alterity of the phenomenal world, which especially confounds narrowly rational, 'academic' attempts to discipline and make sense of it.

Spirit materialises once more in Lisa Freinkel's essay. Drawing on a range of classic and contemporary treatments of the fetish, Freinkel tells how the critique of fetishism as benighted idolatry was informed by Reformation iconoclasm, facilitated Western cultural imperialism, and was powerfully appropriated by Freud. But after Shakespeare and, to a lesser extent, Luther, Freinkel reclaims the fetish in spite of the Freudian critique. Her reading of the remarkable reversals of Sonnet 20 reveals that the young man, within the poet's very fantasy of his creation, is castrated only to be re-endowed. His penis therefore is a fetish already, and is no more 'his' than it belongs to the feminised figure of Nature who dotingly supplies it. The trauma of deprivation and lack is incorporated into a positive efflorescence of human creativity. Freinkel concludes that 'the Shakespearean fetish' is not an idol to vanish in the cold, humiliating dawn of reason, but a position where 'spirit finally matters'.

In the context of contemporary critical thought, *Spiritual Shakespeares* proffers a striking spiritual materialism, where spirituality is not so much an escape from material reality as an immanent chance for something better. John J. Joughin's chapter establishes the interplay between the material and spiritual as the inherent dialectic of dramatic form. Joughin points to the director Peter Brook's conception of 'Holy Theatre' or 'The Theatre of the Invisible-Made-Visible', which makes its metaphysics out of 'common sense'. Like Theodor Adorno, Joughin insists on the political implications of the fact that a play necessarily brings another world to bear on this one by crudely physical means and effects: a stage, a curtain, the materiality of generic conventions and language. He holds up Bottom's dream as a singular epitome of Shakespeare's restless traffic between the human and divine. But Shakespeare doesn't domesticate the spirit so much as he makes the everyday mysterious, as Stephen Greenblatt also avows.[26] What Joughin terms 'Bottom's secret' reminds us of the comical, unfathomable strangeness of the everyday. Drawing also on the statue scene in *The Winter's Tale*, Joughin argues for Shakespeare's rhapsodic power to transport us beyond the losses and narrow identifications of history to a new place where we must 'begin again'.

Spiritual Shakespeares concludes with two new essays on *Hamlet*. The philosopher Richard Kearney begins with the disarmingly simple recognition that '*Hamlet* is a play about spirits'. He considers psychoanalytic explanations of Jacques Lacan and others, the existential account of Søren Kierkegaard, the deconstructive descant of Derrida and the theologically inclined reading of René Girard. Although his philosophical purview doesn't take in *Hamlet in Purgatory* (2001), Kearney's conclusion that Shakespeare's tragedy is not a monument to the 'majesty of melancholy' but 'a miracle of mourning' chimes with Greenblatt's view. However, Kearney's irreducible 'miracle' separates him from Greenblatt. The philosopher leaves us with a vision of universal political significance: 'an eschatological end to the bitter cycle of repetition and revenge' that is all the more appealing amid the turbulence of contemporary global politics.

My own chapter on *Hamlet* takes a different line, arguing that any overriding preoccupation with mourning and the ghost fails to see that the play transcends them in favour of an ambiguous metaphysics of 'rashness'. In an exact reversal of what we might expect, Hamlet's mystical experience turns him from a kind of conscientious objector into the activist who says, 'The readiness is all'. In our present, Hamlet's supposed transcendence of ethics has a sinister flavour of terrorism and the 'War on Terror'. But I argue that Shakespeare's play suggests nonetheless that the present is the place where all time – the legacy of the past and the hopes of the future – can and perhaps must be consummated in action. Perhaps such a metaphysics of rashness is the natural spirituality of drama?

V

Preoccupied with death and the oppressive nightmares of history, recent Shakespeare scholarship has typically sounded a melancholy and depressing note.[27] *Spiritual Shakespeares* is more optimistic. It presents spirituality as an excess of life, as overbrimming fullness, as the transcendence of given material conditions. Consider the following passage from *The Tempest*:

Miranda: What is't? A spirit?
    Lord, how it looks about! Believe me, sir,
    It carries a brave form. But 'tis a spirit.
Prospero: No, wench, it eats and sleeps, and hath such senses
    As we have – such. The gallant which thou seest
    Was in the wreck, and but he's something stained
    With grief, that's beauty's canker, thou might'st call him
    A goodly person. He hath lost his fellows,
    And strays about to find 'em.
Miranda: I might call him
    A thing divine, for nothing natural
    I ever saw so noble.
Prospero: [*aside*] It goes on, I see,
    As my soul prompts it. [*To* ARIEL] Spirit, fine spirit, I'll
        free thee
    Within two days for this.
Ferdinand: Most sure, the goddess
    On whom these airs attend. [*To* MIRANDA] Vouchsafe
        my prayer
    May know if you remain upon this island,
    And that you will some good instruction give
    How I may bear me here. My prime request,
    Which I do last pronounce is – O you wonder –
    If you be maid or no?

                                        (1.2.410–29)

There is an extraordinary existential intensity in a scene that dramatically isolates human being and says, 'What is't?' Miranda suggests Ferdinand is 'a spirit'. Then she affirms that guess: 'Believe me . . . 'tis a spirit'. Undeterred by her father's demystifying explanations – 'it eats and sleeps, and has such senses as we have' – she insists he is 'divine', 'nothing natural'. Prospero's scepticism seems misleading at first. After all, the instant flourishing of love between Miranda and Ferdinand is instigated by his 'soul' and by Ariel, whom the magus calls 'Spirit, fine spirit'. But ideology is involved in Prospero's ambivalence. The mage at least partly wants Miranda and Ferdinand to come together for personal and political reasons, but they exceed these purposes by *activating* the amorous and spiritual content that are the means of Prospero's self-interested promptings. Perhaps it is this as much as paternal anxiety that wrong-foots Prospero into opposing the very spirituality he says he inspired.

In fact, Prospero is not really directing the scene, though no doubt he'd like to be. He is pushed aside by the spiritual conjunction of Ferdinand and Miranda. Even as Miranda is captured by his aura, Ferdinand sees her as a 'goddess'. Having blundered into her realm, he prays she may teach him how to comport himself there. He is beside himself, ecstatic: 'O you wonder'. Filtered though it is through a worldly patriarchal expectation of female chastity, his concluding question intimates desire to be one with her. And Miranda isn't some Marlovian conjuration of Helen but a real, substantial woman who wants Ferdinand back. An instructive pun is at work in Ferdinand's question: Miranda may be 'a maid', but she is also 'made' in the sense of being physically in existence, incarnate. We are dealing with neither the deferral (Derrida) nor the advent (Žižek) of the beyond, nor with its recovery at a more profoundly natural level (new-age religion). The distance between the spirituality that Miranda and Ferdinand perceive and normal life is nil, nothing like the magical superiority Prospero enjoys. The beyond is here already, spirituality an indwelling excess inalienable from being (and that this holds for Caliban as much as any other character is plain from his exquisite dreams and visions earlier in the play).[28]

Ferdinand is *both* the thing that eats and sleeps and the spirit Miranda recognises. Such double-vision isn't a trick of love's drunkenness, as is confirmed at the end when the ideal alterity of human society as such is revealed to Prospero's daughter:

> O, wonder!
> How many goodly creatures are there here!
> How beauteous mankind is! O brave new world,
> That has such people in't!
>
> (5.1.184–7)

Of course, this meets a sceptical paternal put-down, but it is a half-hearted one that can't quite break the spell of Miranda's words. The alternative world of spiritual ultimacy shimmers in her eyes as the other, potential face of our real world. Like Shakespeare, Prospero knows spirituality is just a possibility. But surely the possibility that human beings may thrillingly surpass what we have taken for reality is aesthetically, intellectually and politically irresistible? As Leontes says in *The Winter's Tale*,

> No settled senses of the world can match
> The pleasures of that madness.
> (*The Winter's Tale*, 5.3.72–3)

Notes

1 For a comprehensive account of how new historicism and cultural materialism have avoided considerations of religion and spirituality or silently converted them into terms more amenable to materialist thought, see Ken Jackson and Arthur F. Marotti (2004). The new 'turn' towards religion in criticism described by Jackson and Marotti is predominantly historicist. A large number of critical works – to give just a few examples: Shuger 1990, 1994 and 2001, Diehl 1997, Shell 1999, Dolan 1999 and 2002, Knapp 2002, Lake 2002 and McCoy 2002 – have treated religion as a complex reality of the early modern period and an important dimension of its historical alterity in relation to our own times.

2 For more on 'presentism', see Grady 1991, 1996 and 2002, Hawkes 2002 and Fernie 2005. A few pioneers, including Jackson and a number of contributors to this volume, have begun a theoretical recovery of spirituality as an existential, ethical or epistemological *experience* pertinent, in several ways, to the present: see especially Berry 1999 and 2004, Freinkel 2002, Gallagher 1991, Girard 1991, Jackson 2001, Lupton 1997, 2000a and 2000b, Taylor 2001 and Wilson 2004. As well as surveying the field, Jackson and Marotti attempt to further and consolidate this initiative (Jackson and Marotti 2004). Out of a fastidious respect for the otherness of the past, they fight shy of presentism, but the connections they perceive between early modern religion and postmodern theory belie this – and Jackson is acutely sensitive to the extraordinary resonance between early modern belief and postmodern theory in other work (Jackson 2001). Jackson and Marotti are right to be wary of glibly translating early modern religion into 'acceptable modern forms conformable to our own cultural assumptions' but they don't consider the positive possibility that a presentist criticism might deliberately seek out, and dialectically profit from, the alterity of the past and of literature (see Grady 2002 and Fernie 2005). This collection not only explores the strange connec-

tions between the spiritual vitality of the plays and our contemporary moment, but it also enjoys the recalcitrant challenges that Shakespearean spirituality offers the present. For more on the 'religious turn' in postmodern culture, see, for instance, Berry and Wernick 1992, de Vries 2002 and Caputo 2001 and 2002. See also Badiou 2001 and 2003, Derrida 2002, Irigaray 1993, Joy *et al.* 2002 and Žižek 2000a, 2000b, 2001, 2002 and 2003.

3 On Catholicism see, for instance, Lake 1989, Finlayson 1983, Shell 1999, Marotti 1999, Dolan 1999 and 2002 as well as Dutton *et al.* 2004a and 2004b and Wilson 2004. For a consideration of religious difference with real purchase on the present, see Lupton 1997.

4 See also Newell 2003: 1. It's instructive that a non-academic book picks up on the existential intensity of Talbot's speech.

5 Speaking for the political Left, Fredric Jameson has written of such radical religious figures, 'These dead belong to us' (Jameson 1981b: 319).

6 This connection between literature and spirituality isn't just a Shakespearean archaism. It has been asserted by notable thinkers and writers throughout the modern era. For instance, Martin Heidegger writes, 'Poetic thinking is being in the presence of . . . and for the god' (see Caputo 2002: 66). Echoing Theseus, Salman Rushdie has written more recently that art 'is the third principle that mediates between the material and spiritual worlds' (Rushdie 1991: 415ff.). Richard Rorty has called for 'a religion of literature in which works of the secular imagination replace Scripture as the principle source of inspiration and hope for the new generation' (Rorty 1996: 15).

7 Similarly in *Macbeth*, according to Stephen Greenblatt, 'Shakespeare achieves the remarkable effect of a nebulous infection, a bleeding of the spectral into the secular and the secular into the spectral' (Greenblatt 2001: 194).

8 I am indebted here to Tom Bishop's excellent unpublished essay, 'Othello in the Wilderness', part of his current monograph-in-progress: *Shakespeare's Scriptures*.

9 Knapp 2002 has stressed the spiritual openness of Shakespearean drama. But reading Shakespearean drama 'in conformity with the Erasmian spirit of the English religious settlement – a spirit of uncontentiousness and impartiality, according to its defenders, of apathy and evasiveness, to its enemies' neglects the agonistic intensity and spiritual struggle of the plays that I want to bring out (169).

10 For a more theological definition, see Sheldrake 1992. My definition is meant to be general and inclusive in order to facilitate the broadest possible consideration of spirituality in Shakespeare.

11 Fredric Jameson stressed such potential some years ago, attempting to 'rewrite certain religious concepts – most notably Christian historicism and the "concept" of providence – as anticipatory foreshadowings of historical materialism' (Jameson 1981a: 285).

12 A good description of the new-age movement is provided by Heelas 1996.

13 Dympna Callaghan puts her finger on the way in which this shift has disabled traditional Marxist materialism in Callaghan 2001. See also Bruster 2001 and Stallybrass 2002.

14 For a fuller consideration of Greenblatt's *Hamlet in Purgatory*, see Chapter 8.

15 Muslim intellectuals like Ziauddin Sardar have long advocated Islamic resistance to globalisation and corporate culture (see Sardar 1979: 230).

16 Gallagher 1991, Lupton 2000b and Jackson 2001.

17 This point has already been well made by Kiernan Ryan:

> The culminating moments of concord, 'When earthly things made even/Atone together' (*As You Like It*, 5.4.109–10), also bristle with estrangement effects. These demand that the denouement be grasped as a symbolic fiction, whose mood is subjunctive rather than indicative, and whose satisfactions therefore lie beyond the reach of contemporary society.
>
> (Ryan 2002: 118)

18 See Badiou 2001 and 2003 and Žižek 2000a, 2000b, 2001, 2002 and 2003.

19 Derrida says:

> He is coming now; the messianic does not wait. This is a way of waiting for the future, right now. The responsibilities that are assigned to us by this messianic structure are responsibilities for here and now. The Messiah is not some future present; it is imminent and it is this imminence that I am describing under the name of messianic structure.
>
> (Derrida 1997: 24)

But to the extent that the Messiah is always 'to come', by contrast with Žižek's and Badiou's, Derrida's remains a spirituality of the beyond.

20 Badiou admits that Žižek made the comparison first (Badiou 2003: 2).

21 I am grateful to Patrick Cheney for stressing this point.

22 In a typically elegant and suggestive treatment, Greenblatt rationalises these moments of spiritual pressure in *King Lear* so much that he drains them of their aesthetically and intellectually compelling power to intimate another, more ultimate world that overlaps with the more familiar world of the play (Greenblatt 2001: 185ff.).

23 Wilson argues that the historical Shakespeare was 'a member of one of the most militant recusant families in a town which was a bastion of Elizabethan papist resistance' (Wilson 2004: 1). He brings this into conjunction with contemporary culture when he writes:

And the return of fundamentalism has taught us never again to conflate spirituality with humanism, or to euphemise Protestant-ism, in the old Left tradition, as 'hardly religion at all, but a kind of Christian anarchy'. We know so much more about religious violence than critics before 11 September 2001. For as I write this, on the site of Shakespeare's Gatehouse, the 'Ring of Steel' around Blackfriars and the City, first erected to counter the Catholic IRA, is being reinforced, to seal the precinct even more securely from a world elsewhere.

(Wilson 2004: 7)

24 See Heelas 1996.

25 Ryan 2002 originally appeared in 1989. The political philosophy of hope that Ryan develops out of Shakespeare bears comparison with Derrida's conception of 'the messianic' as well as with the work of Ernst Bloch.

26 See Greenblatt 2001.

27 Terry Eagleton writes in *The Ideology of the Aesthetic*: '[F]ew literary texts are likely to make it nowadays into the new historicist canon unless they contain at least one mutilated body' (1990: 7).

28 Žižek is interested in the possibility of such immanence. In Žižek 2003, he quotes Christ in St Thomas's Gospel, 'That (resurrection) which you are awaiting has (already) come, but you do not recognize it', and comments, 'This is the key "Hegelian" point of Christianity: the resurrection of the dead is not a "real event" which will take place sometime in the future, but something that is already here – we merely have to shift our subject position' (86–7). Yet even this depends on the paradigmatic advent that is the incarnation; spiritu-ality always is more violently eruptive in Žižek than at this point in *The Tempest*. Better theoretical bearings here could be taken from French feminist theoreticians of spirituality, especially Luce Irigaray's notions of a 'sensible transcendental' and 'becoming divine' (see Irigaray 1993 and Joy *et al.* 2002).

1

'Where hope is coldest'

All's Well That Ends Well

Kiernan Ryan

I

In the opening scene of Act II of *All's Well That Ends Well* the heroine, Helen, steps into the timeless, archetypal realm of folklore and fairy tale, and turns into the Clever Wench who stakes her life on curing the King. His scepticism quelled by the force of her conviction, the King wonders whether Helen is possessed by a higher power:

> Methinks in thee some blessèd spirit doth speak,
> His powerful sound within an organ weak;
> And what impossibility would slay
> In common sense, sense saves another way.
>
> (2.1.174–7)

Things that common sense would dismiss as impossible may be perfectly plausible in another sense, which owes nothing to realism or rationality. So flagrantly do such phenomena break the laws of likelihood that they bespeak the intervention in our world of spiritual forces beyond human understanding.

Impalpable powers are repeatedly invoked in *All's Well* to accomplish or account for the incredible. The first striking instance occurs in the speech with which Helen, determined to bridge the chasm of class that divides her from her beloved Bertram, concludes the opening scene of the play:

> Our remedies oft in ourselves do lie
> Which we ascribe to heaven. The fated sky
> Gives us free scope, only doth backward pull
> Our slow designs when we ourselves are dull.
> What power is it which mounts my love so high,
> That makes me see and cannot feed mine eye?
> The mightiest space in fortune nature brings
> To join like likes and kiss like native things.
> Impossible be strange attempts to those
> That weigh their pains in sense and do suppose
> What hath been cannot be.
>
> (1.1.199–209)

Helen begins by refusing to shift the responsibility for our destiny to divine providence or astrological influence. But her assertion of autonomy is swiftly eclipsed by her sense that she is nonetheless in the grip of a power she cannot name or comprehend. This thought prompts the reflection that nature finds ways of dissolving huge disparities of wealth and rank. And that reflection triggers the contention, echoed in the next act by the King, that extraordinary endeavours ('strange attempts') seem futile only to those who try them in the court of common sense and judge them to be not worth the 'pains' they would cost.

All's Well That Ends Well stacks the deck from the start against its characters and the dictates of comedy. The play begins in the shadow of the death of old Count Roussillon, with the Countess, Bertram, Helen and Lafeu dressed in black, and the gloom is deepened by the impending death of the King:

Countess: What hope is there of his majesty's amendment?
Lafeu: He hath abandoned his physicians, madam, under whose practices he hath persecuted time with hope, and finds no other advantage in the process but only the losing of hope by time.

(1.1.11–15)

The hopelessness of the King's plight is underlined by the fact that the only doctor who could have healed him – Helen's father, Gérard de Narbonne – has recently died as well, despite possessing skills almost great enough to vanquish death itself. His daughter regards her secret love for the dead Count's son as equally hopeless:

> 'Twere all one
> That I should love a bright particular star
> And think to wed it, he is so above me.
> In his bright radiance and collateral light
> Must I be comforted, not in his sphere.
> Th'ambition in my love thus plagues itself.
> The hind that would be mated by the lion
> Must die for love.
>   (1.1.80–7)

When the Countess presses her to confess her feelings for Bertram, however, Helen finds sublime solace in the futility of her desire, which she transmutes into a state of spiritual exaltation:

> I know I love in vain, strive against hope;
> Yet in this captious and intenable sieve
> I still pour in the waters of my love
> And lack not to lose still. Thus, Indian-like,
> Religious in mine error, I adore
> The sun that looks upon his worshipper
> But knows of him no more. . . .
>   . . . then give pity
> To her whose state is such that cannot choose
> But lend and give where she is sure to lose,
> That seeks to find not that her search implies,
> But riddle-like lives sweetly where she dies.
>   (1.3.185–91, 197–201)

The very act of striving against hope releases intimations of plenitude and ecstasy that turn lack and loss into fulfilment and death into exquisite life. The last four lines of the speech slip into couplets that charge them with the vatic resonance such riddles require. Their effect, amplified by the switch from the first person to the third, is to make Helen sound as though a remote, impersonal voice, whose origin is as obscure as its import, is indeed speaking through her, as the King later suspects. Beneath the surface of the speech, which revels in its thraldom to despair, deeper tides are stirring.

The strange fecundity of that despair, its power to summon salvation from the void into which it stares, is borne out at once by Helen's revelation that her father has bequeathed her 'a remedy, approved, set down,/To cure the desperate languishings whereof/The King is rendered lost' (1.3.214–16). The means to cure the King, which will provide in turn the means to win Bertram's hand, does not derive its potency, however, from its deviser's genius or its medicinal properties alone, as Helen explains to the Countess:

> There's something in't
> More than my father's skill, which was the great'st
> Of his profession, that his good receipt
> Shall for my legacy be sanctified
> By th' luckiest stars in heaven . . .
>
> (1.3.228–32)

What that something more is, and whether the celestial realm that sanctifies the 'receipt' is Christian or pagan, Shakespeare declines to divulge. Of its startling supernatural virtues, however, Lafeu stands in no doubt when he sets about cajoling the King into trying the elixir on himself:

> I have seen a medicine
> That's able to breathe life into a stone,
> Quicken a rock, and make you dance canary
> With sprightly fire and motion; whose simple touch
> Is powerful to araise King Pépin, nay,
> To give great Charlemagne a pen in's hand,
> And write to her a love-line.
>
> (2.1.70–6)

But before 'Doctor She' (2.1.78) can raise her own sovereign from the dead and revive his virility, she must persuade him to place his trust in the cure he spurns as 'A senseless help, when help past sense we deem' (2.1.122). To this end she adduces divine precedents furnished by the Bible, conscripting couplets again to lift her reasoning to another plane:

> He that of greatest works is finisher
> Oft does them by the weakest minister.
> So holy writ in babes hath judgement shown
> When judges have been babes; great floods have flow'n
> From simple sources, and great seas have dried
> When miracles have by th' great'st been denied.
> Oft expectation fails, and most oft there
> Where most it promises, and oft it hits
> Where hope is coldest and despair most fits.
>
> (2.1.134–43)

Helen's allusions to the precocious wisdom of Daniel and Jesus as children, and to the miracles wrought by Moses when he struck water from the rock and caused the Red Sea to part, are veiled, but the inference they invite the King to draw is clear: Helen is the instrument of 'him that all things knows' and can count on 'The help of heaven' to effect what lies beyond 'the act of men' (2.1.148, 151). Such miracles materialize, however, Helen is at pains to stress, not when we expect them to, but precisely at the point of utter despair, 'Where hope is coldest' and thus, inexplicably, at its most powerful.

Up to this point, Helen's plea to heal the lethal fistula that afflicts his highness has been couched in Christian terms, but the incantation into which she glides to predict the cure's duration springs from another place altogether:

> Ere twice the horses of the sun shall bring
> Their fiery coacher his diurnal ring,
> Ere twice in murk and occidental damp
> Moist Hesperus hath quenched her sleepy lamp,
> Or four-and-twenty times the pilot's glass
> Hath told the thievish minutes how they pass,
> What is infirm from your sound parts shall fly,
> Health shall live free, and sickness freely die.
>
> (2.1.160–7)

The universe this spell conjures up with no sense of incongruity is pagan. Its chanting rhythms, chiming rhymes and ritual repetitions would not sound amiss on the lips of Oberon or Prospero. Helen metamorphoses from 'the weakest minister' of the Almighty into a formidable sorceress, and her readiness to lose her own life should she fail clinches the King's consent.

The curing of the King is displaced from the stage by a bout of parodic badinage between the Countess and her fool, Lavatch. The masking of the act magnifies its mystery. What takes place between the sovereign and the 'Sweet practiser' (2.1.184) to cure his 'past-cure malady' (2.1.119), and whether the potion, Christian prayer, pagan rite or Helen's sexual allure is responsible for his restoration, is left open to surmise. Indeed, the desire to explain things that defy explanation is made the object of Lafeu's scorn immediately after the King's recovery: 'They say miracles are past, and we have our philosophical persons to make modern and familiar things supernatural and causeless' (2.3.1–3). Lafeu is adamant that, far from being commonplace ('modern'), what has transpired is unprecedented, 'a novelty to the world' (2.3.19), which reveals the 'Very hand of heaven' (2.3.30). That Lafeu's view of the matter is already enshrined in the title of the ballad he reads out – 'A showing of a heavenly effect in an earthly actor' (2.3.22–3) – qualifies it as a cliché, as does its parroting by Paroles in his eagerness to ingratiate himself: 'Why,' opines the shallow braggart, ''tis the rarest argument of wonder that hath shot out in our latter times', manifesting in a 'debile minister great power, great transcendence' (2.3.6–7, 33). But this whiff of irony at the expense of the miraculous is not enough to dispel the atmosphere of awe that fills the stage as the resurrected King enters with his redeemer, who states with simple certainty, 'Heaven hath through me restored the King to health' (2.3.61).

For a time, of course, the miracle seems to have misfired as far as Helen's ulterior 'project' (1.1.211) is concerned. Her reward for summoning 'great power, great transcendence' to slay impossibility is to find herself not the fairy-tale bride of the young lord she adores, but publicly reviled by an aristocrat so appalled at being forced to wed 'A poor physician's daughter', who 'had her breeding at [his] father's charge' (2.3.110–11), that he abandons her for the Tuscan wars rather than consummate the marriage.

But the doctor's child is not long deterred by Bertram's brutal rejection, which his own mother deplores as 'the misprizing of a maid too virtuous/For the contempt of empire' (3.2.30–1). The 'dreadful sentence' (3.2.59) Bertram sends her seems to set the seal on the futility of her love and the hopelessness of her plight all over again:

> When thou canst get the ring upon my finger, which never shall come off, and show me a child begotten of thy body that I am father to, then call me husband; but in such a 'then' I write a 'never'.
>
> (3.2.55–8)

Yet as before, by some occult logic that remains opaque, impossibility and the abjection it breeds engender their anti-thesis. In the grip of a Griselda-like swoon of self-sacrifice, Helen steals away in the dark like a 'poor thief' (3.2.129), so that Bertram will feel free to return safe from the wars. But no sooner has she exiled herself than a brighter note is discreetly struck by the speech of the Duke of Florence to Bertram that opens the next scene, the mathematical centre and turning point of the play: 'we,/Great in our hope, lay our best love and credence/Upon thy promising fortune' (3.3.1–3). Without rational warrant, hope rears up again out of hopelessness and, moments later in stage time, the Countess receives a poetic epistle from 'Saint Jaques' pilgrim' (3.4.4). Helen's penitential sonnet adopts the same posture of self-abnegation as the speech in which she portrayed herself as one who 'riddle-like lives sweetly where she dies'. But this time the obtrusive artifice of the verse, read to the Countess by Reynaldo, renders its author even more remote and rarefied; its piety is pronounced and unquestionably Christian ('barefoot plod I the cold ground upon/With sainted vow my faults to have amended' (3.4.6–7)); and the final couplet succumbs less ambiguously to extinction, though with the same paradoxical rush of delight: 'He is too good and fair for death and me;/Whom I myself embrace to set him free' (3.4.16–17).

The death Helen embraces, however, is equally figurative this time, unlike the real death from which she rescued the King. In fact, in this case it is astutely feigned, a subterfuge cooked up with the help of Diana, Diana's mother and 'the rector of the place' (4.3.57) in Saint Jaques le Grand, where she supposedly died of grief. Yet the fact that her death is virtual does not make what ensues less uncanny than it would have been if Helen had died for real. Helen's fabricated death to the world empowers her to devise the means of her deliverance from its adversities, the bed-trick that dupes Bertram into completing their union and making her pregnant. The tenor of that trick, which belongs entirely to the enchanted realm of folk tale, demands a Delphic conundrum to contain its glaring contradictions:

> Let us essay our plot, which if it speed
> Is wicked meaning in a lawful deed
> And lawful meaning in a wicked act,
> Where both not sin, and yet a sinful fact.
>   (3.7.44–7)

The bed-trick is further mystified, like the curing of the King, by the creation of a smokescreen, in this case the entrapment of Paroles, which harbours obvious parallels with his master's fate in Diana's bedroom. Diana keeps Helen's fictitious corpse subliminally in focus by her demeanour and diction. 'You are no maiden but a monument', Bertram complains at their first tryst, 'When you are dead you should be such a one/As you are now' (4.2.6–8). After he departs, Diana even pushes the charade so far as to flirt with the idea of necrophilia: 'He had sworn to marry me/When his wife's dead; therefore I'll lie with him/When I am buried' (4.2.72–4).

Helen's absence from most of the last two acts reinforces the delusion that she is indeed dead. So do the recurrent laments for her demise and the subtextual echoes of it, such as 'When you have spoken it 'tis dead, and I am the grave of it' (4.3.12–13). Their concerted effect is so strong that it takes a conscious effort in the last scene to remind oneself that the King, the Countess, Bertram and Lafeu are deceived, and their indecent haste to hitch Bertram to Lafeu's daughter, 'fair Maudlin' (5.3.69) – 'Be this sweet Helen's knell, and now forget her' (5.3.68) – is misbegotten. Shakespeare's purpose is plain: to amplify the impact on the characters and the audience when 'Helen that's dead' (5.3.78) rises from her grave and materializes in the court at the eleventh hour to solve Diana's riddle. The last scene pulls out all the stops to make us feel as though Helen has truly returned from the dead. The barrage of contradictions with which Diana assaults common sense baffles us into consorting with another sort of sense and surrendering to a transcendent theatrical wonder:

> He knows himself my bed he hath defiled,
> And at that time he got his wife with child.
> Dead though she be she feels her young one kick.
> So there's my riddle; one that's dead is quick.
> And now behold the meaning.
>   *Enter* HELEN *and* WIDOW
> *King:*   Is there no exorcist
>   Beguiles the truer office of mine eyes?
>   Is't real that I see?
> *Helen:*   No, my good lord,
>   'Tis but the shadow of a wife you see,
>   The name and not the thing.
> *Bertram:*   Both, both. O, pardon!
>   (5.3.297–305)

Unlike the King, we witness Helen's resurrection in full possession of the truth. Yet the existence of a rational explanation does not dispel our impression that something 'supernatural and causeless' has taken place that cannot be reasoned away. The King's suspicion that Helen's spirit has been raised by sorcery, and that what he beholds is unreal, is not contradicted by Helen's reply, ''Tis but the shadow of a wife you see,/The name and not the thing', and Bertram's 'Both, both' is not enough to exorcise the ghost of the tragic heroine Helen might have been.

II

From this account of *All's Well That Ends Well* it might be tempting to conclude that the comedy is an early modern miracle play. At every turn it begs to be read as a parable of self-mortification and blind faith rewarded by grace, redemption and the promised conquest of death itself. And nothing would seem to endorse that reading more than the store the play sets by the power of hope, which rises time and again from the ashes of its annihilation. It would certainly be simpler to turn *All's Well* back into the dramatic act of piety early twentieth-century Christian critics believed it to be. But the comedy is too complex to tolerate such simplifications. It is equally impervious, however, to profane approaches that repress its recourse to the discourse of spirituality in order to shackle it to some new historicist precept or poststructuralist creed.

All's Well is clearly not a religious play in the sense that it demonstrates and demands belief in Christian doctrine. It deploys the narrative templates, affective lexicon and master tropes of Christianity, but it does so neither consistently nor exclusively. The ease with which Helen can slip from citing the Old and New Testaments as God's 'weakest minister' to fusing the pagan lore of pre-Christian Britain with the exotic rites of the ancient world is ample evidence of that. Moreover, *All's Well* has plenty of room alongside these metaphysical models of reality for more earthbound conjectures about the mainsprings of human destiny. If we return to the speech in the opening scene where Helen muses on these matters, it is arresting, after all the marvels confidently credited to higher powers, to hear her aver with equal confidence: 'Our remedies oft in ourselves do lie/Which we ascribe to heaven.' She revises that proposition in favour of the notion that what makes us tick is a double act, a tug of war between celestial constraint and individual volition: 'The fated sky/Gives us free scope, only doth backward pull/Our slow designs when we ourselves are dull.' In the process, the ambiguously Christian 'heaven' turns into an unambiguously pagan 'fated sky', which mutates in the next sentence into a nameless 'power', neither Christian nor pagan, whose imperatives Helen must obey.

The provision with which Helen prefaces her healing charm – 'The great'st grace lending grace' (2.1.159) – is no less vague about the source of that grace, notwithstanding the Christian tint of the word. A similar evasiveness marks the King's ascription of Helen's assurance to 'some blessèd spirit'. When we add to these considerations the light burlesque of the miraculous in Paroles's echoes of Lafeu, the play's detachment from its eclectic spiritual discourse can scarcely be overlooked. The strongest proof of that detachment is Shakespeare's concern to keep everything that confounds 'common sense' intelligible in sublunary terms. Unlike the romances for which it paves the way, *All's Well* concocts no spectacular theophany like that of Jupiter in *Cymbeline* to confirm its protagonists' faith in divine intercession. Whatever the characters say, the miracles worked by Helen can also be attributed to material, mortal causes: to the pharmaceutical skill of her father in the first case, and to her own ingenuity in the second.

This is not to undermine or understate the spiritual dimension of *All's Well That Ends Well*, but rather to redefine its role in the comedy as revolutionary rather than religious, as a means to the end of a play obsessed with means and ends. By framing the play's religious discourse as figurative rather than factual, Shakespeare declutches it from dogma, releasing its resources to serve the secular agenda that religion secretes. The dream of salvation, of the self and the world redeemed, doubles as a metaphor for forms of emancipation that as yet can find expression in no other way. The Christian's hope for grace and resurrection houses the indomitable human hope for freedom from misery, injustice and oppression – a hope anchored in realism rather than revelation, a hope that thrives on disappointment and defeat. And the play fosters faith in miracles, not as the props of revealed religion, but as testaments to the poverty of rationality and realism, as mockeries of the empirical mind that sustains the status quo and kills transformation in the cradle. The cynical materialism of those who claim 'miracles are past' is doomed to remain in thrall to the past, from which it draws its conclusions about the limits of possibility. Whereas the spiritual idealism of those who believe that 'what impossibility would slay/In common sense, sense saves another way' is incorrigibly prospective, propelled toward the transcendence of the present by the radical difference of the future it foresees.

For proof that the revolutionary spirit of utopian hope governs *All's Well*, we need look no further than its scandalous central premise. In no other play by Shakespeare does such a wide social gulf yawn between heroine and hero, a gulf that early modern men and women would have found formidably difficult to cross. The breadth and depth of that class divide are brought painfully home to Helen in Bertram's response to her choice of him as her prize for curing the King: 'But follows it, my lord, to bring me down/Must answer for your raising?' (2.3.108–9). However, not only does the penniless doctor's daughter succeed in hooking a husband far above her station, but she does so by taking the sexual initiative from start to finish, in a reversal of patriarchal roles that has no parallel in Shakespearean comedy. So unseemly did Helen's frank desire and forwardness appear to the Victorians that they doctored her part in the play's upending of *The Taming of the Shrew* to make her more demure.

Nor is this inversion of gender roles, which makes a man the helpless object of a woman's choice, the only generic heresy of which *All's Well* is guilty. The parental elders of the play, the Countess, the King and Lafeu, whom convention should have cast as obstacles to such an irregular union, shatter the stereotype epitomized by Egeus in *A Midsummer Night's Dream*. Far from being stony pillars of conformity, this truly sage trio backs Helen and her cause to the hilt. Indeed, so incensed is the Countess by her son's snubbing of his bride that she disowns him and adopts Helen in his stead: 'He was my son,/But I do wash his name out of my blood,/And thou art all my child' (3.2.64–6).

Blood is also the theme of an astounding speech placed in the mouth of the King, whose advocacy of Helen's cause subverts the foundations of his own sovereignty. When Bertram rebuffs his bride-to-be, the King rebukes him:

'Tis only title thou disdain'st in her, the which
I can build up. Strange is it that our bloods,
Of colour, weight, and heat, poured all together,
Would quite confound distinction, yet stands off
In differences so mighty. If she be
All that is virtuous, save what thou dislik'st –
'A poor physician's daughter'– thou dislik'st
Of virtue for the name. But do not so.
From lowest place when virtuous things proceed,
The place is dignified by th' doer's deed.
Where great additions swell's, and virtue none,
It is a dropsied honour. Good alone
Is good without a name, vileness is so:
The property by what it is should go,
Not by the title. She is young, wise, fair.
In these to nature she's immediate heir,
And these breed honour. That is honour's scorn
Which challenges itself as honour's born

And is not like the sire; honours thrive
When rather from our acts we them derive
Than our foregoers. The mere word's a slave,
Debauched on every tomb, on every grave
A lying trophy, and as oft is dumb
Where dust and dammed oblivion is the tomb
Of honoured bones indeed.

                                                        (2.3.113–37)

To hear such Falstaffian contempt for honour and titles as
mere ornaments of rank voiced by royalty is disarming enough.
But this commendable attitude is dwarfed by the King's admission that the 'differences so mighty' over which he presides as
a monarch have no basis in human physiology, which 'Would
quite confound distinction' were we to found society on the
facts of nature rather than the fictions of culture. The fragility
of those fictions is underscored by the Epilogue, when the actor
who has played the King steps forward and declares, 'The
King's a beggar now the play is done.'

   Furthermore, by endowing his heroine with the power not
only to leap the barriers of class and gender, but also to bridle
mortality itself, Shakespeare suggests something far more dis-
concerting: that deliverance from our subjection to death may
depend on our deliverance from structures of social subjection
that feed on the fear of extinction. Certainly the faculty Helen
inherits from her father is described as one which, 'had it
stretched so far, would have made nature immortal, and death
should have play for lack of work' (1.1.18–19). The full significance of that dream of natural immortality, of death robbed
of its terror and made redundant by human art, must be left
to readers and spectators of the distant future to decipher.

   The surest guide to the play's seditious vision is its *spiritus
rector*, Lavatch. In his first line he reminds his mistress that he
is but 'a poor fellow', and, when the Countess responds with
an innocuous 'Well, sir?', he pounces on the word worked so
hard by the title of the play: 'No, madam, 'tis not so well that
I am poor, though many of the rich are damned. But if I may
have your ladyship's good will to go to the world, Isbel the
woman and I will do as we may' (1.3.11–16). Lavatch's pre-
emptive mimicry of Helen's marital ambition weds it to the
damnation of the rich, implying that both share the same

rationale. His confession that his connubial desire is 'driven on by the flesh' and 'the devil' (1.3.24–5), to whom his 'other holy reasons' (1.3.27) play second fiddle, discloses the carnal core of Helen's motives, first glimpsed in her ribald quibbling with Paroles about the best way a woman might lose her virginity 'to her own liking' (1.1.140). One of Lavatch's chief tasks as the play's irreverent *raisonneur* is to flesh out its ethereal energies. At the end of her round of repartee with Paroles, Helen laments 'That wishing well had not a body in't/Which might be felt' to aid 'the poorer born,/Whose baser stars do shut us up in wishes' (1.1.168–70). Lavatch supplies that body to ensure that the longings of 'the poorer born' in this play are viewed as incarnate rather than incorporeal.

Lavatch's mock-religious iteration of the phrase 'flesh and blood' (1.3.31, 41–3) in praise of cuckoldry is crowned by a quip that seeks common ground between the rival tribes of Christianity while debunking the divisiveness of both: 'For young Chairbonne the puritan and old Poisson the papist, howsome'er their hearts are severed in religion, their heads are both one: they may jowl horns together like any deer i'th' herd' (1.3.45–8). Shortly afterwards, Lavatch tacks another poke at the Puritans onto an ironic exclamation that spotlights the anti-patriarchal thrust of the plot: 'That man should be at woman's command, and yet no hurt done! Though honesty be no puritan, yet it will do no hurt; it will wear the surplice of humility over the black gown of a big heart' (1.3.81–4). When the Countess upbraids her fool for being 'a foul-mouthed and calumnious knave', he protests that he is 'A prophet', adding 'and I speak the truth the next way' (1.3.51–2). In one sense he speaks the truth anything but 'the next way', preferring the byways of obliquity to the highway of blunt statement. But in another sense he does deal directly with issues of which the play he glosses fights shy. He is thus like a prophet in his role as revealer of concealed truths, but he also has the vatic task of foreshadowing the ultimate objective of the play.

Consider, for example, the next encounter between the Countess and the Clown, which supplants the miraculous curing of the King. While Helen rejuvenates her monarch off-stage, the Countess puts Lavatch to the proof of his boast that he has 'an answer will serve all men' (2.2.11–12). The basic butt of Lavatch's ridicule is the vacuous idiolect of the fatuous courtier, anxious to deflect questions with his catch-all cry, 'O Lord, sir!' (2.2.36). But the torrent of gross analogies the Clown unleashes to commend this reply – 'as the nun's lip to the friar's mouth, nay as the pudding to his skin' (2.2.22–3) – insinuates that the sovereign's virility is what is really at stake in the occluded scene. Moreover, these lewd shafts of plebeian derision are fired at the court from a standpoint that collapses class distinctions in the name of universal community. The answer that will serve all men 'is like a barber's chair that fits all buttocks' (2.2.14), says Lavatch. 'From beyond your duke to beneath your constable, it will fit any question' (2.2.26–7). The whole scene synchronizes, and thus conflates, the miracle that empowers the poor doctor's girl with the utopian materialism of Lavatch's comic fantasy.

Two scenes later, the misprized maid and the lugubrious fool are overtly allied, when it is Helen's turn to prompt Lavatch to worry the word 'well' to death, this time by inquiring of the Countess, 'Is she well?' The two reasons why 'she's not very well' despite being 'very well indeed' are, Lavatch explains: 'One that she's not in heaven, whither God send her quickly. The other, that she's in earth, from whence God send her quickly' (2.4.1, 9–11). The Clown's equivocation warns us again to treat the term 'well' in the titular proverb, and in Helen's repeated appeals to it, with the utmost circumspection. But it also adapts a routine piety to vent an aggressive *contemptus mundi* on the Countess. This subterranean strain of class animosity camouflaged as Christianity becomes more salient as the play proceeds. It peaks in Lavatch's *sermon joyeux* to his betters on 'the prince of darkness, alias the devil' (4.5.36–7), who is, the fool informs Lafeu, 'as great a prince as you are' (30–1):

> I am a woodland fellow, sir, that always loved a great fire, and the master I speak of ever keeps a good fire. But since he is the prince of the world, let the nobility remain in's court; I am for the house with the narrow gate, which I take to be too little for pomp to enter. Some that humble themselves may, but the many will be too chill and tender, and they'll be for the flow'ry way that leads to the broad gate and the great fire.
>
> (40–6)

It is no coincidence that Helen's comic counterpart enlists Matthew 7:13–14 – 'Enter ye in at the strait gate: for wide is the gate, and broad is the way, that leadeth to destruction' – to launch his final attack on 'pomp' and 'nobility' in the name of the 'humble' just as the 'poor unlearnèd virgin' (1.3.226) and her female companions are converging on Roussillon to rout the noble lord who abhors her.

III

Lavatch binds the numinous vision of *All's Well That Ends Well* to the materialist critique of rank and patriarchy that shadows it. He embodies the points at which the transcendental and the terrestrial, the yearnings of the soul and the claims of the body, fuse in a perspective that incorporates both. *All's Well* understands that the miraculous is meaningless unless it is made flesh through the transmutation of human lives in the material world of history. It is equally adamant, however, that sheer materialism, bereft of the spiritual and the prospect of transcendence, immures men and women in a retrospective present, from which all hope of transfiguration has been banished.

But if Lavatch highlights the alliance of radical humanism and religion that turns *All's Well* into a materialist miracle play, he also bears witness to the anger and hostility that animate that alliance, to the dark side of the dream of Shakespearean comedy. Like its predecessors and successors in the canon, *All's Well* whets our hunger for a new dispensation and excites our hope that it can be created, that what we have been told is unattainable is within our reach. It does so through a theatrical parable in which a poor, despised woman overcomes social and sexual prejudice and fulfils her heart's desire with the help of other women. At the same time, *All's Well* is acutely aware that the spirit of utopia that possesses it and procures its radiant denouement must also be as ruthless as the hope that spurs it on.

Helen hints as much when she tells the King, 'Oft expectation fails, and most oft there/Where most it promises, and oft it hits/Where hope is coldest and despair most fits', which suggests that hope is strongest not only at its lowest ebb, but also at its most cold-blooded. The most revealing remark in this regard is made by Lafeu. Immediately after the curing of the King, as we have seen, Lafeu decries those 'philosophical persons' who 'say miracles are past' and attempt to explain away 'things supernatural and causeless'. But his next sentence makes clear that by miracles Lafeu means something quite different from comforting proof of divine providence: 'Hence is it that we make trifles of terrors, ensconcing ourselves into seeming knowledge when we should submit ourselves to an unknown fear' (2.3.3–5). With these words an abyss opens beneath the comedy that Lafeu's resort to pious platitudes cannot close. Lafeu's reflection invites us to wonder whether our true response to miracles should be terrified submission to a nameless fear of the unknown. However benign its effects may be, a miracle is also a form of terrorism, an arbitrary manifestation of omnipotence, before which mere mortals are helpless. The miraculous is autocratic and coercive: it brooks neither doubt nor discussion, but imposes its will by pure force.

The 'sweet practiser' who performs the miracles of healing and reunion in *All's Well* achieves her goal, after all, through blind obsession and the inflexible exertion of her will. That much she makes plain in the lines that close the first scene of the play: 'The King's disease – my project may deceive me,/ But my intents are fixed and will not leave me' (1.1.211–12). She saves the King, whose doctors could not save him, not for the King's sake, but as a means to secure the power to make Bertram marry her. The suppressed ferocity of the heroine beatified by Coleridge as Shakespeare's 'loveliest character' (Coleridge 1930: 113) and praised by Hazlitt for her 'great sweetness and delicacy' (Hazlitt 1930: 329) suffuses the speech in which she stakes her life:

> Tax of impudence,
> A strumpet's boldness, a divulgèd shame;
> Traduced by odious ballads, my maiden's name
> Seared otherwise, nay – worse of worst – extended
> With vilest torture let my life be ended.
>
> (2.1.169–73)

Bertram's public and private revulsion from his wife – he cannot even stoop to kiss her goodbye – leaves Helen wounded but fundamentally undaunted and finally determined to exact by guile what Bertram refuses to give freely. That her gratuitous passion for Bertram remains unreciprocated does not restrain her from duping him into cementing their marriage by means of what she admits is 'a wicked act' and 'a sinful fact' (3.7.46, 47).

Helen comforts herself and her accomplices by quoting the play's title, inflating it by rephrasing it until it fills a couplet: 'All's well that ends well; still the fine's the crown./Whate'er the course, the end is the renown' (4.4.35–6). But, however often she recites her mantra, it cannot disguise the fact that her 'course' has been to fake her own death and practise a grotesque deceit on a man constrained to wed her. When she next invokes the adage, she glances directly at the dubiousness of her methods: 'All's well that ends well yet,/Though time seem so adverse, and means unfit' (5.1.27–8). And she returns a few lines later to pick compulsively at the word that troubles her as much as 'well' nettles Lavatch: 'I will come after you with what good speed/Our means will make us means' (5.1.36–7). For once, Hazlitt could not have been wider of the mark when he insisted: 'There is not one thought or action that ought to bring a blush to her cheeks, or that for a moment lessens her in our esteem' (Hazlitt 1930: 329).

Even after she has brought Bertram to heel and the comedy to a close, Helen's repressed rage still resonates in her final speech: 'If it appear not plain and prove untrue,/Deadly divorce step between me and you' (5.3.314–15). The unpalatable truth of the matter is that the miracle play of *All's Well* cradles a revenge comedy fuelled by *ressentiment*. If Helen is an angel of redemption, she is also an avenging angel, an implacable base-born fury unleashed on Bertram, the arrogant ruling-class rake, to pursue him the way men pursue women, and to make him pay for refusing to love her by lashing him to her forever. Alongside its more uplifting satisfactions, *All's Well* offers us the unsavoury pleasure of seeing Bertram bamboozled and brought to his knees by a woman who had her breeding at his father's charge.

In his commentary on the play, Dr Johnson wrote:

> I cannot reconcile my heart to *Bertram*, a man noble without generosity, and young without truth; who marries *Helen* as a coward, and leaves her as a profligate: when she is dead

by his unkindness, sneaks home to a second marriage, is accused by a woman whom he has wronged, defends himself by falsehood, and is dismissed to happiness.

(Johnson 1968: 404)

But part of the point of Bertram's undesirability is to expose the callous indifference of Helen's desire as she hunts down and corners her aristocratic quarry. As Johnson's superb phrase 'dismissed to happiness' suggests, Bertram's feelings are of no consequence to his persecutor or the playwright. Bertram is not there, as sentimental moralists suppose, to be redeemed by love, but to be unmanned and unmasked as a despicable object of undeserved love. The trapping and humiliation of Bertram's partner in crime, Paroles, are cross-cut with Bertram's seduction by Diana and the bed-trick to hammer the point home. The prolonging of Bertram's torment in the final scene, where he is arrested on suspicion of murdering Helen and publicly shamed as a lewd, spineless liar, puts the punitive aspect of Helen's plot beyond doubt.

Thinking of *All's Well* as a social and sexual revenge comedy, in which the epitome of patrician misogyny gets his comeuppance, throws light on the Countess's cryptic remark about Helen early on in the play, a remark that proves as prophetic as the gnomic wisecracks of her fool: 'she herself without other advantage may lawfully make title to as much love as she finds. There is more owing her than is paid, and more shall be paid her than she'll demand' (1.3.90–2). How deeply or consciously Shakespeare identified with Helen must remain speculative. But it does not seem too far-fetched to surmise that the glove-maker's lad from the sticks who conquered the London stage, won the patronage of the Crown, acquired a coat of arms, and – as the *Sonnets* attest – knew the pain of loving 'a bright particular star' out of his orbit, had good grounds for empathizing with his heroine's plight and her nailing of Bertram through her own native wit. This surmise is strengthened by the care the dramatist takes to insulate Helen from the slur of vulgar opportunism and vindictiveness her actions threaten to attract. She is partly immunized by her portrayal as a seraphic alien from the parallel universe of folk myth. But she is doubly indemnified by the presence in the play of Paroles, who is, like Helen's other secret self, Lavatch, a character wholly of Shakespeare's invention. A brazen *arriviste* parasitically attached to Bertram, Paroles is coupled with Helen from their saucy banter about virginity in the first scene to his vital betrayal of Bertram in the final moments of the play.

The animus Helen's transgressive triumph might arouse, and whatever guilt Shakespeare felt for letting her flout rank and female decorum, are deflected onto the fawning upstart, Paroles. Hence the King's scolding of Bertram for snobbery and demand that he marry Helen are followed by Lafeu's vitriolic abuse of the bogus gallant, on whom the play can discharge its covert aversion to its heroine. And when Paroles is baited and crushed by his fellow soldiers, his affliction serves not only as a mirror of Bertram's fate at Diana's hands, but also as a punishment of Helen by proxy for what she achieves with impunity. If Lavatch unlocks the utopian import of Helen's apotheosis, then Paroles is the lightning rod for the loathing the parvenu inspires in any hierarchical culture. That Paroles, as his name proclaims, is also the personification of the words the play is forged from makes clear, moreover, the complicity of the wordsmith himself in the coercive wiles of *All's Well*. In so far as Shakespeare perceives in Helen and Paroles caricatures of his own ambition and the art by which he achieved it, his portrayal of 'the manifold linguist' (4.3.224) and 'double-meaning prophesier' (4.3.96) as 'A very tainted fellow, and full of wickedness' (3.2.87) speaks volumes about what comedy has obliged his language to connive in.

In the end, in spite of his collusion with her, Shakespeare's thaumaturgic heroine cannot remain unsoiled by the world in which she works her miracles. Nor can the utopian spirit and the principle of hope she embodies escape contamination by the culture of division, subjection and injustice they seek to destroy. On the contrary, as the creatures of that culture they leave the imprint of its violence and malice on every scene of *All's Well That Ends Well*, as it broods on the means and ends of human happiness. Even the perfunctory formalities of farewell are infected: 'I grow to you,' Bertram assures his comrades, 'And our parting is a tortured body' (2.1.36–7). The play whose title acknowledges the devil's deal struck by comedy knows the cost of the providential closure it contrives, and incriminates itself by virtue of the language it commands. If the 'blessèd spirit' that the King hears speak 'His powerful sound within an organ weak' is Shakespeare, so is the demonic dramatist who stalks *All's Well*, making it a thing of darkness as well as a child of light.

That dramatist ensures that disavowal is not an option for the play's spectators either, by hooking them into its utopian realism. Helen herself reminds us not only that the fulfilment of her fantasy is double-edged, but also that it hangs by a syllable, by a single thread of the language disparaged in the figure of Paroles:

> Yet, I pray you –
> But with that word the time will bring on summer,
> When briers shall have leaves as well as thorns,
> And be as sweet as sharp.
>
> (4.4.30–3)

'Yet' is made to bear enormous weight here, as both adverb and conjunction, for it stresses the play's unresolved openness to the future in which it places its faith, and asks us to place ours. The fragility of the resolution is accentuated by an equally potent slip of a word, 'if', which fronts its conditional clauses, as in Bertram's last lines: 'If she, my liege, can make me know this clearly/I'll love her dearly, ever ever dearly' (5.3.312–13). Indeed, 'yet' and 'if' team up in the final couplet of the comedy, spoken by the King, to strand the ending in the subjunctive mood, at the mercy of reversal:

> All yet seems well; and if it end so meet,
> The bitter past, more welcome is the sweet.
>
> (5.3.329–30)

The axiomatic truth maintained by the title is betrayed by deferral and exposed as a hypothesis, whose validity only the future beyond the play can verify.

That future belongs to the world the audience inhabits, as the Epilogue, addressed to us by the actor who has played the King, compels us to recognize:

> The King's a beggar now the play is done.
> All is well ended if this suit be won:
> That you express content, which we will pay

With strife to please you, day exceeding day.
Ours be your patience then, and yours our parts:
Your gentle hands lend us, and take our hearts.

(Epil., 1–6)

The first line dissolves the difference between beggar and king
in the democratic spirit by which the King of this comedy has
been possessed. Then the second line recycles the penultimate
line of the play, but this time to snare the spectators in its
circumspect syntax and the dilemmas it has dramatized. The
Epilogue makes the audience – and all the audiences that will
succeed it – accountable for the satisfactory resolution of what
it has witnessed. It redefines ending well as an unending
endeavour, stretching off into an indefinite future: 'which we
will pay/With strife to please you, day exceeding day'. And
the closing couplet leaves us in command of that endeavour
by reversing the roles of actors and audience. It puts us on the
stage in their place with their hearts, and turns them into
witnesses of our struggle to make their fairy tale come true.

2
Harry's (in)human face
David Ruiter

Harry, Prince Hal, Henry V: he's quite a character. And in the end – whereas many of Shakespeare's principals trespass strangely into the sphere of the human – a character is all Hal becomes. This chapter examines him through two philosophical lenses: the first provided by Martin Buber's paradigm of the "I-You, I-It" duality of human, relational existence, and the second taken from Emmanuel Levinas' theory of "face" and "character." Both of these theories, Levinas' knowingly following Buber's, understand humanity and the possible creation of authentic human existence in terms of relational opportunity and responsibility. My main aim is simply to see how Hal/Henry V relates to others – even to "the Other." I start with his easily overlooked dealings with Francis, the apprentice drawer at the tavern, whose limited but repeated appearance in the *Henry IV* plays provides a template upon which to begin mapping the Prince's relational life, which is what life essentially – yes, essentially – is according to Buber and Levinas. Ethics for these thinkers has a numinous coloring. As what is other to habitually selfish life and what is ultimately significant and valuable, it is, to use the terms of this volume, their version of spirituality.[1]

Most critics who examine Hal ultimately determine whether he treats Falstaff ethically, especially when the newly crowned Henry V chooses a very public rejection for the fat knight. We learn later that this rejection "kills" Falstaff (*Henry V*, 2.1.110ff., 4.7.37ff.), but the same act seems to open the door for the new, improved Hal to become "the mirror of all Christian kings" (*Henry V*, 2.0.6). Of course, the rejection of Falstaff, no matter how one views it, is just one moment in Hal's dramatic life, but that it is traditionally taken to be *the* moment is a reminder that we are compellingly confronted with the ethics of Shakespeare's plays and with the ethical choices of Prince Hal in particular.[2]

Paul Dean writes:

> Shakespeare seems to show, in the Histories, and above all in the figure of Prince Hal in *Henry IV* and *Henry V*, something contrary to the determinism of contemporary theory: that it is what we do and wish to be which shapes the universe we live in.
>
> (1997: 35)

Individual identity is more complex than simply the "is" and "was" of existence. It entails the hope of what "could be" and even the wish to live up to what "should be." These aspirations are achieved or fail in action – with, as Dean emphasizes, real consequences for the world. Criticism should pay heed to Hugh Grady's recommendation of a more "Machiavellian" understanding of character, which begins with what characters are rather than what they should be.[3] But Shakespeare dramatizes Hal's potential for becoming something else, for finding the ethical mode which is, as Levinas would say, "otherwise than being" (Levinas 1981). I will describe Hal's relational existence as it is before going on to what should be, but "could" and "should" do become inevitable because seeing Hal's ethical potentiality creates a reasonable curiosity as to whether and how that potential will be realized, which contributes richly and involvingly to the drama.

As mentioned, I use the Hal–Francis relationship as a foundation for my argument. The ordinariness of Hal's contact with a barman seems to me especially revealing of his ethical and even spiritual conditions: another main contention of this chapter is – God is or isn't in the details, as it were. There has been a relative abundance of criticism on the basic (ir)relevance of the short scenes with Hal and Francis. For example, several critics, including Fredson Bowers (1975–6: 18–20), Joseph Porter (1979: 69–70), J. McLaverty (1981: 107), and Lois Potter (1999: 289–90) see Francis as relevant in the sense that he is a representation, in miniature, of Hotspur, because of the linguistic monotony each demonstrates – Francis shouting, "Anon, anon," and Hotspur equally committed to repeating the name "Mortimer"; thus both appear to be single- and simple-minded in comparison to Hal. J. D. Shuchter offers a more elaborate comparison, one that shows Francis as a puny Hal in his paralysis created by "conflicting obligations," and as a tiny Hotspur in terms of his potential rebellion against a master (1968: 130). In each of these cases, Francis is interpreted as a figure for someone else. G. L. Kittredge sees the relationship between the waiter and the Prince as essentially pointless, except in terms of fun (in Bowers 1975–6: 139). Eugene Wright, similarly, sees the Francis scenes as aesthetically useless, except for filling time until Falstaff arrives (1975–6: 65–7). More pertinently to my emphasis on relationship and responsibility, Stephen Greenblatt sees significance in the historical politics of the interaction, writing, "the prince is implicated in the production of this oppressive order [and] in the impulse to abrogate it" in his conversation with Francis (1985: 44). Also speaking historically, Charles Whitney asks, "what does the truant Prince Hal have in common with the many apprentices who in the 1590's were regularly committed to Bridewell for tavern-haunting?" (1999: 455). But Greenblatt and Whitney take it for granted that Francis has no interest *in himself*, which is ethically and politically questionable and which, I argue, is precisely what is at stake in Hal's reactions to him.

When we first encounter Prince Hal in the Boar's Head Tavern, he is aglow with enthusiasm for his newly established relationship with the "drawers," the tavern's apprentice tapsters and waiters (*1 Henry IV*, 2.5). It is a complex moment dramatically, partly because the Prince is discussing his relationship to his supposed social and political inferiors, the drawers, with another of his supposed inferiors, Poins. Moreover, the discussion occurs after Hal has delivered his "I know you all, and

will awhile uphold/The unyoked humour of your idleness"
speech, in which he promises to use the Boar's Head community – including Poins and Falstaff – for political advantage
(1.2.173–95). These factors complicate what can be gathered
about Hal's relationships from the following lines. He says that
he's been:

> With three or four loggerheads amongst three or fourscore
> hogsheads. I have sounded the very bass-string of humility.
> Sirrah, I am sworn brother to a leash of drawers, and can
> call them all by their christen names, as "Tom", "Dick",
> and "Francis". They take it already, upon their salvation,
> that though I be but Prince of Wales yet I am the king of
> courtesy, and tell me flatly I am no proud jack like Falstaff,
> but a Corinthian, a lad of mettle, a good boy – by the
> Lord, so they call me; and when I am King of England
> I shall command all the good lads in Eastcheap. They
> call drinking deep "dyeing scarlet", and when you breathe
> in your watering they cry "Hem!" and bid you "Play it
> off!" To conclude, I am so good a proficient in one quarter
> of an hour that I can drink with any tinker in his own
> language during my life. I tell thee, Ned, thou hast lost
> much honour that thou wert not with me in this action.
> But, sweet Ned – to sweeten which name of Ned I give
> thee this pennyworth of sugar, clapped even now into my
> hand by an underskinker, one that never spake other
> English in his life than "Eight shillings and sixpence", and
> "You are welcome", with this shrill addition, "Anon,
> anon, sir! Score a pint of bastard in the Half-Moon!" or
> so. But, Ned, to drive away the time till Falstaff come, I
> prithee do thou stand in some by-room, while I question
> my puny drawer to what end he gave me the sugar, and
> do thou never leave calling "Francis!", that his tale to me
> may be nothing but "Anon!" Step aside, and I'll show thee
> a precedent.
>
> (2.5.4–29)

The Prince speaks first of some "loggerheads", but he then
potentially gives the members of that group personal identities, calling them by their supposed "christen names of 'Tom',
'Dick', and 'Francis'." There is a question, of course, as

to whether "Tom" and "Dick" are the actual names of the other apprentices, or whether the Prince is jocularly using an identity-denying cliché – every "Tom, Dick, and Harry" – but substituting the name of the actual "Francis" for his own, as Kiernan Ryan suggests (1995: 108).[4] On the other hand, at least one of the trio, Francis – the very one who breaks the "Tom, Dick, and Harry" cliché – is in the tavern and will shortly appear. Hal's throwaway line seems casually to credit the possibility of Francis' singularity at the same time as it undermines it.

In his complicated attempts to establish his own identity in relation to Francis and the drawers, Hal fluctuates between two relational positions that exemplify precisely the dialectical condition that Martin Buber describes as inherent to human, relational existence. Hal is demonstrably "human" in Buber's terms; however, despite the Prince's seeming desire to relate in the mode of what Buber calls the "I-You," he fails really to acknowledge Francis. And his bluff contempt for supposed inferiors surely rebounds on Poins; in fact, in calling Poins "Ned," Hal again signals the particular and generic identity of one of his Boar's Head associates, as "Ned" is both an abbreviation of "Edward" and a general label for a petty criminal.[5] Recognition of and responsibility for the Other is what Levinas posits as necessary for the achievement of ethical subjectivity. While Hal manages to demonstrate his human potential through his dual attitude to others throughout the Second Henriad, his being human is frustratingly impeded by his failure to fulfill the ethical life he can imagine and has opportunity to attain. The pathos of this is not blunted but sharpened by the humdrum quality of a barroom encounter, which suggests that the most important issues of human ethics and ontology are dramatized and decided in the infinite series of forgettable moments that comprise the everyday.

After naming the drawers, Hal sways again towards the conglomerate perspective of apprenticeship, repeatedly referring to the drawers as "they" – "so *they* call me," "*They* call drinking deep 'dying scarlet'," etc. But even while speaking of the apprentices *en bloc*, Hal seems genuinely excited by the sense that the experiences he shares with them prove his ability to relate: "To conclude, I am so good a proficient in one quarter of an hour that I can drink with any tinker in his own language during my life."[6] But this enthusiasm is complicated, most notably when Hal says:

> They take it already, upon their salvation, that though I be but Prince of Wales yet I am the king of courtesy, and tell me flatly I am no proud jack like Falstaff, but a Corinthian, a lad of mettle, a good boy – by the Lord, so they call me; and when I am King of England I shall command all the good lads in Eastcheap.

The apprentices' appraisal of Hal as being "a lad of mettle, a good boy" might be authentic praise or simple flattery; either way, Hal appears to take it as an extended hand, an invitation to join their group. But if it is such an invitation – rather than just a means of enjoying an evening on the Prince's tab, utilization of others not being exclusively available to the powerful, as Nina Levine makes clear (Levine 2000: 414–15) – Hal nonetheless sees the apprentices' utility to him. The seriousness of his apparent casualness is always explicitly an issue after "I know you all" (1.2.173–95) and here it emerges powerfully, even brutally. Says Hal in effect, "I am Prince of Wales; while I drink with them, they think that I am a good boy and a peer of sorts: all the better to rule them with – when I am King I will *command* such 'good lads' as these". As Jeffrey Knapp demonstrates, this political method contrasts starkly with that of Henry IV:

> While Hal's father Henry IV ineffectually struggles to resolve "intestine" conflict by reminding his people of the Crusades and their lapsed duty to Christendom, Hal finds companionship in an alehouse, and then finds a way through the alehouse to rid England of civil war, recover its empire, and strike a "Christian-like accord" with France – all as the "king of good fellows."
>
> (Knapp 2002: 57)

Here, Hal's method is only beginning to take shape, but it does appear to be working: the "good lads" name him a "good boy"; he places them as affectionate future subjects.[7]

However, as soon as we realize the political benefits of Hal's relationship with this group, he turns his attention to one of its individual members. Only at this moment do we realize for sure that "Tom-Dick-and-Francis" is not *simply* a mocking cliché for the apprentices, but that there is an actual "Francis" at work in the Boar's Head; this same Francis will also be the butt of Hal's attempted joke. Shortly, the Prince calls Francis to his table and seems to take an interest in him – asking how much time remains to serve out the terms of his apprenticeship, suggesting that Francis might be interested in breaking this bond and running away, inquiring after the waiter's age (2.5.37–49). Hal even promises extraordinarily generous reciprocation for the gift of the sugar, saying, "but hark you, Francis. For the sugar thou gavest me, 'twas a pennyworth, was't not? [. . .] I will give thee for it a thousand pound. Ask me when thou wilt, and thou shalt have it" (2.5.53–7).

This promise is fraught with difficulties of the kind that Ken Jackson, building on the work of Marcel Mauss (1990) and Coppélia Kahn (1987), discusses in his thoughtful essay on *Timon of Athens* (2001). The reader might be willing to see Hal's apparently absurd generosity as matching that which Francis has shown; that is, given their economic difference, a pennyworth of sugar to Francis may be similar to a thousand pounds to the Prince. Or perhaps Hal's generosity should be seen as ethically and impressively excessive. But the economic difference between prince and waiter is nonetheless highlighted, and maybe even aggressively, as Hal not only makes the offer, but also suggests the ease with which he can produce such a handsome sum by encouraging the waiter to come and ask for the thousand pounds at any time. Jackson would likely see this gesture as an example of Mauss's concept of "potlatching," whereby a chief would provide a huge gift in order to "prevent any reciprocation and establish his superiority [. . .] by demonstrating his different social position in the exchange network" (2001: 38). In this case, the fact that Hal (Big-Chief-in-Waiting) doesn't even produce the actual gift but only the offer of the gift (a sort of rain check) turns Francis from a free gift-giving agent into a supplicant; and it potentially subjects the waiter to scorn and humiliation for believing a joke to be an honest offer. This is not to suggest that Francis' "gift" is entirely free of "economy" – a situation Jacques Derrida argues is logically impossible (in Caputo 1997b: 140–51) and Ivo Kamps, relying on Marx, demonstrates to be historically so (1996: 96). But it would seem that we are encouraged to see Hal's gift as significantly poorer than the tapster's.[8]

Still, Francis appears to take the Prince's questions and offer at face value, which only makes him all the more confused when Hal begins speaking his "leathern-jerkin, crystal-button, knot-pated" nonsense (2.5.64–6). When the bewildered waiter asks what Hal means, the Prince roughly reminds him of his subordinate position, saying, "Away, you rogue! Dost thou not hear them call?" (2.5.73). Hal here treats Francis with the contempt of a royal customer towards an apprentice waiter. When he next calls the waiter, Hal receives the customary, waiterly response of, "Anon, anon, sir!" (2.5.90). This comment concludes the Hal–Francis interaction in *1 Henry IV* with the relational positions of each apparently clarified: Francis is the waiter, Hal the master.

To summarize, in fewer than a hundred lines of text, Hal happily describes his relationship with the drawers, makes clear their political utility, enters into personal conversation with Francis, then treats him in a manner that clarifies the difference between royal customer and apprentice waiter. The dramatic situation is brief, involves four speakers (Hal, Poins, Francis, and the vintner), is all prose, and is certainly not sentimental moralizing; instead, it has both the tone and the significance of real speech, of everyday language, right down to the barroom specifics of drink orders and seating arrangements. Yet the lines also repeatedly evoke the difference between treating others as subjective individuals or as objects to be used for one's own advantage. I am arguing that the passage is, perhaps paradoxically, *more* ethically compelling because it doesn't involve any extraordinary "fear and trembling." We can recognize ourselves in this exchange, and in the ethics of casualness, of relaxation, of contingent rather than ultimate situations that define our lives. I also suggest that if any spiritual issues can be shown to hang on Hal's failed barroom joke, then spirituality may be more of an issue in ordinary life than we might think.

At the end of these lines, it seems that Hal withdraws into a view of Francis as a bought man rather than an individual. But such a view will not hold entirely because Francis appears again in *2 Henry IV* (2.4), and again he alone receives special attention as the only named person in a group of three drawers.

Though Hal this time does not exchange words with Francis, he does borrow the waiter's uniform and attempts to fill Francis' position. That is, Hal attempts in some way *to be* Francis – though less than successfully. In this second situation, in which Francis again appears as individual and as member of the apprenticeship conglomerate, the text explicitly replays Hal's dual attitude as if to underline that Hal's relationship with the apprentices, and with Francis in particular, is not reducible to a single orientation.

Prince Hal and Buber's "I-You" paradigm

Martin Buber's *I and Thou* provides a helpful basic construct by which to understand the natures of Hal's relationships with Francis and others.[9] In his opening line – "The world is two-fold for man in accordance with his twofold attitude" (Buber 1970: 53) – Buber suggests that humans live, essentially, in two relational positions – the position of "experience/utility," which he characterizes as the "I-It," and that of true relationship, which he calls the "I-You." These positions are distinct but are also simultaneously at work. The "I-It" position, says Buber, is realized when a person

> perceives the being that surrounds him, plain things and beings as things; he perceives what happens around him, plain processes and actions as processes, things that consist of qualities and processes that consist of moments, things recorded in terms of spatial coordinates and processes recorded in terms of temporal coordinates, things and pro-cesses that are bounded by other things and processes and capable of being measured against and compared with those others – an ordered world, a detached world. This world is somewhat reliable; it has density and duration; its articulation can be surveyed; one can get it out again and again; one recounts it with one's eyes closed and then checks with one's eyes open.
>
> (82)

This "I-It" position, I suggest, is the one from which Hal formulates his prodigal-prince-to-powerful-king prognostica-tion early in *1 Henry IV*, and it is also from this relational

position that Hal understands the political value of his
association with the apprentices as a group. The world is an
objective reality outside himself that Hal is going to refashion
for his own purposes. But that is not quite the whole story of
the way he relates to the apprentices, as we have seen.

The "I-You" position is much different. Buber says that in
this attitude a person

> encounters being and becoming as what confronts him –
> always only *one* being and every thing only as a being.
> What is there reveals itself to him in the occurrence, and
> what occurs there happens to him as being. [. . .] The
> encounters do not order themselves to become a world,
> but each is for you a sign of the world order. They have
> no association with each other, but every one guarantees
> your association with the world. The world that appears to
> you in this way is unreliable, for it appears always new
> to you, and you cannot take it by its word. [. . .] It cannot
> be surveyed: if you try to make it surveyable, you lose it.
> [. . .] It does not stand outside you, it touches your ground;
> [. . .] you can make it into an object for you and experi-
> ence and use it – you must do that again and again – and
> then you have no present any more. Between you and it
> there is reciprocity of giving.
>
> (83–4, Buber's italics)

The shift from "him" to "you" exemplifies the interplay between
the two positions Buber describes. The "I-You" position is
evident in Hal's questions regarding Francis' apprenticeship
and in his promised reciprocation for Francis' gift of the sugar;
as seen in the quotation earlier, reciprocity of giving is, in fact,
the central ethical component of Buber's "I-You" construction.
I suggested that Francis' confusion results largely from his belief
in the authenticity of this aspect of his relationship with the
Prince. We may categorize this belief, and Francis himself, as
simple or even "mindless," as does Bowers (Bowers 1975–6:
20). From one point of view, no doubt it is, but if we follow
Buber's thought then the drawer's belief is also indicative of
an ethically and existentially *superior* mode of being, one which
stunningly reverses the positions of the prince and the pauper.
Even if we choose to pass off Hal's moment of generosity as

being ego or alcohol induced, the "I-You" position also comes into view in Hal's delight at being "sworn brothers" to the drawers. Ultimately, through the seeming casualness and insignificance of this dramatic moment in a pub, another dimension shows through. Our first real glimpse in this chapter, perhaps, of spirit.

Still, it seems easy to decide that Hal's "I-You" relationships turn out to be phony or hypocritical. The shifting back and forth from the personally engaged to the instrumentally political is really only symptomatic of Hal's relationships with everyone, and especially with Falstaff. But if Hal does reject his "I-You" relationship with Falstaff, the Boar's Head gang, Francis, and the drawers, then the "I-You" relationship does, or at least did – or at least *could* – exist. I suggest that the oscillation in Hal between "I-You" and "I-It," between understanding and perhaps desiring true relationship with Francis or Falstaff and utilizing them, creates a dramatic environment that is less than completely, less than theoretically stable or straightforward, but is convincingly, ambiguously human, in a way that would satisfy Buber.[10]

On relationship Buber writes in terms that take on a strong spiritual and essentialist coloring:

> [. . .] the longing for relation is primary, the cupped hand into which the being that confronts us nestles; and the relation to that, which is a wordless anticipation of saying You, comes second. [. . .] In the beginning is the relation – as the category of being, as readiness, as a form that reaches out to be filled, as a model of the soul, the *a priori* of relation; *the innate You.*
>
> (1970: 78)

Such a desire imbues the speech I have focused on earlier. Consider not only Hal's warm exuberance, but also his value-laden, sometimes explicitly spiritual diction: "humility," "sworn brother," "christen," "salvation," "Corinthian," "by the Lord," "drink with any tinker in his own language." All of these words and phrases are suggestive of relationship. For example, brotherhood is a form of, often a synecdoche for, relationship, whereas drinking with a tinker in his native tongue suggests generous, other-directed solidarity. The dramatic setting for all this, let us recall, is the Boar's Head. In a sense, the episode is absurd, as it's doubtless meant to be. But it also suggestively plants what otherwise would only be mock-pious irrelevancies in the soil of real existence. Here, as I have suggested, spirituality is another dimension of ordinary life itself.

Significantly, Hal's personal conversation with Francis and later borrowing of Francis' outfit occur in the context of attempted jokes, indicating that the Prince is trivializing his knowledge of the "I-You" relationship and clarifying his superior position by temporarily drawing close to the drawer. Nonetheless, in order to be effective, each joke involves a certain emptying out of that very superiority. That is, Hal has to step down from his princely position and into the place of Francis and the other drawers. In the first instance, he does this by attempting to learn the loggerheads' "language." In Part Two, Poins indicates that all that is required to change from prince to apprentice is costume – "leather jerkins and aprons" – and professional behavior – "wait upon [Falstaff] at his table like drawers" (2.2.149–50). Hal takes note of his stepping out of position, saying, "From a God to a bull – a heavy declension – it was Jove's case. From a prince to a prentice – a low transformation – that shall be mine; for in everything the purpose must weigh with the folly" (151–4). When the Prince mentions the "purpose" of the joke, he once more highlights his tendency toward utilization. But Jove descended into the form of a bull from desire: the comparison keeps the possibility of relationship in play.[11] And the disguise offers an image of identification and solidarity. In his transformations into a sort of everyman/drawer, Hal's attempt to utilize is mixed up with an effort and a *desire* to relate that lean toward ethical/spiritual possibility even in the midst of self-orchestrated political history.

On several other occasions, Hal demonstrates this desire for true relationship. We might consider three of the most memorable:

- Hal's desire for small beer (*2 Henry IV*, 2.2.1–23). Is the draw for the Prince really toward Falstaff and the old gang (and beer), or away from his troubled relationship with his father and the pressing politics of the kingdom? Most likely, both are the case. Hal utilizes Falstaff and his father, but he appears to desire relationship with both. As evidence, moments later he wishes to show concern regarding his father's illness (2.2.29–54) – a desire which Poins might not see as hypocritical if only the Prince had spent time administering to his relationship with his father prior to this moment when the King's death is so fully equated with Hal's rise to power. Once again it is in the complexity, the detail, the "undecidability" of this moment that its ethical credibility is felt.

• Henry V's pain as the result of Scroop's betrayal (*Henry V*, 2.2.90–141). This moment is almost shocking in its re-humanization of Hal/Henry V. After the rejection of Falstaff, one senses that Hal has become the "Great User," a perspective strengthened by his spurious spiritual sanction for a war with France – the battle abroad that his father had suggested would end the British civil war. And yet, Henry V asks us to believe that he is both stunned and sorrowed by the fact that Scroop attempted to "ha' practiced on [the King]" (2.2.96). He even says that Scroop's treason "is like/Another fall of man" (2.2.138–9). If the first fall of man ended the perfect relationship between humans, their environment, and God, this second fall perhaps indicates the King's near despair of authentic relationship even on a limited basis. But has he not himself created this twice-fallen world of the Second Henriad?

• Still, Henry continues to try to relate, as is evinced by his desire to move among the soldiers on the night before Agincourt (4.1.24–211). This effort fails but merits consideration. Henry again disguises himself and attempts to communicate with the common people, as he did in donning Francis' apron at the tavern, but Bates and Williams remind him that the King's politics are inextricably bound up with his and their personal and spiritual relationships: if they die, they will leave wives and children behind, and the King will be responsible. Henry strains to deny this responsibility, but the burden of their words stays with him. He cannot reach them, cannot authentically relate to them, because he's already using them for his kingly advantage.

As Hal moves through his politically successful kingship, he moves deeper and deeper into the more surveyable but inert landscape of what Buber calls the "I-It." Buber says, "However the history of the individual and that of the human race may diverge in other respects, they agree in this at least: both signify a progressive increase of the It-world" (1970: 87); furthermore, "the improvement of the capacity for experience and use generally involves a decrease in man's power to relate" (89). As we witness in Hal's dismissal of Francis, his "crown-theft" while supposedly attending to his dying father (*2 Henry IV*, 4.3.150–311), the chilly deaths of Falstaff and Bardolph (*Henry V*, 2.1.73–116, 2.3.1–37; 3.6.89–103), and the ultimate disappearance of Francis and Poins, Henry's increased "capacity for experience and use" and decreased ability in the "power to relate" is painfully evident. According to Buber, this makes him a paradigmatic figure of modernity.[12] However, even so late as in Henry's late-night chat with Bates and Williams, designed by the King as an "I-It" experience preparatory to the battle, there remains a flicker of the urge to relate, uncomfortable now for Harry as Williams essentially forces the issue of being understood as a "You," rather than as one more soldierly "It." Though this urge is left unfulfilled in Henry, elsewhere in Shakespeare – for example, in Lear's relationships, especially with the Fool, and in Richard II with his last "friend" the groom – it is possible for the "I-You" between king and subject to be discovered or rediscovered after a period of latency. Therefore, we see that Shakespeare's texts tend to maintain both relational integers, the "I-It" and the "I-You," even in obviously hierarchical contexts, although as Buber suggests, "it is not as if these states took turns so neatly; often it is an intricately entangled series of events that is tortuously dual" (69).

Hal and Buber's being-in-relationship

In Buber's terms, Hal demonstrates the dual attitude indicative of the divided human condition, as well as the requisite longing for relationship, and these characteristics do much to vitalize the drama. But we also remember how excited Hal was to be viewed as a "good boy" and a "sworn brother" to the drawers, terms that establish the desirability of sustained ethical relationships to others. There is more than just a desire simply to *experience* ethical life here. We seem instead to glimpse, even through Hal's cynical humor, a desire *to be* ethical by moving into what Buber calls the "lived actuality" of the concept of being-in-relationship (136).

Buber's "I-You, I-It" structure concedes the necessity of the "I-It" world, largely because this is the world in which events and experiences can be psychologically, politically, and historically organized, and made generally reliable through a certain detachment (82). There must be an accommodation of the "I-It," because it is simply not possible to live exclusively in the "I-You" (83–4). However, Buber states of the two positions: "The It is the chrysalis, the You the butterfly" (69) and "without It a human being cannot live. But whoever lives only with that is not human" (85) and is "buried in nothingness" (83). While Hal's desire for true relationship appears time and again throughout the tetralogy, there is the question of whether or not the move towards true relationship is actualized at any time, whether Hal unfurls into a fully human being, an example to us all such as a "mirror of all Christian kings" might be.

If a moment of actualization does occur, it perhaps is found in the Prince's relationship with Falstaff. From the moment we first see these two in *1 Henry IV* (1.2), there is a sense of at least a verbal fraternity between them. Initially, their discussion is mostly made up of light banter concerning whoring, thieving, drinking, and eating: again, not a very promising starting-point for a spiritualized ethics, we might think. But this banter, as is the case in Shakespeare's texts elsewhere (perhaps most notably with Benedick and Beatrice in *Much Ado*), does indicate a certain closeness of feeling, a camaraderie, a desire for and pleasure in the Other. The lines quoted below continue this significant tone and begin to absorb more explicitly if ambiguously spiritual content:

Falstaff   Thou hast the most unsavory similes, and art indeed the most comparative, rascalliest sweet young Prince. But Hal, I prithee trouble me no more with vanity. I would to God thou and I knew where a commodity of good names were to be bought. An old lord of the Council rated me the other day in the street about you, sir, but I marked him not; and yet he talked very wisely, but I regarded him not; and yet he talked wisely, and in the street too.

Prince Harry   Thou didst well, for wisdom cries out in streets, and no man regards it.

Falstaff   O, thou hast damnable iteration, and art indeed able
to corrupt a saint. Thou hast done much harm upon me,
Hal, God forgive thee for it. Before I knew thee, Hal, I
knew nothing; and now am I, if a man should speak truly,
little better than one of the wicked. I must give over this
life, and I will give it over. By the Lord, an I do not, I am
a villain. I'll be damned for never a king's son in
Christendom.

Prince Harry   Where shall we take a purse tomorrow, Jack?

Falstaff   Zounds, where thou wilt, lad! I'll make one; an I do
not, call me villain and baffle me.

Prince Harry   I see a good amendment of life in thee, from
praying to purse-taking.

Falstaff   Why, Hal, 'tis my vocation, Hal. 'Tis no sin for a
man to labour in his vocation.

(1.2.70–93)

The familiar nicknames suggest a sort of easy "I-You" mode.
In addition, there is a relishing affection in Falstaff calling Hal
the "rascalliest sweet young Prince" and "lad." And, as with
Hal's speech regarding the drawers, there are strange, even
overwhelming spiritual connotations: "God," "wisdom cries out
in the streets,"[13] "corrupt a saint," "God forgive thee," "By the
Lord," "I'll be damned for never a king's son in Christendom,"
"Zounds," "good amendment of life," "praying," and "sin."
Though it dances in complex, not easily decipherable measures
with his humor and general audacity, Falstaff's skewed, weird
but persistent spirituality appears from these first moments in
1 Henry IV to the last we hear of him in *Henry V*, and it often
occurs in conversation with, or concerning his relationship
with, Hal.

   Opportunity for the "I-You" again surrounds Hal here,
this time in the person of Falstaff, and in a performative and
improvised manner the Prince participates; shortly later, this
participation will be even more fully realized in their play-acting
scene (2.5). The earlier passage associates Falstaff with suffering
virtue and Hal with sin and temptation until they both join in
an enthusiastic spiritual "vocation" of thieving! What I am
hinting at – what I am suggesting that *the play* hints at – is that
the dramatic warmth and pathos of knockabout Falstaff and

Hal is a revelation of a strangely ethically and spiritually creative mode of being that is not carried into Henry's kingship and is beyond conventional piety.

In their initial scene, Hal concludes their interaction with the "I know you all" speech; similarly, the play-acting ends with Hal's ominous "I do; I will" promise to banish Falstaff (2.5.439). And what's really unnerving is that Hal *knows* that in banishing plump Jack he's banishing all the world. And yet, the fact that Hal is using Falstaff does not rule out the continuing chance for authentic relationship. Although Falstaff's (like Francis') optimism for developing true relationship with Hal is ultimately unrealized and even misplaced, his understanding of Hal's human, relational being is nonetheless far from stupid: in its unworldliness and reckless independence from the selfish desire usually associated with Falstaff, it is even rather heroic. As for Hal, the fact that he utilizes Falstaff and Francis and others does not cancel the Prince's *potential* to realize honest relationship.

This potential is later enacted as the worried Henry V attempts to turn toward God. On the night before the battle of Agincourt, immediately following his conversation with Bates and Williams, Henry decides to pray, to (in Buber's terms) enter into the ultimate "I-You" relationship. In this attempt, the King asks that God give his soldiers courage and that his familial guilt for the death of Richard II not be considered at this historical moment, for after all, Henry points out, he has demonstrated great penitence for that death. But he ends the prayer with the realization that his good works are worthless because he retains the kingship, the lasting benefit of Richard's murder (4.1.271–87). This allows us to see that Hal/Henry V, who to some resembles Hamlet,[14] is also related to the prayerful Claudius. Like Henry, Claudius guiltily frets that his desire for forgiveness and atonement with God will remain unrealized because he retains the benefits of his murder of Old Hamlet. And while Claudius suffers from "the primal eldest curse" (3.3.37) – that is, Cain's curse for having murdered Abel – Hal's inherited responsibility for the death of his cousin Richard has a similar result. To gain a crown, Claudius killed a brother and thereby stifled his possible relationship to God. As heir to his father's crown as well as to his guilt for the death of a kinsman, Henry finds himself frustrated in his efforts to realize true relationship with his "sworn brothers," his brothers-in-arms, and God.

Hal's attempt at prayer is also interesting when read more explicitly through Buber's comments. Buber states:

> One cannot divide one's life between an actual relationship to God and an inactual I-It relationship to the world – praying to God in truth and utilizing the world. Whoever knows the world as something to be utilized knows God in the same way. His prayers are a way of unburdening himself – and fall into the ears of the void.
>
> (156)

Buber's concept of God is at least partly comprised in the idea of "absolute relationship" or the "true You [. . .] that cannot be restricted by any other and to whom [one] stands in relationship that includes all others" (127, 124). The philosopher understands God as a kind of quintessence of personality. A relationship with God is implied and realized in ordinary ethical life, and vice versa (172–82).[15] This clearly has a bearing on my "spiritual" reading of seemingly mundane moments in the Second Henriad. If, as Hal does, one utilizes one's fellow humans and puts aside the actualization of the "I-You," then one does the same with God, both in the moment of utility and when attempting to relate to God in prayer. And this process of utilization is draining to one's humanity; in that respect, and considering Henry's prayer as merely one more attempted "piece of shrewd diplomacy," Una Ellis-Fermor says:

> Neither we the readers nor Henry himself nor his God ever meets the individual that had once underlain the outer crust that covers a Tudor monarch, for there is nothing beneath the crust; all has been converted into it; all desires, all impulses, all selfhood, all spirit.
>
> (1946: 46)

This idea is precisely realized as Henry finishes the prayer, now basically talking to himself (4.1.284–7). He clearly is not transforming from chrysalis to butterfly, but instead is coming to recognize the It-world as the world that presently matters to him. It is an existentially fraught moment. To Buber, it would signify a mere departure from the pole of ethics, but the dramatic spotlight shines so powerfully on Hal's inwardness here as to suggest that lasting damage has been done. In other words, Henry's distancing of relationship has corrupted and degraded his being, his "I," and reduced him to his utilitarian value, his "It." Disrespect for others manifests and results in a harmful disrespect for the nature of his own being, his being-in-relationship. It is a failure by Henry V to achieve his own inherent potentiality, to realize the fullness of the "I-You."

Hal and Emmanuel Levinas

Through the lens of Levinas, Hal's failure is seen somewhat differently – not simply as failure in self-actualization (a failure of the "I"), but as failure for the Other (for the "You"). For Buber, the "infinite" exists as personal potentiality (1970: 136, 167), but for Levinas it exists as responsibility.

Before moving on briefly to consider Hal/Henry V in relation to the ethics of Levinas, it is important to point out that Levinas is acutely aware of Buber's "I-You" paradigm,[16] and in significant ways values this model even while changing both the terms and the ethical ideal it enshrines. As to the terms, what Buber refers to as the "I-You, I-It" duality of humanity, Levinas compasses under his theory of the Other. The Other is experienced as either the "face" or as a "character," which Levinas defines as follows:

> The face is signification, and signification without context. I mean that the Other, in the rectitude of his face, is not a character within a context. Ordinarily, one is a "character": a professor at the Sorbonne, a Supreme Court justice, a son of so-and-so, everything that is in one's passport, the manner of dressing, of presenting oneself. And all signification in the usual sense of the term is relative to such a context: the meaning of something is in its relations to another thing. Here, to the contrary, the face is meaning all by itself. You are you. In this sense one can say that the

face is not "seen". It is what cannot become a content, which your thought would embrace; it is uncontainable, it leads you beyond.

(Levinas 1985: 86–7)

In Buber, the "I-You" is what is uncontainable, what leads one beyond, while the "I-It" is very much a content within a context. But despite the similarity of their foundational terms, it is apparent even at this cursory level that Levinas' ethics are differently focused, not so much oriented toward the development of the "I" as to the responsibility for the Other. In this respect, while Buber focuses on the issue of reciprocation in relationship for full development of the "I," Levinas focuses on response to and responsibility for what is outside the self.

Although Levinas makes clear that the desire for what he also calls the "Infinite," for authentic relationship (1985: 82), is as crucial as Buber claims it to be, Levinas also believes that this desire "nourishes itself on its own hungers and is augmented by its satisfaction" (92). This may explain how relational desire appears to decline in Hal over the course of the tetralogy. That is, as Hal turns away from authentic relationship with his father, Falstaff, Francis, Poins, Scroop, and others, his desire for actualizing authentic relationship begins to wane, and while he may have the impulse towards the "Infinite," his longing for true relationship is consistently smothered by his commitment to utilizing others as "characters" within his ultimately socio-symbolic network, rather than responding to them as "faces," as what immediately confronts his subjectivity in and even *as* the Other below or above any social description.

Levinas believes that in taking note of the existence of the "face," one immediately becomes responsible "for him, without even having *taken* on responsibilities in his regard; his responsibility *is incumbent on me*" (96, his italics). The reason for this, in Levinas' view, is that "subjectivity is not for itself; it is [. . .] initially for another" (96). In fact, says Levinas, "[f]or every man, assuming responsibility for the Other is a way of testifying to the glory of the Infinite, and of being inspired" (113). In this regard, Hal's dismissal of opportunities for authentic relationship is not just a matter of failing to achieve his potentiality. Rather, this pattern of turning away is grossly irresponsible. By desiring true relationship, longing for the "I-You" – even while living in the "I-It" – Hal demonstrates that he has the dual attitude inherent to humans, but by refusing responsibility for the Other, by not responding to the "face," he becomes buried in nothingness and fails to achieve a subjective, ethical agency.

Nowhere is this lack of humanity more pronounced than in Henry V's last moments in the tetralogy, the scene of his "wooing" of Catherine (5.2). Here, Henry's instrumentalization of others manifests itself once again, and he has now become so brazen in this relational mode as to refer to his future wife – in front of both herself and her parents – as "our capital demand" (5.2.95–7). In addition, he decides to act the part of a plain soldier with Catherine (5.2.145–62) even though this role does not square with our experience of Hal/Henry V throughout the larger part of the tetralogy. When Catherine leaves the room after Henry's most flagrant failure to relate, the King attempts to keep up his bluff soldierly role when he speaks with Burgundy, but this "character" quickly fades to be replaced by something akin to the Boar's Head Hal, who roughly banters about the similarity between women and flies (5.2.262–94). Here, at the closing of the Second Henriad, having reduced everyone else to the function of "character" in his personal political drama, and having played a vast array of roles himself, Hal confirms that he has ultimately buried his own ability to respond to the "face," buried the responsibility for the Other, and therefore his own humanity, lost his own face and become a mere "character."

Maybe this loss is in some ways inevitable for Hal/Henry V, as kingship in Shakespeare appears generally to result in greater utilization of others and a reduced ability to relate and respond; in that regard, along the way I have mentioned Richard II, Lear, and Claudius, and other ready examples might include Henry IV and Macbeth. But Hal is a special case, partly because his opportunities to relate occur so frequently and under a dramatic spotlight, and his turnings away, especially from Falstaff, create a more devastating sense of what is lost in the process of achieving abundant political gains. Despite his many maneuverings as prince and king, Harry somehow always seems on the verge of becoming, of entering or rediscovering a new mode of being-in-relationship. Although my emphasis has been on Hal's ethical conditions in this chapter, I do not wish to oppose private ethics to public politics. A politics of ethical responsibility toward all others is the "undeconstructible" inspiration for deconstruction that many of the chapters in this volume explore. God's love for everything in creation may be the most concrete image of such politics.[17] Henry V's kingdom cannot compare. In the Second Henriad, Hal does demonstrate that he is a man, even has the necessary "stuff" – potential, desire, and opportunity – to become an ethical human being and ruler. But the roles that he chooses to play, those many "characters" – prince, thief, drinking buddy, benefactor, son, brother, king, soldier, suitor, etc. – while allowing for position and power, cost him his shot at the "Infinite." Harry is in the end all-too-human and, as a result, not really human at all, because bereft of that extra, precious, spiritual element that defines humanity and yet is engendered in a vital responsiveness to ordinary life. The strange truth of spirituality is that when we look in the mirror we should see *someone else.* Were this "Christian king" to look in the mirror, he might well see one of his gratifyingly successful "characters" smiling smugly back at him, but he wouldn't see a Levinasian "face," the face of the Other that is also his own, the meaningful authentication of the "could be" and "should be" of his life.

Notes

1 There has been no lack of interest in the religious issues of the Second Henriad, especially in regard to the Catholic, Protestant, and Reformation ideologies found within the plays. For interesting reading on these issues, see, among many others, Poole 1995, Hunt 1998, and Hamilton 2003. But I would distinguish this work from the sorts of spiritual/ethical matters I am discussing here.

2 For a sampling of the variety of impressions concerning the ethics, politics, and propriety of Hal's rejection of Falstaff, see Bradley 1909, Newman 1966, McGee 1984, Bloom 1998, and Amirthanayagam 1999.

3 See Grady 2000.

4 The *OED* notes the common use of the names "Tom", "Dick", and "Harry" both as nicknames for the Christian names of "Thomas", "Richard", and "Henry" and as the generic naming "for any male representative of the common people." Shakespeare also uses the names of "Tom" and "Dick" in this generic way in Winter's song at the conclusion of *Love's Labor's Lost* (5.2.887–902).

5 The *OED* includes other possibilities for "Ned," as well, among them "a general term of disapprobation."

6 Steven Mullaney 1983 writes thoughtfully on the nature and utility of Hal's language lessons in the tavern.

7 Harry Levin states, the Boar's Head event demonstrates the politically useful idea that the "dissolute playboy seems at heart to be a fun-loving boy-scout. [. . .] Harry's youthful fraternization with Tom, Dick, and Francis will have made him more humane as head of state than his aloof and crafty father has been" (1981: 6–7). Eugene Wright more bluntly asserts, "Hal is, and this scene proves it, a man who acts according to his present political needs [. . .]" (1975–6: 67).

8 Though outside of my parameters here, it is tempting to discuss Derrida's concept of the gift much further, especially as it is addressed by both Jackson 2001 and Caputo 1997b. Desire for the gift is relevant to Hal's interaction with Francis, and possibly with many others in the Second Henriad. Derrida's idea that gift (at least as an impossibility) and economy are always with us, and therefore demand that decisions and choices are made in regard to both, has several interesting parallels and intersections with Buber's "I-You/I-It" paradigm, and also, as Caputo suggests (150), with Levinas' concept of responsibility for the Other.

9 For more on the spiritual and sociological implications of Buber's work, see Friedman 1955, Kohanski 1982, Murphy 1983, and Silberstein 1989. I wish to thank Alfonso Morales for many productive discussions on the sociological application of Buber.

10 See Buber 1970: 82.

11 I am indebted to Bruce Louden for discussion of Jove/Europa. See Books Two, Six, and Eight of the *Metamorphoses* (Ovid 1965).

12 For much more on the instrumentalization of others in Shakespeare as part of the onset of modernity, see Grady's *Shakespeare's Universal Wolf*, especially Chapter Three, "*Othello* and the Dialectic of Enlightenment: Instrumental Reason, Will, and Subjectivity" (1996: 95–136).

13 This phrase comes from Proverbs 1:20: "Wisdom crieth without; she uttereth her voice in the streets."

14 For some thoughtful comparisons between Hal and Hamlet, see H. D. Janowitz 2000, H. MacLean 1987, and D. R. C. Marsh 1983.

15 These ideas are made especially clear in the referenced pages, which were added by Buber in 1957 in his Afterword to the second edition.

16 For more on Levinas' understanding of Buber, see Sean Hand's *The Levinas Reader*, especially Chapter Three, "Time and the Other," and Chapter Four, "Martin Buber and the Theory of Knowledge" (1989: 37–74). Correspondence between Buber and Levinas can be seen in Levinas 1976: 51–5.

17 See Lupton 2000b.

3

Waiting for Gobbo
Lowell Gallagher

The cascade of revelations at the close of *The Merchant of Venice* achieves the effect of a cinematic close-up, calling attention, one last time before morning dawns in Belmont, to the unsettled semantic range and ideological mooring of gifts and gift-exchange in the play-world at large. Three gifts appear, brought forth from as many origins: happy coincidence (unexpected news of the return of Antonio's argosies); civil law (safe conveyance of Shylock's deed of gift to Lorenzo and Jessica); and providential care (Lorenzo's grateful invocation of biblical manna). However one judges the worth, and the cost, of these gifts, there is more than meets the eye in the ensemble. There is an absence: the Gobbo family, Old Gobbo and his son, Launcelot. The absence is easy to overlook, for several reasons. The Gobbos belong to the periphery of the play's social world, and what we know of the story of their lives dissolves into white noise when pitched against the dominant key of the pre-marital banter in the final act. Yet their absence discloses something that anthropologically driven notions of the logic of the gift, which have dominated the subject of gift exchange in *Merchant* criticism, fail to see.

For the Gobbos have their own forgotten gift to give. Its vanishing tacitly proclaims the essential component of the gift to be nothing – literally, no thing. In gift-giving, it's the thought that counts, the excessive, gratuitous spirit of the gift, not the thing itself. The gift soundlessly but persistently mocks materialism's investment in empirical and quantifiable measures of the real. By no coincidence, the most telling indicators of this provocation surface in the Gobbos' forays into the main action. Their comic wordplay generates intuitions of the gift that challenge the play's dominant religious, ethnic, and social partitions (Christian/Jewish enclaves, landed vs. mercantile economies, and the shifting choreography of friends, lovers, neighbors, rivals, and enemies).

Taking its cue from the Gobbos' accidental insights and suggestions, this chapter examines the radical nature of *Merchant*'s rendering of the spirit of the gift. To this end, it follows the question of the gift's intangible essence into the contested peninsula of twentieth-century philosophical thought on the gift – outside the play's local frames of reference – where contemporary phenomenologies of religion and incarnational theologies converge. The Gobbos' wayward exchanges, I argue, find illuminating counterparts in the philosophical debates between Jacques Derrida, Jean-Luc Marion, Emmanuel Levinas, and Alain Badiou over the defining terms of the gift and its conditions of possibility.

Beyond gift exchange

Where mainstream Shakespeare scholarship is concerned, the four thinkers just named occupy a place strangely reminiscent of the Gobbos' in the final tableau of *Merchant*. Though acknowledged as significant participants in the community of discourse on the gift, their speculative labors have by and large gone unrecognized in *Merchant* criticism. This is so, in part, because of the visceral immediacy of the play's depiction of an urban, and urbane, social world and the raw urgency of its antagonisms. No wonder the play has lent itself with such ease to materialist inquiry and to sociological and anthropological theories of gift exchange: these are the prevailing critical idioms for addressing the immanence of the real. However, the quarry I seek – the imaginary place where the Gobbos' witticisms speak to the arguments of Continental philosophers of the gift – does not lie as far afield as one might think.

The route opens from an established crossroads in *Merchant* criticism. The play's reiterated oscillations between a concocted memory of feudal usury and a waking dream of mercantile capitalism evince prescient intuitions of one of Marcel Mauss's foundational contributions to anthropological discourse on the gift: the distinction between gift and commodity. For Mauss the distinction turned on a surplus element he found to be characteristic of the gift rather than the commodity (unlike Karl Marx, who famously discovered "the secret of surplus value" in the capitalist system of commodity exchange (Yan 1996: 5)). On Mauss's account, the surplus element – the spirit (*hau*) of the gift – generates relations of exchange and reciprocity, without being reducible to them. By and large, subsequent anthropological writing rejected Mauss's intuition of the spirit of the gift, erecting in its place a logic of immanent reciprocity, as in Bronislaw Malinowski's "principle of give and take" (Yan 1996: 6), and Claude Lévi-Strauss's gift economy, in which the exchange of women constitutes both origin and paradigm of sociality. In a well-known essay on the dynamics of gift exchange in *Merchant*, Karen Newman accounts for the legibility of the Lévi-Straussian "traffic in women" paradigm model in the play, even as she contests its viability.[1] What is striking about the critique, from the standpoint of Mauss's legacy of thought on the gift, is what it passes over in silence: notably, the vexed relation between legible structures of reciprocity or exchange and the gift's "spirit" or unquantifiable surplus.

Discerning excess

Mauss's thought is strategically important to my argument because it gives rise to two basic questions on the gift: does the gift appear only in acts of reciprocity (however diffused these might be over space and time), and does the component of reciprocity nullify any conceivable surplus to the gift?[2] *Merchant* raises these questions, too. Their impact can be felt not only in the eye-catching spectacles of the casket scenes and the pound of flesh but also, more tellingly, in the suburbs of the main action – the Gobbos' world – where encounters of little consequence nonetheless appear charged with implication. Consider, for example, the strange career of the gift Old Gobbo produces in Act II, the "dish of doves" (2.2.134). We will return to this scene later, but for the moment I want to indicate how some of the subliminal provocations produced by Gobbo's gift help redirect the basic questions arising from Mauss's anthropological horizon.

Carried in a basket, the dish of doves hardly seems an ostentatious gift, though in view of the likelihood that Gobbo is not a wealthy man it seems fair to say that the gift is not *nothing*, either. Materialist inquiry would first seek to ground the reference in a relevant historical context by assembling data from Renaissance cookbooks and food practices, but such information alone does not account for what happens to the dish of doves in the scene: its drift into the elusive domain of "no thing." We should recall here that Old Gobbo's first mention of the gift identifies it as a "present" (2.2.89) for Shylock and that Launcelot, appalled at the thought of giving any present to "a very Jew" (2.2.93), orders his father to give the dish of doves to Bassanio instead. Given Launcelot's earlier decision to change masters, trading Shylock for Bassanio, it is easy enough to assume that the gift has tactical value from Launcelot's standpoint. He says as much, voicing the hope that Bassanio will reciprocate by hiring him as a servant (giving him one of his "rare new liveries" (2.2.97)). Launcelot's candor (or naked ambition) raises more questions than it answers, however. Does the integrity of the gift – its freely given character – depend on the extent to which the gift's conformity to a rule of reciprocity is not known – that is, not given to consciousness? If so, whose knowledge is at issue: the giver's, the recipient's, the onlooker's? Is the gift Old Gobbo prepares to give Bassanio the same gift he intended to give Shylock? The material substance – the cooked dish – is unchanged at the end of the scene, but it is far from clear how many – or whether any – gifts have actually transpired.

The questions raised by Gobbo's gift are not confined to anthropology's investment in mapping patterns of social behavior. They also speak to phenomenology's project to describe the "given" character of the world and to discern the range of perceptual frames or horizons through which specific, more than material events – such as gifts, or love, or terror –

come to be recognized as such.[3] In addition, these questions are susceptible to theological inflection, insofar as theology is expressly concerned with the gifts of creation and divine presence and involvement in human affairs. The fact that Gobbo's dish is made of doves is not without interest here, given that doves figure conspicuously as covenantal signs of divine care in both Jewish and Christian traditions. Gobbo's dish of doves, then, provides a suggestive index of what we can expect to find at large in the world of the Gobbos. Not only do we find an interrogation of the nature of the gift and of its ties to "no thing." We find this by observing how the manner of the interrogation – the Gobbos' farcical misadventures and miscommunications – exposes the fault line, the shifting and uncertain boundary, between phenomenological and theological concerns with givenness.[4]

To better grasp the shape of this concern in the Gobbos' world, I turn to a crucial parting of ways between Jacques Derrida's and Jean-Luc Marion's respective thoughts on the essential character of the gift.[5] Both thinkers are inclined to discount the role of reciprocity and to rekindle interest in the speculative question of the gift's surplus element. But their ways of framing the question diverge significantly. For Derrida, the gift crucially transcends its material conditions. From this follows Derrida's controversial aporia of the gift: the "conditions of possibility of the gift . . . designate simultaneously the conditions of impossibility of the gift . . . For there to be gift, it is necessary that the gift not even appear, that it not be perceived or received as gift" (Derrida 1992: 12, 16). If the gift were to appear as such, this would only generate indebtedness, raising the expectation of repayment and nullifying its character as gift. In the 1997 Villanova roundtable discussion on the gift, Derrida tries to quell the confusion apt to arise from such logical sleight-of-hand by insisting that the statement "the gift as such is impossible" does not mean that there is no gift (Caputo and Scanlon 1999: 60). Rather, it attributes to the word "gift" a spirit, a "no thing," that transpires in excess of knowledge, "beyond" the "economic circle" of gift exchange and beyond what can be seen or put into words (ibid.: 60).

As we have already seen, this is the basic problem posed by the dish of doves. But the problem has two faces: it addresses both Derrida's concerns and those of his main interlocutor at the Villanova roundtable, Jean-Luc Marion. For Derrida, the gift's spirit is a subtraction or withdrawal from our everyday phenomenal world.[6] Yet precisely because it is not an apprehendable thing – because it is, strictly speaking, impossible – it creates a space from which new things or events may emerge. The transcendent trajectory of the gift pulls towards a different and better future. For Marion, the gift's impossible excess works otherwise: not by withdrawing from the world, but by exposing it to a "new horizon," one of unconditioned, superabundant givenness (Caputo and Scanlon 1999: 61). Through this gesture, the gift enters the domain of what Marion calls the "saturated phenomenon." Such a phenomenon can be seen, heard, tasted, touched, or smelled, and it can be thought or made present to consciousness. But it cannot be comprehended by any of these horizons, because its essential trait is nothing other than its capacity to give *"more, indeed immeasurably more"* than either mind or body can grasp (Marion 2002: 197). By definition, then, the saturated phenomenon is irreducible to description either as object or thing or as being. Nonetheless, saturated phenomena surround us, Marion explains, in the inexhaustible character of historical events and works of art, in the profound intimacy of the human sensorium with its environment, in the elusive constitution of interpersonal relations, in the giving of time, of one's attention, one's word, one's life, and, crucially, in the possibility of divine revelation.

Both Derrida's and Marion's accounts of the gift's impossibility see beyond the habitual determinism of cultural history, whether by imagining a deferred or a manifest excess in lived experience. To judge from their standoff at Villanova, however, the difference between the deferred and the manifest appears irreconcilable, not least because Derrida's "no thing" lies outside sociality and representation, to the point of abstraction, whereas Marion's not only saturates the world of appearances but also appears ultimately to do so on behalf of a particular religious tradition.[7] The standoff warrants mention because *Merchant*, too, aligns the question of the gift with the logic of a zero-sum game. Think again of the conundrum posed by the dish of doves, which seems to mutate into either too many gifts or none at all. Crucially, however, *Merchant* also sees beyond such divisive maneuvers – that is, it asks whether the gift's essential trait resides precisely in its capacity to incarnate, within the social lineaments of gift exchange, the profound intimacy between opposing dimensions of the gift's "no thing" – between what remains categorically out of sight and mind, and what is so immediately present as to confound comprehension. Such insight, as the Gobbos' misadventures suggest, seeks to reawaken wonder at the strangeness and vulnerability of what is given in the world.

To indicate more precisely what is at stake in this line of inquiry, I turn to two thinkers who were not present at the Villanova roundtable, Emmanuel Levinas and Alain Badiou. Ethics, rather than the question of the gift per se, is their principal concern, and their respective accounts of the ethical relation could not be more different, if you consider Badiou's well-known objections to Levinas's ethics of alterity, which on Badiou's account mistakenly privileges the transcendence of the Other and underestimates the ethical solvency of conditions of likeness and solidarity – the sphere of the Same (Badiou 2001: 18–19). Nevertheless, these thinkers' respective meditations on eschatology and universalism fruitfully expose a common intuition – which the Gobbos share – of the profound connection between the gift's impossibility and the possibility of a radical ethics: an ethics not content with dutiful observance of given norms but mindful, instead, of the "no thing" that subsists in social relations and challenges all settled forms of knowledge and behavior.

For Levinas, eschatology refers not to a stage in history (a messianic "End-time," for example) but to the sudden breach made in totality by the "infinity" of desire and responsibility for the Other (Levinas 1969: 23). As Richard Kearney reminds us, Levinas "confronts us with the paradox of the infinite which is inscribed *within* our historical experience of totality," within the warp and woof of the everyday (Kearney 2001: 63). Hence the ambiguity of one of Levinas's key terms for the event that gives eschatological desire its ethical charge: the "face" of the other. Rather than simply denoting physical features, "face" calls attention to what is singular in the face-to-face encounter and thus irreducible to the horizons of objectivity and being. By "exceeding the idea of the other in me," the "face" issues a call to compassion and care which is both inexhaustible and fragile: impossibly present, one could say, yet easily ignored (Levinas 1969: 50). In sum, to encounter the "face" of the other is to discover that the social other – whether neighbor, stranger, or kin – compels attention because it eludes cognitive mastery, though it may be mastered in other ways. Shylock, for example, is mastered by the Venetian court: he is brought into a determinate civic identity whose prerequisite is religious conversion. Yet Launcelot's astonishment at the dish of doves Old Gobbo intends, without explanation, for Shylock – an impossible gift – suggests that Gobbo's gesture acknowledges, however fleetingly, the "face" of Shylock, an aspect that does not coincide with any of the names used to define him (Jew, usurer, father, alien, etc.) but rather belongs to and indicates his singular, irreducible personality.

Badiou mounts a comparable provocation by drawing out the ethical and political challenge of the visionary thinker whose writings constitute a significant proof text for *Merchant*: St Paul. It should be said that the Paul at issue here is not the Paul known as the font of Christian orthodoxy and tacitly presented as such in the confessional antagonisms informing the main plot of Shakespeare's play. Instead, Badiou's Paul is a non-denominational thinker of the gift. We might call this Paul the patron saint of the Gobbos, in the sense that the Gobbos' antics, performed on the margins of Christian, Jewish, and mercantile Venice, express a core insight remarkably similar to what Badiou finds in Paul. At the heart of Paul's thought, Badiou discovers a radical intuition: that universality is "organically bound to the contingency of what happens to us, which is the senseless superabundance of grace" (Badiou 2003: 81). Badiou's reading of a key passage from Romans develops the implications of this intuition: "'for you are not under law, but under grace' (Rom. 6:14)" (Badiou 2003: 63). The statement indicates that grace is "neither a bequest, nor a tradition, nor a teaching," because these belong to the domain of law, which is "always predicative, particular, and partial," whereas grace is "supernumerary relative to all this and presents itself as pure givenness" (Badiou 2003: 76, 63). In consequence, the division indicated by the "not . . . but" turn of phrase occurs not *between* social, ethnic, or religious groups (the divisions with which contemporary thought has been so preoccupied, and which the trial scene in *Merchant* famously broods over), but within the subject of grace. Indeed, this division constitutes the subject.

Badiou and Levinas share with Paul (as do Derrida and Marion) the conviction that subjectivity is not, as it is for cultural historicism, socially determined: it is exactly what exceeds social determination. In other words, the subject is "no thing" other than the process through which the sheer excessiveness of grace disrupts and alters the entire field of the given – the received horizons of everyday experience, the realm of the possible. And it is this very process, born of the "suddenly emerging singularity" of grace, which founds the universal – that is, the categorical possibility for everyone of unmooring from social conditions (Badiou 2003: 36). On this account, the event of grace is *necessarily* unrelated both to the historical Jesus (whom Paul did not know) and to the Christ of ecclesiological and doctrinal history (who postdates Paul). As Badiou puts it, Jesus is "the name for what happens to us universally," and what happens is not induction into a new way of marking sectarian differences, but fidelity to what Badiou calls the "strong, simple idea that every existence can one day be seized by what happens to it and subsequently devote itself to that which is valid for all" (Badiou 2003: 60, 66).

Fidelity to the truth of a "pure event," to its charisma, may be a strong, simple idea with heroic associations beyond a couple of Shakespearean antics, but it is also a precarious one. In fact, Paul's discourse on grace insists on the contradiction: "whenever I am weak, then I am strong" (2 Cor. 12:11).[8] Strength resides in the "completely precarious having-taken-place" of the event of grace, detached from the "logic of signs and proofs," so that its "real content," its truth, will be "nothing but what each can see and hear" (Badiou 2003: 54, 53). But what can this "real content" be, since it clearly has nothing to do with empirically or logically verifiable knowledge or received opinion? The gist of Paul's argument is that what can be seen and heard is nothing – no thing – but the excess, or "charism," of the received gift, which interrupts the horizons of object-ivity, being, and constituted knowledge. As Paul says, this is the treasure held "in clay jars" (2 Cor. 4:7), in vulnerable embodiment.

Kenosis

One of the running jokes in *Merchant* has the Gobbos repeatedly stumbling across the "no thing" to which Paul's image of the treasure held in "clay jars" alludes. To get the joke, however, we must recognize that *Merchant* harbors a memory of another Pauline word for the gift's impossibility, and that the play's most challenging insights on the gift turn on the ways in which varied implications of this word are deployed. The word, from Paul's epistle to the Philippians, is *kenosis*.

> Look not every man on his own things, but every man also on the things of other men. Let the same mind be in you that was even in Christ Jesus, Who being in the form of God, thought it no robbery to be equal with God: But he made himself of no reputation [*heauton ekenosen*, "emptied himself"], and took on him the form of a servant, and was made like unto men, and was found in shape as a man. He humbled himself, and became obedient unto the death, even the death of the Cross. Wherefore God hath also highly exalted him, and given him a Name above every name.
>
> (Phil. 2:4–9)[9]

For Paul, kenosis, the gesture of self-emptying, describes the ultimate theological gift: the descent of God into human form. It also constitutes a radically selfless new ethics. The depiction of Christ's person as exalted in self-emptying discloses an altered concept of personhood, where personhood refers not to a historically determinate set of properties, but instead to an ongoing process of separation from familiar contours of identity, and consequent exposure to further, unexpected vistas of responsiveness and responsibility.[10] *The Merchant of Venice* offers its own fraught comedy of kenosis when Launcelot outrageously tells his blind father his son Launcelot has died, and then has to struggle to persuade him that he is Launcelot himself. In between, Launcelot is deprived of all the social specifics of his accustomed identity. He plummets into a condition of bare or pure personhood, from which he must renegotiate his position in the world. It is a theme Shakespeare will take up again in *King Lear*, when Edgar loses his identity as his father's son and is obliged to forge a new one out of sheer destitution.

In both cases, tragic and comic, I am arguing that the shocking appearance of the destitute human being is also a positive manifestation of human being as such, as it is given before and beyond socialization.

It is no accident that Derrida, Marion, Levinas, and Badiou should all invoke the word kenosis in their ruminations on the gift, for the event it describes – the enigmatic crossing of destitution and plenitude – speaks to their common ambition to describe the challenge to thought (whether in social, political, aesthetic, or spiritual domains) generated by the gift's impossible "no thing." With the possible exception of Marion, none of these thinkers writes from Paul's presumed Christological perspective, yet collectively they maintain the arc of Paul's thought on kenosis by testifying to the word's continuing power to evoke a generosity of vision and action, which is given body – made operative – through a counterintuitive grasp of the real.[11] Kenosis strips the social specifics of identity, to reveal that which is essentially unexplainable, unwarranted, a gift.

Merchant's investment in the thought of kenosis is closer in spirit to these thinkers than it is to the word's early modern reception. While the incarnational mystery suggested by the Philippians passage text was much rehearsed and debated in sixteenth-century Christology, contemporary English devotional cultures retained only something of the ethical intuition couched in Philippians, partly because most vernacular translations (like the text from the *Geneva Bible* cited earlier) deflected the theological conundrum of the emptying deity by emphasizing the more legible act of humility.[12] To claim that such emphasis did no more than endorse ostensibly Christ-like acquiescence to social hierarchies would be reductive, yet even modern discussions of humility – to say nothing of their early modern antecedents – are marked by a normalizing ethos that does little to indicate how the spirit of kenosis might actually undo existing social hierarchies in the service of a broader vision of sociality.[13] This, however, is the very question posed by the four philosophers we have considered. And by the Gobbos.

What's in a name?

In a classic essay on *Merchant*, Walter Cohen observes the purpose of Launcelot Gobbo's designated role as master of malapropisms: "On the one hand, his nonsense parodically demystifies; on the other, it uniquely combines archaic memories and utopian vistas" (Coyle (ed.) 1998: 60). With only slight adjustment, Cohen's assessment points up Launcelot's unique contribution to the question of the gift. Parodic demystification, archaic memories, and utopian vistas name mutually interpenetrating parts of a single constellation of wit, but the whole makes of Launcelot the unwitting vessel of a searching inquiry into the very limits of what the thought of kenosis can bear.

Consider, for starters, his two names. In "Launcelot Gobbo" the ineffable and the commonplace converge, which is to say that the name alone spells out the essential grammar of the incarnational theology housed in the Philippians passage. "Launcelot" harbors a memory of the Grail legends woven into Arthurian romance, certain strands of which read incarnational and, more pointedly, Eucharistic significance into the Grail.[14] The Arthurian Launcelot is arguably more closely linked with Guinevere than with theological speculation, but the patronymic of *Merchant's* Launcelot brings the latter question into focus. If the colloquial word "gob," conjuring a mouthful of food or stash of money, points up the ambiguity of Launcelot's social reality – is he ravenous from hunger or greed, or both? – the cognate "gobbet" raises the stakes. "Gobbet," which means "raw flesh," belongs to the reformist lexicon of slurs on the Eucharistic doctrine of transubstantiation.[15] Launcelot's name, in other words, is provocatively invested with a specifically Eucharistic variant of the incarnational question: Where is the body of Christ? As the semantics of "gob"/"gobbet" suggest, contemporary answers to the question favored the partisan logic of "either/or," claiming Christic presence to be manifested either in the sacramental bread or in the believing community.[16]

Launcelot's first malapropism, in his comically tormented effort to find moral sanction for running away from Shylock (2.2.1–25), discovers an answer literally unthinkable to religious orthodoxy, which is to say thinkable only as nonsense. He names "the Jew ... the very devil incarnation" (2.2.21–2) instead of the devil incarnate. Principally, the conjunction of "incarnation," "devil," and "the Jew" confects a garbled memory of the equation of Jews with devils in the vice tradition, where the word "incarnation" can only make sense as a mangled attempt to assert the self-evidence or sheer givenness of the equation – that which is incarnate being for all eyes to see. But Launcelot's accidental foray into incarnational theology also expresses further nuances to the questions already lodged in his name: How does the person of Christ manifest itself? What are the attributes of Christic identity?[17] By suggesting a secret proximity between Christ's kenosis and regions associated paradigmatically in Christian orthodoxy with the refusal of grace ("the fiend," "the Jew"), Launcelot's tongue, fabricator of perverse affinities, briefly – and daringly – suspends the historical and theological justifications for confessional antagonism and communitarian partisanship which are axiomatic in the play-world and in Shakespeare's culture at large. Astonishingly, Launcelot's nonsense revives or reinvents the gift of grace as that which extends universally, even to an identification with "the very devil."[18]

Fathers and sons

For all that, Launcelot's tongue is also barbed in obvious ways. The most flagrant, perhaps, appear in his several rehearsals of the play's sedimented anti-Judaism, beginning with the intended attack on Shylock just described and ending with the sobering advice he gives Jessica concerning her prospects as a viable Christian (3.5.1–21). These incidents document Launcelot's function as casual witness to the play's regnant Same/Other dichotomy. But Launcelot's nonsense consistently works to undo this structure of thought. In Launcelot's world, otherness is not simply synonymous with social or religious difference; it is what animates and sustains sameness, beyond all considerations of difference. It is the excess of the given.

Consider the joke Launcelot plays on Old Gobbo. After he sees that his "sand-blind" father has failed to recognize him, Launcelot seizes the opportunity to "try confusions," (2.2.29–30) by claiming that the son the father seeks has died. While the joke no doubt carries an edge of oedipal aggression, what should give pause is the full measure of "confusions" triggered by Gobbo's turning a blind eye, so to speak, to Launcelot's ensuing efforts to drive home the joke's punch line – to stage his resurrection, as planned, and reclaim his "true" identity as Gobbo's son. In the unsettled moments of comedy and panic before

Launcelot finds his way out of the inadvertent trap he has sprung, the thought of kenosis takes visceral shape, by reducing the objectifying force of biological and culturally legible orders of filiation. While Launcelot helplessly watches and hears Gobbo mourn the loss of his son, categories of father and son are emptied of given, normative significance in a way that is reminiscent of Badiou's reading of Paul.

What, indeed, is a father, or a son? Launcelot restores viable communication with his father only through exasperated and uncalculated proclamation of equivalent intimacy with a Jewish paternal body and a Christian maternal body : "I am Launcelot, the Jew's man, and I am sure Margery your wife is my mother" (2.2.90). The identity Launcelot seeks here owes its life to a bond and a kinship deemed, from the point of view of Christian patriarchal social order, either contingent and undesirable or relatively inconsequential. Two bodies are also summoned into a glancing type of union that would be dubious at best from the play's anthropological horizon, given its admixture of Christian triumphalism and atavistic horror at the thought of reversion from Christian to Jewish dispensations. Launcelot's "born-again" identity equalizes and dissolves salient differences between Christian and Jew, employer and employee, male and female. It is vested not just in the patriarch but also in the webbed givenness of all relationship.

Perhaps Launcelot's transient disorientation expresses an involuntary memory of Paul's use of the word "son" to mean "apostle" or messenger: the discourse of the son is the position taken up by the subject of grace who gives apostolic witness to the (Pauline) truth of the resurrection, where resurrection refers not to a biological event in defiance of the "law" of nature, but to subjective exposure to an unsought intuition of what it takes to be reborn – that is, detachment from all the social specifics we think of as the substance of our selves.[19] Accordingly, while Launcelot and Gobbo do not come to see quite the same thing, their face-to-face encounter rediscovers the thrilling ethical charge of kenosis: its capacity to disclose the transfiguring claims of the Other within the Same, a perception which undermines the legislation of social, ethnic, or confessional difference. Bereft of his conventional identity, the play's most conspicuous clown flashes for a moment with a more precious and essential kind of being. Had this enlightenment not been excluded from the play as a whole, Shylock's fate might have been very different.

Doves and more

The kenotic subtext to Launcelot's joke assumes an even wider compass in the career of the dish of doves. Leo Rockas is right to observe that the gift Gobbo carries with him appears in, and as, the play's "most inconsequential" moment (Rockas 1973: 348). As we found in my initial review of Gobbo's gift, it is perhaps best thought of as a vanishing event, where diverse intuitions of gift-giving cross each other without coalescing into a stable entity. Pre-eminent among these are the gospel accounts of the revelation at the baptism of Jesus, where the "Spirit of God" descends from the heavens in the form of a dove, while the voice of the Father identifies Jesus as the "beloved Son" (Matt 3:16–17).[20] Given the specific trajectory of Gobbo's gift, doves carry collateral significance as metonyms of the anti-Judaizing edge to the gospel accounts of Jesus's repudiation of Second Temple sacrificial practices: the over-turning of the money changers' tables and the "seats of those who sold doves" (Mark 11:15).[21] What is overturned in *Merchant*, as noted earlier, is Gobbo's intention to give the doves to Shylock. Launcelot substitutes Bassanio for Shylock, voicing the hope that his prospects for hire by a new, Christian master will be enhanced by the grace note of a gift.

It is easy enough to see in the substitution the elemental figure of the play's ambivalent narrative of Christian triumphal-ism, whereby the Jewish body is both expelled from and incorporated into the Christian fold. But the play's triumphalist gesture is not everything. In this case, its alignment with Launcelot's caprice shows more than the play can say. What remains unsaid is the spirit of Gobbo's gift. It would be tempting to say that what Gobbo offers is the gift of simple kindness. But kindness is rarely simple, not least because it translates readily into liberal humanist complacency. So, rather than calling it simple, let's call it impossible. The spirit of Gobbo's gift is the impossible thought of unconditioned giving. It is a thought harbored by Christian *agape* – Paul's word for the animating power of love – and by *agape*'s parent, the Levitical instructions to love the neighbor as well as oneself. Without question, this thought can be construed merely as an index of social interest in the symbolic capital to be accrued by gift-giving (this is the anthropological argument on behalf of reciprocity), or as symptom of the mystifying subtleties of Christianity's supersessionist ambition (consider the manifold ironies of Portia's legal discourse on mercy). But it is irreducible to these prescriptive imperatives.

One detail conveys the point. From where Gobbo stands, the dish of doves is no more and no less of a gift for Bassanio than it would have been for Shylock. Nominally, Gobbo's "suit" (2.2.121) is to appease Launcelot's master, whoever he may be. But Launcelot's confused tongue – calling the suit "impertinent" (2.2.122) instead of "pertinent" – discerns the truth of the matter. As Bassanio indicates, the suit is indeed impertinent, because Shylock and Bassanio have already worked out the details of the transaction. The intended suit shears off from the gift, and with it goes the determinative character of the master–servant bond. The dish of doves fades from view, but not before its self-evident fields of reference – the master–servant bond, as well as the confessional and social differences known as "Christian" and "Jew" – have been vacated, if only for a moment. In that moment flickers the mystery of giving – not as servants currying favor with their master, not as Christians mollifying a superior Jew, but *for its own sake*. The dish of doves, still visible as object but only uncertainly so as gift, expresses the precarious proximity of Derrida's and Marion's opposing views of the gift's impossible surplus. Is the dish no more than a standing but strangely empty promise of the gift, as Derrida might say? Does its identity as gift thoroughly saturate its material form to the effect that it is indistinguishable from it, as Marion would have it? Each prospect sees a future worth striving toward, the former by holding fast to the thought that its advent is not here, not yet, and the latter by soundlessly descending into what is already at hand, needing only the further impulse of grace (Paul's "not . . . but") to be revealed and declared. *Merchant* does not, perhaps cannot, choose between the two. Indeed, it is precisely the indeterminacy of the dish of doves that enables it to disclose the gift's excess as a "no thing" charged with eschatological and ecumenical desire: the possibility of impossibility.

The prickly exchange between Launcelot and Lorenzo in Act 3 ventures even further into this domain. Jessica has just repeated to her husband the lesson Launcelot has taught her: that their marriage is anathema in every imaginable way. Lorenzo's attempt to chastise the meddlesome servant takes the form of a reminder that Launcelot has trespassed the bounds of propriety and decency by consorting with the Moor and, through "the getting up of the Negro's belly" (3.5.32), giving body to the specter of miscegenation. Launcelot's laughing reply to the accusation: "It is much that the Moor should be more than reason; but if she be less than an honest woman, she is indeed more than I took her for" (3.5.34–6).

The aim of recent commentaries on the pun has been to quarry the ideological ironies of Launcelot's quibble on "Moor" and "more," as in Kim Hall's reading of the manner in which the quibble exacerbates rather than neutralizes the cultural anxieties driving the accusation. On this account, Launcelot's pun conjures the "image of the black woman as both consuming and expanding" (Coyle (ed.) 1998: 97). The depicted intimacy of these contrasting actions says more about the unresolved contradictions informing the triumphalist narrative, whether Christian or colonialist, than Lorenzo can bear to listen to. The Moor's pregnant body promises "not resolution, but the potential disruption of Europe's imperial text, because in *Merchant*'s Venice – and Elizabeth's England – the possibility of wealth only exists within the dangers of cultural exchange" (Coyle (ed.) 1998: 110).

Though compelling, this approach maintains the figural scope of the Moor's body under the material conditions of the triumphalist gaze and its structural antagonisms. On these grounds, the conclusion that the "possibility of wealth only exists within the dangers of cultural exchange" would likely see its theoretical endgame in the anthropological emphasis on reciprocity as the key to the gift. Which is to say that it would *not* likely push the question of "cultural exchange" into the phenomenological hinterlands of "possibility" and "wealth" all too often discounted by materialist critical practice.

Yet Launcelot's pun invites just such an excursion. The proposed consanguinity of "Moor" and "more" recognizes more than the perturbation to the Venetian state caused by the visible sight of the Moor's pregnant body. Playing on the extensive mental and interlocutory exercise of the adjective "pregnant" in the early modern lexicon (quickness of wit, imaginative resourcefulness, and sheer receptivity), Launcelot's pun figures the nature of his personal relation to the Moor as well. The "more" factor conjures up the capacity of interpersonal relations to be aerated by the excess, or charism, of a "no thing." In other words, the pun proposes that the ultimate paradigm of the excluded relation in Venice carries particular evidence of the gift's impossibility. The pun remembers the "face," the irreducibly personal singularity, of the unnamed Moor.

The pun also reminds us of the profound kinship between the Levinasian face, Marion's saturated phenomenon, and the grammar of kenosis, which transfigures the shape of the real by emptying the given of its familiar horizons so as to uncover the plenitude and infinity of "no thing." Where least expected, in Launcelot's scorned sexual relations with "the Moor," Shakespeare's text recognizes that eschatological desire does not concern a distant utopian vista, but rather the present, active "work of love."[22]

And it recognizes in such work the presence of the Eucharist. This is not the Eucharist of theological debate and liturgical practice, and it is owned by no particular religious denomination or tradition. It is not owned, period. It is found in the genuinely radical implication of kenosis, which is the thought that the Other and the Same subsist in a profound though precarious intimacy, within each social group, each particularity, and each person. The name for this intimacy is the universal: the "no thing" that is given to all and that makes possible, universally, a transfigured perception of the real, outside the bounds of what can be incorporated or manipulated as knowledge.

From this perspective, it is no accident that the exchange between Lorenzo and Launcelot concludes with a comic Eucharistic allusion: they reconcile by quibbling over the proper way to "prepare for dinner" (3.5.46). In *Merchant*'s Venice, where the question of hunger is never far from the question of excess, whether gourmandizing or cannibalizing, the banter touches more than one nerve. Transposed to matters of state polity, the essential question raised by the banter is this: can all, without exception, receive the spirit of the gift? The question gives way to the trial scene's revelation of the impossible literalism of the pound of flesh, and to the ensuing disavowals of the universality of that revelation. Hence the partisan force of the "difference" the Duke shows in the Christian's "spirit" (4.1.363), by commuting Shylock's death sentence while making the pardon contingent on the exchange of Antonio's pound of flesh for Shylock's forced conversion and the Venetian state's de facto extortion of the deed of gift.

Yet in Act 3, before dinner is served, Launcelot's quibbling art once again, and for one last time, sees past the seductions of the play's historical and anthropological horizons and the differences these horizons insist upon to articulate their domains of knowledge. "Prepare," he insists, is not quite the right word; "'cover' is the word" (3.5.44). "Cover" is the word because it allows Launcelot to disclose several different senses in which to prepare for dinner: setting the table, wearing proper head-gear, keeping meat warm before dinner is served. But "cover" is also exactly the right word in the sense that it suggests the play of concealment and disclosure whereby the spirit or excess of the Eucharist – the spirit of the gift – makes itself felt through the material "accidents" of a communal meal, of supper, of bread and wine. "Cover" knows the substance of what it means to be brought to the table and to eat. It knows that what is substantial sustains and turns on what is unapparent in embodiment, and given unconditionally.

That such insight in *Merchant* remains for the most part "covered" in a further sense – isolated from the principal concerns of the plot – indicates the particular historical and cultural circumstances which both shape and limit the play's field of vision. Not least among these is the emergent logic of the mercantile spirit, which partly accounts for the ease with which Antonio, at play's end, equates "life" with "living" in giving thanks for the unexpected bounty of the returned argosies, just as Lorenzo, moments later, sees "manna" in the deed of gift's promise of solvency (5.1.284–5, 293). The equivalencies drawn by Antonio and Lorenzo pre-emptively cast the spirit of the gift in material and measurable terms. But it cannot be said that their seemingly instinctive interpretive preference is confined to Shakespeare's early modern location.

The meat on Lorenzo's table is still covered.

Notes

1 I refer to Newman's second version of this essay (Newman 1996). The earlier appeared in *Shakespeare Quarterly*: 38 (1987): 19–33.

2 See the concise account of these issues in Horner 2001: 12–14.

3 A helpful review of the central preoccupations of phenomenology's key figures, Edmund Husserl and Martin Heidegger, is in Horner 2001: 19–44.

4 From this vantage point, *Merchant* speaks to a pressing question in our current epoch of globalization: whether intuitions of the "spirit" of the gift can be meaningfully translated across specific cultural and confessional traditions without being converted into instruments of a hegemonic drive toward mere uniformity (as the "spirit" of capital would suggest, for example).

5 For an argument that advances interests broadly sympathetic to mine, though different in focus, see Jackson 2001. Jackson brilliantly traces the secret affinity between Derrida's aporia of the gift, as shaped by Derrida's readings of Søren Kierkegaard and Jan Patočka in *The Gift of Death* (see Derrida 1995b), and the crisis of gift-giving in *Timon of Athens*.

6 Derrida recurrently identifies the gift's excess with what he calls *khora*, one of his favorite names for the "absolutely universal place" (or, more accurately, non-place) that comes before all distinctions between presence and absence (Caputo and Scanlon 1999: 76).

7 Derrida, to be sure, is not alone in questioning the "theological turn" in phenomenology. See Janicaud, *et al.* (2000). An impressive, and more sympathetic, review of the issues is in Horner (2001).

8 Unless otherwise indicated, biblical citations are from the NRSV, Metzger and Murphy (1994).

9 *Geneva Bible* (1599 ed.) at http://www.genevabible.org/Geneva.html (28 June 2004).

10 The word's currency in contemporary philosophy is directly related to the word's position as matrix of thought in the history of incarnational, Trinitarian, and Eucharistic theologies, to say nothing of the concept's deployment in the grammar of sublation in Hegelian dialectic, and its genetic link to "death of God" a-theologies in modernity. Lucid accounts of these developments are in Coakley 1996, Ward 1998, and Ward 1999.

11 Representative examples of each thinker's use of the image of kenosis are in Derrida 1995a: 50; Marion 2004: 62, 78; Levinas 1994: 114–15, 126; Levinas 1998: 53–5; and Badiou 2003: 110.

12 The 1582 Rheims New Testament tries to preserve the theological notion of emptying through the use of a neologism concocted from the Latin term for kenosis in the Vulgate. Thus Phil. 2:8 reads "He exinanited himself."

13 Important contributions to the debate within feminist theology over the relative merits of an ethics of humility are in Hampson 1996,

and Frascati-Lochhead 1998: 149–209. Levinas' remarks on the relation between kenosis and humility are relevant here (Levinas 1998: 53–60).

14 Loomis 1991: 28–9, 60–1.

15 *OED*, "gob," n. 1.2, "A large sum of money"; n. 1.3a, "A lump or large mouthful of food"; "gobbet" n. 1b, "A piece of raw flesh." A secondary sense, from the Italian "gobbo," suggests the hunchback's deformity. *OED* "gobbet" n. 1b, "A piece of raw flesh." Famously, in the den of Errour, Spenser's Redcrosse Knight discovers the monstrous figure of Errour spewing poison "Full of great lumps of flesh and gobbets raw" (Spenser 1977 1.1.20). For a discussion of the scene's Eucharistic argument, see Gregerson 1995: 96.

16 The presiding force of such logic partly explains why the central antagonism in *Merchant* (Shylock vs. Antonio) has lent itself to a double reading, as reflection of the historical division between Jewish and Christian orthodoxies and as symptom of further divisions within the Christian church wrought by Reformation controversies over the nature of the Eucharist. A helpful account of the fundamental issues in Eucharistic debates, from patristic culture to modernity, is in Milbank 2003: 122–37.

17 For a lucid account of the theological range to these questions in Christian discourse on kenosis, see Coakley 1996.

18 The well-known prohibitions of sacramental and theological representation on the early modern English stage virtually guarantee that *Merchant's* investment in theological argument will be oblique. The more germane point, however, is that the factor of obliqueness also enables the play's turn from historical horizons to phenomenological intuitions of the "no thing" which kenotic theologies contemplate as well.

19 See Badiou 2003: 42–5.

20 Further gospel proof-texts: Mark 1:9–11, Luke 3:21–2, John 1:31–4. While the Trinitarian implications of Gobbo's dish of doves do not rise to the level of theological argument in the play, the Trinitarian element suggests how the idea of *thirdness* marries well with the gift's impossible surplus. Thirdness is what disrupts the closed field or restricted economy of binary relations. An account of the important relation between Trinitarian theology and kenosis is in Ward 1998. On a different register, Salerio's impatient and cynical mention of the erotic caprice of "Venus' pigeons" (2.6.5) reasserts the fragility, if not the aporia, of the gift, transposed to the lexicon of humanist mythography.

21 See also Mark 11:15, John 2:13–16.

22 Žižek 2000b: 129–30.

4

'Salving the mail'
Perjury, grace and the disorder of things in *Love's Labour's Lost*
Philippa Berry

I

Often described as Shakespeare's most courtly but also most obscure play, *Love's Labour's Lost* is much preoccupied with the riddling word-games that appear to have been fashionable at the Elizabethan court in its last decade. The comedy's explicit posing of textual 'enigmas' has famously prompted several critics to pillage it in search of secrets, in the form of allegorical references to contemporary aristocrats as well as writers and thinkers; since the 1970s, however, it is the secondary meanings that appear to be secreted in the text's wordplay that have attracted most critical attention. In its focus upon the play's evident interest in the affinity between the materiality of signification and bodily desire, my chapter owes an important debt to the latter kind of study, in particular to Patrica Parker's essay, 'Preposterous Reversals' (Parker 1993). But in the specific context of this collection, my aim is to foreground how Shakespeare's 'pleasant conceited Comedie' (as it is described in the quarto of 1598) invites us to look beyond its self-conscious staging of solipsistic word-games, together with the amorous courtships undertaken by its love-struck male characters, and to reflect upon what kind of 'end', natural or unnatural, may follow or come after 'the posterior' or latter end of man's brief play-time.

Biron confirms in Act 5 that 'Our wooing doth not end like an old play./Jack hath not Jill' (5.2.851–2). And in its obstruction of the lords' quest for erotic gratification, the play's closing deferral of comedic resolution also emphasises the ambiguous affinity between the ostensibly different 'ends' of sexuality and mortality. At the start of the play, significantly, it is a mortal 'end', rather than sexual consummation, that is anticipated by Navarre in his appeal to his male courtiers to join him in studious seclusion: 'Let fame, that all hunt after in their lives,/ Live registered upon our brazen tombs,/And then grace us in the disgrace of death' (1.1.1–3). Navarre evokes a tomb that he aspires to have posthumously dignified by a 'registered', textually recorded form of 'grace': specifically, that of intellectual fame. But this is a worldly 'grace' whose value the plot of *Love's Labour's Lost* explicitly questions, in part through insistent repetition of the word. In its concluding act, the shallowness of the lords' language-games is exposed as 'maggot ostentation' (5.2.409), while the inherent corruption of scholarly memory that converts the 'registered' fame of dead heroes to unintentional comedy is emphasised by the concluding pageant of the Nine Worthies.

Parker has brilliantly explicated the sexual and scatological implications of the 'preposterous' trope of coming after that is introduced in the first scene of the play (Parker 1993). Yet in reconsidering the comedy's implicit question of what kind of grace may follow man's surrender to 'sin' (here associated with a breaking of oaths due to erotic desire), I read the play as intertwining the comedic motif of courtship with a distinctive dimension of sacrality.[1] And my contention is that the self-referential materiality of Shakespeare's play-text is imbricated with a riddling and distinctly heterodox meditation upon the grace and salvation that may – or may not – follow man's mortal 'end'. In this respect *Love's Labour's Lost* can be read as anticipating or achronically intersecting with late modern or postmodern meditations upon subjectivity – as a being-in-the-world that discovers, in the very materiality of that experience, an opening to non-human modes of alterity. In anticipation of thinkers who have written in the wake of phenomenology, the play substitutes for the abstract study proposed in its opening scene a different, phenomenal or 'natural' model of knowledge, allied to both desire and death. In this 'end of study' the putative stability and singularity of the human is unsettled – stirred or 'keeled', like the 'pot' evoked in the final song of Hiems – through a fuller engagement with the mutability of the phenomenal world, and specifically, with what Michel Foucault identified as the order of things.[2] This redefinition of courtly grace through talking 'greasily' (4.1.133), or with bawdy wordplay, undoes the seeming oppositions of courtly and non-courtly, grace and grease, cerebral and bodily, salvation and sin.

The exaggerated self-referentiality of this early comedy has a notably metadramatic dimension, expressed not simply in the form of the courtly and rustic entertainments that are staged in the last act of the play, but also in the play's striking preoccupation with using texts as props. The circulation of multiple texts within the plot draws insistent attention to the work's status as a play-*text*. These textual props include a written 'schedule', the petition presented to the King by the Princess, numerous love-letters, Nathaniel's 'table-book' or commonplace book, and the 'paper' that is the script for the pageant of the Nine Worthies. Yet the simultaneous substantiality and mobility of words in this play, which attests to their implication in the mutable world of material things, is given further emphasis by the figurative imbrication of these textual props within an extensive network of other material or non-human objects. Here it is the disorder of things that reveals the limitations of 'taffeta phrases' (5.2.406). For like the misdirected letters of Biron and Don Armado, each of these things – plants, animals, birds, coins and favours, ointments, shields and scutcheons, and textiles including smocks and shirts – has a mobile, and sometimes even an uncanny, potency. And as a nexus of puns reveals, and briefly elides, the porosity not just of bodies but also of things, the oscillating significance of the play's cluster of inorganic and organic objects produces meanings that are both material and suggestively metaphysical. The phenomenologist Martin Heidegger called for 'the step back from the thinking that merely represents – that is, explains – [things] to the thinking that responds and recalls', declaring in a riddling idiom of his own that as 'the thing things world', and we know its 'nearness', then 'earth and heaven', 'divinities and mortals' are no longer experienced as separate, but as joined (Heidegger 1971: 181). Heidegger coined the term a 'gathering' for the expanded significance that can inform the things that touch us, and through which we are touched, not simply by others, but by the difference of the inorganic, of the everyday world.

To Biron's question in the first scene – 'What is the end of study, let me know?' – the King replies, 'Why, that to know which else we should not know'. Biron explicates and supplements this definition with '*Things* hid and barred, you mean, from *common sense*?' (1.1.55–7, my emphasis). A decade or so after the publication of *Love's Labour's Lost*, in the works of seventeenth-century philosophers such as René Descartes and Sir Francis Bacon, a reassertion of the distinction between matter and human intellection was posited as the key to a new order of knowledge. Both these writers placed particular emphasis upon the objective empirical truths afforded by 'things'. Of his opposition between *res extensa*, raw matter, and *res cogitans*, thinking substance, Descartes comments that 'there being only one truth of each thing whoever finds it knows as much about it as can be known about it' (cited in Benjamin 1993: 54). But in the cultural ferment of the 1590s, when the accelerating expansion of English commodity-culture was being paralleled by the equally rapid augmentation of the English vernacular, the excessive and often grotesque rhetoric of authors such as Thomas Nashe and Gabriel Harvey was stimulating a vogue for literary interrogations of the curious effects of things – or objects – upon human subjects. In establishing strange affinities between humans and 'things', the literary texts of the 1590s appear to anticipate a strikingly anti-Cartesian comment by Blaise Pascal, in which complex variety is seen as a property common both to the human soul and to 'things': 'Things have diverse qualities, and the soul diverse inclinations, for nothing of that which is offered to the soul is simple and the soul never offers anything simple to any subject' (cited in Benjamin 1993: 75).

In its comedy of mistaken props, *Love's Labour's Lost* can be read as affording an interesting parallel to the chiasmic reciprocity of Pascal's notion of the soul as a thing and the thing as soul-like. In the simple yet shrewd mind of the rustic Costard, the Spanish knight Don Armado's letter to Jaquenetta becomes a 'mail' (3.1.63); this was a bag in which ointment was carried by a 'quacksalver', but the word also homophonically evokes the amorous male. In the imagination of Biron, woman is like a German clock 'never going aright' (3.1.175–6), and the dark Rosaline is also compared to ebony – 'O wood divine!' (4.3.244). In the concluding courtship scene, when the masquerading Lords have been condemned as perjurers once again by the ladies' misplacing of their favours, Biron imagines his 'silken terms precise' as a luxurious range of fabrics that have corrupted his core humanity, like maggots breeding in the wool of sheep:

> Taffeta phrases, silken terms precise,
> Three-piled hyperboles, spruce affectation,
> Figures pedantical – these summer flies
> Have blown me full of maggot ostentation.
> I do forswear them, and I here protest,
> By this white glove – how white the hand, God
>   knows! –
> Henceforth my wooing mind shall be expressed
> In russet yeas and honest kersey noes.
>   (5.2.406–13)

A few lines later, Biron warns the mercurial Boyet, who has mocked their page, 'Die when you will, a smock shall be your shroud' (5.2.479). And this motif of repentance or purgation as a return to the simple things and materials that denote our bare humanity reappears at the end of the pageant of the Nine Worthies, when Costard wants to fight Armado in his 'shirt', only to find that Armado has no shirt at all.

The timeliness of redirecting critical attention to the materiality of objects within Renaissance culture, and simultaneously of beginning to articulate new relations between subjects and objects, was emphasised in *Subject and Object in Renaissance Culture*, edited by Margreta de Grazia, Maureen Quilligan and Peter Stallybrass. In their introduction to this volume the editors suggest that:

> Reading 'ob' as 'before' allows us to assign the object a prior status, suggesting its temporal, spatial and even causal *coming before* . . . So defined, the term renders more apparent

the way material things – land, clothes, tools – might constitute subjects who in turn own, use, and transform them. The form/matter relation of Aristotelian metaphysics is thereby provisionally reversed: it is the material object that impresses its texture and contour upon the noumenal subject. And this reversal is curiously upheld by the ambiguity of the word 'sub-ject', that which is *thrown under*, in this case – in order to receive an imprint.

(de Grazia *et al.* 1996: 5)

However, my reading of Shakespeare's paronomastic exploration of things, and of the human's relations both to and through them, differs from that of these critics in its emphasis, first, upon the perceived mutability of things (not simply as props, but also as imagined and reconfigured solely by language); and second, upon the subtle, implicitly uncanny and even soul-related, effects that are attributed to the supplementary slipperiness – or the 'greasiness' – of these mutable objects, as they reveal hidden flaws in the human subject.

In the mid-nineteenth century, Karl Marx wrote of the 'mystical' character and the strangely spectral secrecy of the commodity-form, which Jacques Derrida redescribed as 'it ghosts' (*Es spukt*) (Derrida 1994: ch. 5). In *Love's Labour's Lost*, the uncanny affinity of things with a 'ghostly' set of meanings that can affect man's spiritual destiny is indicated from the very start of the play, when the 'schedule' signed by the King and his lords allies literary signification (both writing and the 'study' of books) with a spiritual version of legality: this is the quasi-monastic oath of three years' celibate study that is taken by the group. Subsequently, each of the numerous texts embedded within the play emphasises the affinity between the textual attempt to fix meaning and some form of vow, debt or obligation that results in deviation or transgression. Like the love-letters on the one hand or Armado's missing shirt on the other, the play's interest in the recurrent errancy of trivial 'things' exposes a 'naked' human fallibility that does not merit grace, but hopes for it none the less. So Armado finally admits: 'The naked truth of it is, I have no shirt. I go woolward for penance' (5.2.694–5).

In the first scene of the play, Biron voices his scepticism about the four noblemen's heroic pledge to oppose 'the huge army of the world's desires' by studying in Navarre's 'little academe' (1.1.10, 13): 'For every man with his affects is born,/ Not by might mastered, but by special grace' (1.1.149–50). As a result of their rapid enslavement to erotic desire, neither Navarre and his companions, nor Costard or Armado, are able to keep this oath even for a day. In consequence of their perjured oaths – but also because of their gracelessness in the arts of amorous courtship – the lords gradually discovery their mistaken relationship to both words and things, as they admit to needing 'some salve for perjury' (4.3.284). It quickly becomes clear, therefore, that the entire community lacks Biron's 'special grace', which plausibly alludes to the Calvinist conception of 'particular' grace, or election. The European and implicitly Catholic character of this all-male community (especially given its quasi-monastic character) appears thereby to be highlighted.[3] But in spite of its seeming topical reference to the recent conversion to Catholicism (in 1593) of the French king, Henri IV (formerly King of Navarre), the comedy cannot simply be read as a critique of Catholicism. The play's structural opposition between 'his grace' and 'her grace' – that is, between the King of Navarre's entourage and that of the Princess of France, who ends the play as 'Queen' – accords figurative and material shape to a heterodox mode of grace, natural as well as supernatural, whose supplementary (Marian?) character seems far more Catholic than Protestant, as does its metonymic association with the play's female characters.

On her first entrance to sue for the restoration of Aquitaine, Boyet praises the Princess of France as a repository not just of all the graces (in a reference to the female Graces of classical culture) but of a 'dear grace' that is apparently unique. Yet he appeals to her to bestow this grace 'prodigally', or lavishly:

> Be now as prodigal of all dear grace
> As nature was in making graces dear
> When she did starve the general world beside
> And prodigally gave them all to you.
>
> (2.1.9–12)

Christ as the word of God was defined by St Paul as the free gift of love that suspends the (letter of the) law of divine judgement:

In that yee are manifest, to be the Epistle of Christ,
ministred by vs, and written, not with yncke, but with the
Spirite of the liuing God, not in tables of stone, but in
fleshly tables of the heart. And such trust haue we through
Christ to God: Not that we are sufficient of our selues, to
thinke any thing, as of our selues: but our sufficiencie is of
God, Who also hath made vs able ministers of the Newe
testament, not of the letter, but of the Spirite: for the letter
killeth, but the Spirite giueth life.

(2 Cor.3: 3–6)[4]

In *Love's Labour's Lost*, however, it is a feminised and sexualised
model of grace that initiates the revelatory process which shows
the limitations both of the men's law and of their letters, and
ends by imposing a different law upon them.

II

The complicated relationship between textuality and different
forms and temporal contexts of 'salving', or healing, is a
dominant, albeit puzzling, trope in the comedy's central scene
and act. Here a sequence of cryptic puns seems to foreground
a textualised as well as sexualised form of supplementary grace:
this is evoked by the rustic Costard's enigmatic allusion to 'no
salve in the mail' (3.1.63), which anticipates the Lords' desire
for 'some salve for perjury' after the breaking of their oaths.
In this riddling exchange between Costard (identified in the
play-text as either a swain or a clown), the 'man of fire-new
words' (1.1.176), Armado, and his page Mote, masculine subjectivity is troped as wounded or fallen – as 'broken in a s[h]in'
(3.1.61), but also as much preoccupied with an ambivalent
conception of end(s). Although a lowly 'swain', Costard carries
a heavy weight of allegorical significance in this play, since his
name was not only the slang term for a 'head' but also signified a rib as well as an apple. Thus not only does he appear
to personify man's Adamic nature on the point of a sexual fall
(in the production of Eve from his rib and the temptation by
the apple); Costard also parodies the intellectual pretensions
that make Navarre and his courtier-scholars liable to a second

fall. Through interlingual punning, the central scene equates a love-letter with a medical salve, via the Latin for a greeting, 'salve'. But Costard's assertion that there is 'no salve in the mail' initiates a witty discussion about the beginnings and endings of texts that seems to pose a question about appropriate healing for the soul as well as for the body. Mistakenly identified by Costard with a 'l'envoi' – part of a literary text that comes not before but after – his 'salve' initiates a meditation upon endings that concludes by alluding to concepts of 'purgation', 'enfreedoming' and 'remuneration' which have an obvious spiritual as well as a bodily and sexual implication.

The pivotal passage begins some 70 lines into Act 3, when Mote enters with Costard, who is to be an 'envoi' or messenger for Armado. Costard has been apprehended in the opening scene of the play for 'following' the country wench, Jaquenetta. Now he is in a physically and emotionally distressed state, seemingly because of his love for the same wench to whom Armado is sending his love-letter:

Mote   A wonder, master! Here's a costard broken in a shin.
Armado   Some enigma, some riddle; Come, thy *l'envoi*. Begin.
Costard   No egma, no riddle, no *l'envoi*, no salve in the mail, sir. O, sir, plantain, a plain plantain! No *l'envoi*, no *l'envoi*, no salve, sir, but a plantain!
Armado   By virtue, thou enforcest laughter – thy silly thought my spleen. The heaving of my lungs provokes me to ridiculous smiling. O, pardon me, my stars! Doth the inconsiderate take salve for *l'envoi* and the word '*l'envoi*' for a salve?
Mote   Do the wise think them other? Is not *l'envoi* a salve?
Armado   No, page, it is an epilogue or discourse to make plain Some obscure precedence that hath tofore been sain.
I will example it:
    The fox, the ape and the humble-bee
    Were still at odds, being but three.
There's the moral. Now the *l'envoi*.
Mote   I will add the *l'envoi*. Say the moral again.
Armado
    The fox, the ape and the humble-bee
    Were still at odds, being but three.

Mote

    Until the goose came out of door,
    And stayed the odds by adding four.

. . .

    A good *envoi*, ending in the goose. Would you desire more?
Costard The boy hath sold him a bargain, a goose, that's flat.
    Sir, your pennyworth is good an your goose be fat.
    To sell a bargain well is as cunning as fast and loose.
    Let me see: a fat *l'envoi* – ay, that's a fat goose.
Armado Come hither, come hither. How did this argument
    begin?
Mote By saying that a costard was broken in a shin.
    Then called you for the *l'envoi*.
Costard True, and I for a plantain: thus came your argument
    in. Then the boy's fat *l'envoi*, the goose that you bought,
    and he ended the market.
Armado But tell me, how was there a costard broken in a shin?
Mote I will tell you sensibly.
Costard Thou hast no feeling of it, Mote. I will speak that
    l'envoi.
    I, Costard, running out, that was safely within,
    Fell over the threshold, and broke my shin.
Armado We will talk no more of this matter.
Costard Till there be more matter in the shin.
Armado Sirrah Costard, I will enfranchise thee.
Costard O, marry me to one Frances! I smell some *l'envoi*,
    some goose in this.
Armado By my sweet soul, I mean setting thee at liberty, enfree-
    doming thy person. Thou wert immured, restrained,
    captivated, bound.
Costard True, true, and now you will be my purgation, and
    let me loose.

                              (3.1.61–116)

    In this intricate allusion to the ways in which texts aspire
to touch upon the most intimate of bodily matters, Costard
makes overt reference to different kinds of medical as well as
literary innovation. His initial mishearing of the word '*l'envoi*',
in conjunction with the Greek *enigma*, converts an artful literary
device into a 'salve in the mail'. Possibly misunderstanding
'enigma' as another Greek word, *enema*, Costard may also

mishear '*l'envoi*' as 'lenify', a verb first imported from Latin in 1568.[5] The word alludes to the softening or mitigation of a physical condition, often through the application of a purgative substance that lenifies or softens, and that is applied inwardly or outwardly as a lenitive or 'salve'. Thus a literary greeting at the text's end is converted, through the pun on *salve* (Latin for 'hello'), into an ointment carried in a bag or 'mail' by a 'quacksalver' or mountebank, whose basic constituent would be grease, and which could be applied inside the body, in the form of a clyster or enema, or externally, to a wound.[6] Salves could be made from a single herb or 'simple', but in the Paracelsan or 'chemical' medicine that was then the subject of fierce debate, they were typically prepared from chemical compounds.[7] It is this practice that Costard initially rejects when he calls instead for 'a plain plantain'; this herbal remedy for bruising may also connote that Costard wants a 'plain', or sexual, treatment for his ambiguous 'broken shin'.[8]

But the wordplay in this scene also draws our attention to the self-referentiality of *Love's Labour's Lost*, through its use of the literary device of the *envoi* or *tornada*. Derived both from the Italian *canzone* and from French troubadour verse, the *envoi* was enjoying renewed popularity in English verse of the mid-1590s, where it was appropriated by learned poets such as Edmund Spenser and George Chapman as well as by Gabriel Harvey and Thomas Nashe. Equated with the closing lines or final stanza of a poem, the *envoi* was a literary device through which the poet, in turning inwards and self-consciously commenting upon his text, could also speak directly to his addressee or to other poets. This conflation of inside and outside, text and recipient, figuratively anticipated the process of the poem's transmission in the world, and thus the question of literary ends.[9] In Shakespeare's text, however, the structural singularity of the *envoi* is significantly multiplied. Not only does an *envoi* make a paradoxical appearance in the middle of the play-text (albeit at the end of the witty exchange), as the last two lines of a brief beast-fable involving fox, ape, 'humble-bee' and 'ending in the goose'; a doubled *envoi* is also used to end the play, in the two songs of the owl and cuckoo. At both junctures, a human 'envoi' or messenger is used to personify and implicitly to comment upon the literary *envoi*'s meaning.

In Act 3 Costard is eventually reconciled to '*l'envoi*' as the witty completion of an act of communication, along with the mysteriously material and greasy benefits – 'remuneration' – that are seemingly encoded in and attendant upon it: 'Let me see: a fat *l'envoi* – ay, that's a fat goose'. The interlingual pun on the '*oi*' ending of '*l'envoi*' alludes to the French word for goose, *oie*, in seeming reference to the male's 'end' or objective of obtaining sexual favours in the form of a greasy greeting or reception from a 'fat goose' – a fertile or sexually available woman. Goose grease was frequently used in the preparation of salves, but was also commonly used to lubricate bodily orifices (whether vaginal or anal) for sexual intercourse. Armado's '*l'envoi*' 'ending in the goose' may additionally pun on the Latin for goose, *anser*, since 'goose' is the *answer* to his riddle. (Indeed, when Armado's letter is delivered to the Princess' entourage after it has been mistakenly substituted for that of Biron, its feathery metamorphosis is completed, since it is received as a 'capon' whose 'neck' or seal must be broken and which must be carved in order to be read (4.1.56–9).)

Like the greasiness of the 'fat goose', the capacity of salves, plasters, or enemas to be externally or internally applied to the human body depended primarily upon their greasy contents. And in its additional play upon the release of secret 'matters', as discharges or secretions, from the greasy ends of humans as well as things, this central scene reconfigures the materiality of everydayness, investing it not simply with a shifting, multi-faceted character, but also with a suggestive dimension of hiddenness that may imply pollution, given the possible allusion to syphilis in 'goose' and 'shin'.[10] Indeed, the wordplay in Act 3 seems also, more ambitiously, to be reopening – or tenting – a painful and highly contemporary set of spiritual wounds, in an allusion to theological concerns about the relative merits of Calvinist theories of special grace or predestination versus Catholic concepts of penance and purgation. Although the precise date of *Love's Labour's Lost* is not certain, it now seems likely to have been written after 1594, in a period when Shakespeare was to quibble explicitly on the doubtfulness of grace as 'prologue', when Falstaff comments to Hal in *1 Henry IV* that 'grace thou wilt have none . . . not so much as will serve to be prologue to an egg and butter' (1.2.15–18).

In the Lambeth articles of 1595, the Church of England had adopted strict Calvinist doctrine on election and 'absolute predestination'. But during this decade predestination was also beginning to be vocally challenged by anti-Calvinist divines who anticipated Arminianism in arguing for universal grace.[11] On the other hand, among Elizabethan Catholics belief survived in grace, not as prologue, but as epilogue to man's life, in doctrines of the efficacy of penance, Purgatory and the merciful intercession of the saints – above all, in the intercession of the Blessed Virgin. Eamon Duffy observes:

> The Mother of Mercy was one of Mary's most resonant medieval titles, unforgettably carved, painted or engraved, extending her sheltering cloak over the suppliant faithful and enshrined in the most haunting of Marian prayers, the 'Salve Regina'. All over Europe the singing of the 'Salve' each night after Compline had become a popular devotion, and English testators left bequests for lights, incense, and musical accompaniment to dignify this most tender of tributes to the Virgin Mary.
>
> (Duffy 1992: 264)

Invoked in the 'Salve Maria' or 'Hail Mary' that begins the rosary prayers, Mary was also greeted at the end of the rosary prayers with an especial 'l'envoi', a recitation of the antiphon of the 'Salve Regina', which appealed to Mary as a holy queen. Like use of the rosary, the singing of the 'Salve Regina' and all other traces of the cult of the Virgin Mary had been banned by Archbishop Cranmer in 1547.

By inviting us to anticipate a 'salve' that is not a 'salve' – a greeting that paradoxically comes at the end, and that is both like and unlike a healing ointment, the comedy connects erotic courtship with man's quest for salvation, in a heterodox meditation upon the temporality of grace and the possible destination of the soul. And in anticipating the lords' desire for 'some salve for perjury' the artful 'salving' or healing that is viewed so dubiously by Costard glances proleptically toward the play's equally curious conclusion, which makes repeated reference to the terminus of death. The name of Mercadé, the French envoi who arrives bearing news of another king's death, evokes not only the god Mercury, as messenger and psychopomp of souls, but also the Latin word *merces*, meaning reward, price, recompense, remuneration or punishment (*magna mercede* meant 'at great cost') and hence death as the ironic reward or 'remuneration' that is accorded to fallen man. In this respect this second human *envoi* has an obscure relationship to the first *envoi* in the play, Costard, the punning significance of whose name seems to denote the fall of man in relation to the temptations of (sexual) knowledge. But it is a literary *envoi* that concludes the play, in the songs of Ver and Hiems. Here riddling allusions to two 'fowls' or birds foreground the marked ambivalence of the play's conclusion. For the cuckoo and the owl emblematise both the uncertainty of marital endings (which are implied to be vulnerable to the mutability, the 'foulness' or 'greasiness' of an errant female agency that can manifest at either 'end' of the year), and also the uncertain meaning of life's beginning and end. While the song of Ver alludes to the fear of female erotic infidelity that haunts the married man, in the final song, that of Hiems, a dense sequence of non-human objects – a wall, a nail, logs, a hall, milk, a pail, a pot, crabs and a bowl – is figuratively allied with the deviation and frustration of erotic desire. Each verse of the owl's song culminates with the otherworldly, folkloric image of 'greasy Joan' and the cooking 'pot', that she is 'keeling' – stirring or skimming in order to cool: 'a merry note,/While greasy Joan doth keel the pot' (5.2.893–4, 901–2). Given earlier references in the play to Joan as a non-courtly object of desire, this pot seems figuratively to correspond to that greasy feminine end, or 'fat goose', in and through which Costard earlier hoped to be 'enfranchised'. But like the penalty-imposing ladies of France, the materiality of a pleasure-affording feminine end is here invested with a purgative or punitive quality, in an imposed cooling of desire that parallels the ladies' refusal of 'courtesy' to their male suitors. Given the lords' painful awareness of their double perjury, these forms of female-directed 'keeling' or purgation appear to correspond to a process of supernatural judgement that is also, paradoxically, an intimation of the future possibility of grace. Indirectly identified, in the central scene, with man's eventual 'remuneration' or receipt of a 'guerdon' for good works or penance (3.1.120ff.), the feminine grace in question seems to require above all a quasi-theological, quasi-medical purgation of the *grace*ful or witty language of the male courtier and humanist scholar. Through the mutating meanings of ostensibly stable things in this play – as Armado's letter mutates into *l'envoi*, 'salve', 'mail', 'goose', and finally, on its receipt by the ladies, 'capon' – we are reminded of the seeming inevitability of deviations from and of the word. Thereby, both the noblemen's perjury (which may imply a rejection of justification by faith) and the 'miscarrying' of the language of desire (in the form of the love-letters soon to be misdelivered by Costard) are implied to be an inevitable process.

The quasi-culinary agent of this natural grace is not the poet, however, but rather the strangely emblematic figure of 'greasy Joan'. She is imaged as substituting for the erotic touch a paradoxical act of stirring which implies that both pleasure and purgation, both the incitement to and the obligatory cooling of sexual desire, are necessary ingredients in the poet's figurative concoction of a textual salve. This is a 'fowl' or 'greasy' mode of salvation, to be dispensed by a female or feminine source of mercy whose future 'remuneration' or 'guerdon' is seemingly both sacred and profane. For this errant feminine salve is also implied to be closely allied to the peculiar effects that are engendered by the disorder of things.

Notes

1 In this preoccupation with the ambiguity of bodily ends, my chapter builds upon the argument set out in Berry 1999.
2 The redisposition of 'things' in the modern *episteme* was brilliantly anatomized by Michel Foucault in Foucault 1991.
3 'For why is one person more excellent than another? Is it not to display in common nature God's special grace, which in passing many by, declares itself bound to none?' (Calvin 1961: 276).
4 The reference is taken from the *Geneva Bible*.
5 See the New Penguin edition of John Kerrigan (Shakespeare 1982).
6 The *OED* lists the first usage of 'mail bag', as a bag of letters, as 1670 (*Mail* sb. 3 2), but it seems clear that Shakespeare is using the word in this sense, as well as in reference to a bag holding ointment.
7 See Hoeniger 1992.
8 See Rubinstein 1989 for the possible bawdy overtones of 'plain', 'shin' and 'matter'.
9 For an account of the function of this device in troubadour verse, see Phan 1991. I am indebted to Bill Burgwinkle for directing me to this essay.
10 See Williams 1997.
11 For details of this opposition, see Tyacke 1987.

5

The Shakespearean fetish

Lisa Freinkel

What Freud discovers in the fetish is the emptiness of the object.
Freud, in this at least, is the true heir of Protestantism.

(Stallybrass and Jones 2000: 32)[1]

For an astonishingly long time in the contentious modern
history of literary criticism – for a full quarter century, an entire
lit-critter generation – we've been telling ourselves essentially
the same story about psychoanalysis, gender, religion and
Renaissance lyric poetry.

The story is a powerful one; it explicates "Petrarch's characteristic descriptive moves – fragmentation and reification"
(Vickers 1985: 112) by way of the self-consciously idolatrous
stance of the poet-lover. The Petrarchan lover's praise unfolds
in *rime sparse*, in "scattered rhymes," parceling out the beloved
in emblazoned bits "of hand, of foot, of lip, of eye, of brow"
– piecing out upon a pedestal the catalog that Shakespeare
calls "the blazon of sweet beauty's best" (Sonnet 106: 5–6).
And, as we've further come to understand, such idolatrous
fragmentation amounts to nothing less than *fetishism*.

It behooves us, however – we chroniclers of "spiritual Shakespeares" in particular – to consider this story of the Petrarchan fetish a bit more carefully: especially given our discipline's current surge of interest in what's coming to be known as "the new materialism."[2] For a number of recent critics, the cultural history of fetishism has afforded an important vantage point from which to re-assess early modern materialities. Peter Stallybrass' and Ann Rosalind Jones' discussions have been exemplary in this vein, and have proved singularly influential in foregrounding the cultural critic William Pietz's work on the history of fetishism.[3]

Pietz charts the evolution of the pidgin term *fetisso* from its sixteenth-century origins in the intercultural context of the West African gold and slave trades, to the modern day concept of the fetish as used in anthropology, political economy and psychoanalysis (see Pietz 1985, 1987, 1988). As Pietz demonstrates, the origin of the term is difficult to characterize. The complex of usages comprised by the word cannot be simply derived from the nearest etymological root (namely, the Portuguese characterization of West African religion as witchcraft, or *feitiçaria*). Nor can we trace the array of discrete cultural artifacts that *fetisso* comes to designate, back to a single conceptual or discursive field – or even to a single colonial power or colonized people. Instead, the *fetisso* only evolves in the course of translation and transaction *across* competing cultures, practices, spiritualities. *Fetisso* mediates between Portuguese Catholic, Iberian Jew, Dutch Calvinist, Islamicized as well as non-Islamicized African.

For scholars like Stallybrass and Jones, Pietz's account offers a chapter in the history of the modern individual as "private" or *privé* self: i.e. as disencumbered, as *deprived* of material entailments.[4] According to this account, the *fetisso* helps a nascent European capitalism define itself and its commodities, over and against a benighted ethnic Other: an Other incapable of recognizing the "true" value of objects. For the European, the *fetisso* emerges somewhat paradoxically as the expression of an inexpressive materiality – of the material world in all its brute and meaningless density. It is this literally *stupid* world that the savages venerate, and thus their *fetissos*, defined by the Europeans as worthless stuff, enable a critique of unsublimated materiality. As Pietz explains, the truth of the *fetisso* "resides in its status as a material embodiment." Importantly, the *fetisso* is hence no idol, "for the idol's truth lies in its relation of iconic resemblance to some immaterial model or entity" (Pietz 1985: 8). In contrast, the *fetisso* resists spirit, resists the "elsewhere" of the material world. The *fetisso* finds itself, then, on the *other* side of the emerging classical divide between mind and body, participating in the new discourse of the classical subject. By the eighteenth century, it will come to epitomize all that a self must bracket, in order to realize "his" disembodied and fully rational autonomy. In this manner, the early modern *fetisso* paves the way for the Enlightenment. The secularization that *fetisso* bespeaks, augurs progress – albeit a progress only achieved at the expense of a demonized Other. As Pietz argues: "The discourse of the fetish has always been a critical discourse about the false objective values of a culture from which the speaker is personally distanced" (Pietz 1985: 14).

For critics who are critical of this Enlightenment critique, the reappraisal of fetishism – the effort, as Stallybrass and Jones put it, to find "the utopian moment of the fetish" (Stallybrass and Jones 2000: 32) – proves uniquely helpful. The question of the fetish lies at the intersection of matter and spirit; to study the history of fetish is to study the very question of sublimation itself, of spiritual transcendence. Its reappraisal is essential not only for scholars of the "new materialism" but also for those of us intent on a newly "spirited," as it were, discourse. Nonetheless, I remain dubious of utopian fetishism – if only for the simple reason that, logically speaking, *there can be no positive discourse of fetishism*: the discourse of the fetish is irreducibly and originally *negative*. As Pietz argues, the discourse "always posits this double consciousness of absorbed credulity and degraded or distanced incredulity" (Pietz 1985: 14). In the twentieth-century psychoanalytic language of fetish, this doubled consciousness finds its theory within the psyche, in the "double attitude" of Freudian *Verleugnen*, or disavowal: a simultaneous denial and asseveration (Freud [1927] 1957: 203).

I argue that the fetish is better understood as the vehicle of a *triangulated* perspective – not a doubled one. Indeed, its discourse of critique, I argue, always entails *three* positions: (1) the stance of the fully credulous; (2) the stance of the disillusioned; and (3) that of the disillusioned who nevertheless suspend their disbelief.[5] It is only this last position that embodies the doubleness of *Verleugnen,* but such duality logically entails the first two dichotomous positions of total credulity, on the one hand, and unremitting skepticism on the other. Moreover, it is just this triangulation in the context of belief that the Protestant Reformation brings to a traditional iconoclast discourse. *Pace* Stallybrass and Jones, it is not Protestantism per se that supplies the appropriate perspective on the fetish, but rather the triangulated viewpoint of *Luther's* Protestantism in particular. For Luther, the world of the faithful is split into three camps: the naively idolatrous Papists; the skeptically iconoclast radicals; and the true believers (like him) who recognize iconoclasm as idolatry in another guise. Indeed, according to Luther, the iconoclasts are the worst idolators of all, since their fanatical destruction of images now entails an absolute – if absolutely negative – investment in material form.

In other words, Luther triangulates a traditional discourse of idolatry – and in so doing, I argue, he generates an early modern precursor to fetish discourse. In the final section of this chapter, with my reading of Shakespeare's "thing" – *"that one thing to my purpose nothing"* (20:12) – it is toward such triangulation, and toward the decidedly *non*-utopian "something-nothing" at its center, that my reappraisal of the fetish will turn.[6] Shakespeare's "thing," I will suggest, also splits the world into three camps: the haves; the have-nots; and those who have enough to know that they have not.

Silencing Diana . . .

At stake in discussions of Petrarchan fetishism is the alignment between rhetorical strategies, spiritual pieties, and gender politics. Specifically at stake is the logic of "descriptive dismemberment" (Vickers 1982: 109) that Nancy Vickers identified so cogently and influentially more than twenty years ago. Vickers built upon arguments advanced in the 1970s by Robert Durling, John Freccero and Giuseppe Mazzotta – arguments that accounted for Petrarch's "poetics of fragmentation" (the phrase is Mazzotta's) in terms of the poet-lover's self-conscious idolatry.[7] Freccero's formulations are notably pithy: the "fundamental strategy of the *Canzoniere*," he writes, is to transform "the *thematics* of idolatry . . . into the *poetics* of presence" (Freccero 1986: 31). No matter how self-abasing it may seem,

the idolatrous love of Laura proves poetically efficacious.
Tracing out a laudatory circle from *Laura* to *lauro* (laurel), the
poet effectively crowns himself poet *laureate*. Thematic self-
abasement translates into rhetorical self-promotion.

At the same time, the self-reference of Petrarch's rhetoric
precisely mirrors a patristic analysis of the semiotics of sin.[8]
In a universe where the Word of God is both origin and
eschaton – both that divine intention that precedes all creation
and that transcendental signified that secures its final meaning – the idolator's error is to mistake *signs* for *things*. He eschews
the rightful referentiality of the Creator's creatures, enjoying
as a thingly end-in-itself that which rightly only *signifies* the
one true End. The idolator errs, in other words, by refusing
signification; he literally *re*-ifies, makes *thing*-like (*res*), the
signs (*signa*) of God.[9] Here, Freccero's formulations are again
noteworthy:

> [I]f the gentiles, in the Jews' interpretation of them, sought
> to make their gods present by reifying their signs, then we
> might say that Petrarch sought to reify his signs, objectify
> his poetic work, by making his 'god,' the lady Laura, the
> object of his worship.
>
> (Freccero 1986: 27)

Petrarch's reified signs, no less than the idols of the pagan gods,
thus pervert an incarnational logic. Instead of salvation, these
signs-made-thing offer what Freccero calls "a kind of fetishism":
they offer, that is, the worship of a "sign" that has been voided
of all significance. In turn, such fetishes can only yield a poetry
of fragments: to treat signs as *things* is to disarticulate them
from that "principle of intelligibility" (ibid.: 29) which transforms
a collection of parts into a unified whole. Without reference to
the divine Signified – to God as Word, as *telos* or *summum bonum*
– Petrarch's *Laura* quite literally dis-integrates.

The Petrarchan fetish is thus a part without a whole. It is
a member disarticulated from its body, joint by joint.[10] And
yet, such dismemberment just may be the price of immortality.

> So it is with Laura. Her virtues and her beauties are
> scattered like the objects of fetish worship: her eyes and
> hair are like gold and topaz on the snow, while the outline

of her face is lost; her fingers are like ivory and roses or oriental pearls. . . . Like the poetry that celebrates her, she gains immortality at the price of vitality and historicity.

(ibid.: 29)

We're at the core of the idolatry argument now. Let's push this logic a bit further yet. To say that Laura is "fetishized" is not to say in any simple way that she has been "objectified," treated as an object to be used rather than as an end in herself. Such instrumentalization, after all, is precisely what *should* happen in an Augustinian universe of signs. But instead, precisely, the poet *refuses* to objectify Laura in this sense; he rejects the use of Laura as sign, hoarding the nuggets of a well-mined semantic field as if the lifeless hunks of earth were in and of themselves things of value. Gold, topaz, ivory, pearl. In their dead weight, wrenched from their living and historical context, such signs "forget" their use, and instead are scattered "like the objects of fetish worship."

And so the Petrarchan idolator is also a hoarder: one who lays up his treasure in this world. His problem isn't that he won't defer his pleasure; the idolator differs, in that respect, from the glutton. Rather, the idolator seems to take pleasure *in deferral itself.* Thus, for instance, the shivery erotic charge delivered by the fetish of *Rime* 52: that delicate metonym of the pretty little veil, the *leggiadretto velo* watched as it's washed in a mountain stream. *Non al suo amante più Diana piacque. . . .*[11] The poet surveys the scene in delight, no less pleased by this rustic laundry vision, than Acteon was by his chance glimpse of Diana naked in the pool. And yet, it is not nakedness that pleases here. As metonym – as synecdoche, even – the veil pleases by obscuring. It is simultaneously representation and impediment; it signifies by displacement. Instead of Laura herself, the poem's metonymic chain yields a signifier at least three removes distant from the Lady: a "cruel" shepherdess keeps us from the graceful veil while she protectively bathes it; the veil itself stands between the lovely blond head of hair and the breeze; and finally, *il vago et biondo capel*, the lovely blond head itself, stands in for the Lady in her own, whole person. And yet even so, trembling with an "amorous chill," the poet avails himself of this chance encounter with a thrice-removed signifier, taking delight in that distance which precisely should impede his pleasure.[12] The mediation of signs becomes itself a source of *im*mediate gratification. Petrarch's veil thus "functions as a fetish, an erotic signifier of a referent whose absence the lover refuses to acknowledge" (ibid.: 31). Insofar as the idolator takes pleasure in that which should forestall pleasure, his sin reveals itself as erotic perversion. Theology unveils itself as psychoanalysis.

When Nancy Vickers, for her part, picks up the thread of this narrative, she establishes an even clearer reference to psychoanalysis. Reminding us of *Rime* 52's opening conceit (*Diana didn't please her lover more* . . .), Vickers addresses the analogy between Acteon's "voyeuristic pleasure" and the speaker's "fetishistic" delight. The two satisfactions are not as incongruous as they might seem; what links the poem's two stories is in fact a third story: the mythic scenario of taboo and transgression at the heart of the castration complex. In this light, as Vickers explains, the Acteon–Diana encounter

> reenacts a scene fundamental to theorizing about fetishistic perversion: the troubling encounter of a male child with intolerable female nudity, with a body lacking parts present in his own, with a body that suggests the possibility of dismemberment. Woman's body, albeit divine, is displayed to Actaeon, and his body, as a consequence, is literally taken apart.
>
> (Vickers 1981: 273)

That *amoroso gielo* of *Rime* 52, that amorous chill of vision, is as much shudder as orgasmic release; if it marks arousal, it also registers shock and horror. This is a vision that both pleases and petrifies, as if the price of delight were destruction. And indeed, so it is, within the castration narrative that Vickers recounts, where the longed-for vision is quite literally the site or sight of trauma. Yet, at least in fantasy, the possibility remains of holding a space open between longing and trauma, between prohibited seeing and threatened dismemberment. The *Rime sparse*, Vickers argues, hold open just that "median time" (ibid.: 270) by projecting the threat of dismemberment on to the vision itself. Disarticulated into the language of fetish, the body of woman enables man to articulate himself.

Vickers' argument is a potent one, made all the more intuitive by its tacit appeal to a now-familiar critique of modern visual culture. Let us make no mistake: for Vickers, Petrarch's gaze doesn't merely reprise that of an Acteon; more importantly, it prefigures "the gaze" of a Laura Mulvey.[13] When Vickers invokes the "theorizing about fetishistic perversion," the theorizing she has in mind has already been focused through the lens of "psychoanalytically influenced feminist theory" (Mulvey 1993: 3). All the same, and despite the fact that Vickers' reading of the *Canzoniere* has become all but canonical, her debt to feminist psychoanalytic theory has remained unchallenged and untheorized – even though she herself is explicit about her assumptions: "Silencing Diana is an emblematic gesture; it suppresses a voice, and it casts generations of would-be Lauras in a role predicated upon the muteness of its player" (ibid.: 278–9). Vickers leaves no room for doubt here: in her view, to read Petrarch aptly is to read him emblematically. It is to interpret his terms from the standpoint of the future: from the vantage of generations of always-already silenced women.

The problem with Vickers' account is not simply the hermeneutic circle it entails – that circle of the always-already, where the vantage point of the women who will have been silenced determines the poetry's "original" status as emblem. Far more problematic than the paradoxes of the future anterior, is the logical hole at the argument's center. On the one hand, Vickers explicitly builds upon the account of Freccero and others, for whom the Petrarchan fetish is vestigial: an idol or relic that metonymically signifes, as Freccero puts it, an "absence the lover refuses to acknowledge" (Freccero 1986: 31). At the same time, and on the other hand, Vickers invokes the fetish as Freud comes to understand it: as a monument that fills the amnesiac void of trauma, memorializing the horror of castration. Vickers' argument requires both accounts, yet offers no bridge between them. Indeed, in the last analysis, what remains most problematically untheorized in her argument is not her use of theory, but instead this gulf at the heart of her theory: the gap that lies between vestige and trauma – between *relic* and *monument*. Nonetheless, what her discussion thereby neatly reveals is the very same hole at the center of the history of fetish: that epistemic break that, for William Pietz for instance, separates a pre-modern discourse of idolatry from a modern discourse of fetish.[14]

Curiously enough, we find the same hole at the heart of Freud's discussion of fetish. It is the break that separates his early writings on the subject from his later ones.

When the fetish comes to life . . .

In Freud's earliest discussions (e.g. 1905–10), the fetish functions a bit like a religious relic: its power and its value can be traced back to a specific moment in early childhood – i.e. a particular sexual encounter or impression – with which the future fetish was originally associated, and for which it will later be substituted. The fetish, in other words, is a *metonym*: linked to the original sexual object by the tenuous threads of contiguity and contingency, its allure is both easily dismissed and easily understood (see Freud [1905] 1975: 19). It's only, after all, a pretty little veil . . . ah, yes, but it's *Laura's* veil![15] The fetish, properly considered, *belongs* somewhere – belongs to *someone*. No matter how "inappropriate" the object is for the aims of sexuality, a sense of property – of where and to whom it belongs – tempers its impropriety.

And thus, it comes as little surprise that in his 1905 account Freud is unable to draw a clear distinction between normality and pathology: "A certain degree of fetishism is . . . habitually present in normal love, especially in those stages of it in which the normal sexual aim seems unattainable or its fulfillment prevented." Significantly, Freud illustrates this point with a quote that summons Petrarchan categories in all their glittering, apostate allure. He quotes Goethe's Faust, fresh from the Witches' Kitchen: "Get me a scarf from her breast, or the garter of my love's desire!" (Freud [1905] 1975: 20). If the lover is sufficiently deluded (Faust has just been given a love potion) so that the beloved is sufficiently overvalued (as Mephistopheles tells us: Faust will now see Helen of Troy in every woman) – in other words, if one's discourse is sufficiently Petrarchan – then it's only normal to fetishize. In a pinch, any Gretchen can become a Helen, and any old garter or scarf will serve your *Liebeslust* quite nicely.

Garter, scarf or little veil: Freud's early theory of fetish explicates the utility of such Petrarchan part-objects very well. Like the material fragments of sacred history ("the comb of Mary Magdalene, the fingernails of St. Sebastian . . . the bloody

and lice-infested hair shirt of Thomas Becket")[16] – fragments
around which a reliquary of precious metals might be fashioned,
and a cathedral built to house it; so, too, do the metonymic
relics of Petrarchism become a break point for our investments,
damming up and redirecting libido like a kayaker's "cushion":
that bulge of water that builds up over river rock.[17] The fetish
thus conceived articulates the semiotics of idolatry perfectly: as
relic, the fetish becomes the cultic locus of our enjoyment,
rather than the mediating sign that directs us to that enjoyment. Nonetheless, from Freud's account of the fetish-relic, it
would seem that such idolatry is not necessarily perverse –
if by "perversion" we mean behavior that departs from (and
doesn't merely delay) normative sexual aims. A certain degree
of fetishism, Freud here suggests, is not merely "habitually"
but indeed quite *essentially* entailed in the "normal" course of
things, thanks to the "psychologically essential overvaluation
of the sexual object, which inevitably extends to everything
that is associated with it" (ibid.: 20). We're *all*, ultimately,
Petrarchists.

Or so we would be, if Freud's story ended here. That ending
would leave us with the idolatrous logic of the reliquary, but
without that "scene fundamental to theorizing about fetishistic
perversion" (Vickers 1981: 273): the primal scene of the castration complex. It isn't until Freud develops the concept of
disavowal (*Verleugnung*) in the 1920s that he's able to articulate
a coherent theory of the fetish as "memorial" or "monument"
– as *Denkmal* – to the "horror of castration" (Freud [1927]
1957: 200). In the earlier theory, the fetish-character of the
object derived from the historical weight of its moment of
origin: from that original sexual encounter and sexual object,
in all their possible specificity and detail. Registering the "after-
effect" (Freud [1905] 1975: 20) of this intense immediacy, the
fetish-as-relic takes the place of this historical whole (e.g. the
body of the beloved); the member replaces the body, to which
it once literally belonged.

> What is substituted for the sexual object is some part of
> the body ... or some inanimate object which bears an
> assignable relation to the person whom it replaces and
> preferably to that person's sexuality (e.g. a piece of clothing

·or underlinen). Such substitutes are with some justice likened to the fetishes in which savages believe that their gods are embodied.

(Freud [1905] 1975: 19)

Now, in the later 1927 discussion, the fetish object also bears an "assignable relation" to that which it replaces; the principle of the object's selection is still metonymic, following a logic of spatial contiguity. "Thus," as Freud tells us in that later essay, "the foot or shoe owes its attraction as a fetish" to the fact that the curious little boy used to "peer up the woman's legs towards her genitals" (Freud [1927] 1957: 201). But, even so, now our efforts to trace this metonymic chain back to its origin will fail. The pun is unforgivable, but irresistible: at the origin of this chain of metonymies is a *hole* instead of a whole. The fetish as Freud finally comes to define it, is memorial instead of relic, and further, it is a memorial that commemorates quite literally nothing. It erects itself as *Denkmal* (both memorial and monument) to an event that cannot be remembered (e.g. the traumatic sight of castration), and to a loss that we can never lose (e.g. the missing maternal penis).

More specifically, Freud explains that the monumental/ memorializing fetish emerges to negotiate a compromise between avoidance and acknowledgement of the mother's lost penis. The boy, of course, is unwilling to see the "fact" of his own possible castration, but he is also unable simply to obliterate what he's seen – in part because there's literally nothing to obliterate. The boy has not seen *a thing*. The only possible compromise is, somehow, to adopt both positions: to see and not to see. As *Penisersatz*, the fetish substitutes for a missing penis that was never lost. "[T]he fetish is a substitute for the woman's (mother's) phallus which the little boy once believed in and does not wish to forego" (ibid.: 191). At the same time, however, this replacement part can't help but foreground the fact that there's nothing to replace. Freud explains: "The horror of castration sets up a sort of permanent memorial to itself by creating this substitute" (ibid.: 200). The fetish serves as castration's *Denkmal* neither in spite of, nor alongside, its role as penis-replacement. Indeed, it is precisely *because* it replaces nothing that the fetish is the perfect memorial. As a monument that literally stands for nothing, the fetish cannot help but memorialize that loss it hopes to lose. As *Denkmal* the fetish, then, is perhaps less relevant to us for the meaning it *bears* – i.e. as a sign or a symbol – than it is for the meaning it *performs*. The *Denkmal*, with its interpellating name (*Denk mal! Just think!*), prompts, points, marks. . . . It functions, that is to say, at the level of its utterance: as performative. As *Denkmal* the fetish is a speech-act. A disavowal, in short: simultaneously a denial and an admission.

If the *Denkmal* defines the fetish as signifying form, its signifying content takes shape as the *Penisersatz*: the replacement piece that is neither dildo nor prosthesis. The logic that governs the substitutions of this substitute-penis, is not, exactly, mimetic; not, exactly, representational; not even, exactly, a matter of distribution or compensation. There's nothing absent to be re-presented; nothing hidden that must be re-produced; nothing out of balance that must be set right.

> One would expect that the organs or objects selected as substitutes for the penis whose presence is missed in the woman would be such as act as symbols for the penis in other respects. This may happen occasionally but is certainly not the determining factor. It seems rather that when the fetish comes to life, so to speak, some process has been suddenly interrupted – it reminds one of the abrupt halt made by memory in traumatic amnesias. In the case of the fetish, too, interest is held up at a certain point – what is possibly the last impression received before the uncanny traumatic one is preserved as fetish.
>
> (ibid.: 201)

Freud's *Penisersatz* is not a symbol, although occasionally and coincidentally it may look like one. The object in which that last impression is preserved may, sheerly by coincidence, be the sort of object that in other contexts would act as penis-symbol. But in this context, those semantic links are interrupted.

So, the *Penisersatz* is not a symbol. But it certainly *is* a figure, since its emergence marks a moment of displacement and substitution (*Ersetzen*): a moment of trope. And yet this moment is strangely asymmetrical, oddly static; the moment is devitalized and frozen, almost before it begins. *It seems that when the fetish comes to life . . . some process has been suddenly interrupted. . . . the last impression . . . is preserved as fetish.* . . . The problem, of course, is that in general, symbolic discourse works by presenting one thing in the place of another. Symbols (let's just call them *signs*) stand in for *things* in their absence; but what that truism really means – at least from our standpoint, we makers and readers of signs – is somewhat more balletic: as *x* comes to stand for *y*, *y* fades out, and *x* pulsates into view. In fact, it is this dance of scintillating presence that drives the engine in a universe of signs, insuring that the presence of what *is* keeps passing from us, even as what *is not*, dances into view. But the *Penisersatz* wakes into presence, and has nowhere to go. It is not a penis-symbol; not a prosthesis. It is not meant to replace a penis that is absent. Instead, as Freud so carefully explains, this fetish is a substitute for a penis *whose absence is missing.*[18]

Classical rhetoric offers us a ready way to understand the oddities of this trope. As a substitution for nothing, the figure at work in Freud's fetish looks a bit like metonym – a bit like Laura's veil or the scarf of Faust's Gretchen. But if this is metonym, it is acephalic metonym: headless metonym. Where we expect to find the origin-cause of trauma's rippling after-effects, where the displacements of trope should find their closure: instead, we find a void. Amnesia. A process that simply comes to a halt. On the other hand, because of this hole at the heart of signification, the substitution entailed by Freud's *Penisersatz* demands a certain leap across semantic discontinuity: a synaptic spark arcing across disparate points. In this sense, the rhetorical structure of the *Penisersatz* looks a bit like the flash of metaphor.

The figure I have in mind here is neither, strictly speaking, a form of metaphor nor of metonymy. If it is anything, it is the figure that arises when metaphor crashes into metonymy, and vice versa. It is the figure called *catachresis* by the Greek rhetors, or *abusio* in Latin. In George Puttenham's Elizabethan English, this is the "figure of abuse":

> [I]f for lacke of naturall and proper terme or worde we take another, neither naturall nor proper and do vntruly applie it to the thing which we would seeme to expresse . . . it is not then spoken by this figure *Metaphore* . . . but by plaine abuse.
>
> (Puttenham 1589: 3.17.9)

For Puttenham – who follows Quintilian closely in this respect – catachresis marks an abuse of language, a misapplication of a name, although the abuse may well be commendable. Catachresis acts in the absence of a "naturall and proper terme"; it fills the gaps in a lacking lexicon, "adapting the nearest available term to describe something for which no actual term exists" (Quintilian [88] 1959: 8.6.34). Catachresis thereby names an abuse that is practically unavoidable; it tropes the lacunae of a symbolic order into neologism. In this way, the figure that is *not* metaphor, nonetheless functions like it. Like metaphor – or *translatio*, as the Latin rhetors call it, from the past participle of *transfero* – catachresis *transfers* a proper name from one object to another. At the same time, however, catachresis also functions like metonym, since the principle that guides the transfer is one of contiguity or propinquity – adapt the "*nearest* available term" – rather than mimetic likeness.

If the rhetorical structure of Freud's monumental fetish is catachrestic, it is so because it too "vntruly applies" the ersatz where the natural should be – and yet, it does so almost commendably, since, indeed, there is nothing "naturall and proper" to be found in place beforehand. The *Penisersatz* fills a signifying gap not because it takes the place of something else, but because it takes the place *of the gap itself.* Like all good catachreses, the *Penisersatz* substitutes for *nothing.*

That one thing to my purpose nothing . . .

Elsewhere I have argued that Shakespeare's response to the traditional Petrarchan blazon – to those "lip, eye, brow" catalogs that he mocks in Sonnet 106 – is the kind of catachresis we see in his most triumphant, most highly anthologized lyric image: "thy eternal summer shall not fade" (18: 9).[19] The image is "vntruly applied" (as Puttenham might say): neither the young man's beauty, nor a summer's day, is eternal, for as Sonnet 18 also tells us: "every fair from fair sometime declines" (18: 7). Nothing beautiful lasts forever. And yet, what is beauty if not an ideal, and *as such* unchanging and immortal? And so, despite the blatant untruth that Sonnet 18 advances – "thy eternal summer shall not fade!"[20] – the sonnet *does* speak true: beauty is not beauty that alters when it alteration finds. In a world where all that lives must die, and where everything holds in perfection but a little moment, the proper name for beauty is already "vntrue." Neither "naturall nor proper," our most direct designations of beauty are already figures of speech, for they ascribe eternity to that which is bound to time. Every fair *from fair* declines: beauty is, indeed, also *not* beauty. Thus, if Shakespeare's version of the Petrarchan blazon looks a bit perverse, if the poet offers denials and negations as readily as affirmations – e.g. "every fair from fair sometime declines" *or* "my love is as fair/As any mother's child, though not so bright/As those gold candles fixed in heaven's air" (21: 11–12) *or* "my mistress' eyes are nothing like the sun" – if he disavows, in other words, his own visions of beauty, he does so because his sonneteering has shifted from a logic of relic to a logic of memorial – from holy vestige, to monumental loss.

I am, in short, suggesting that we simply take Shakespeare at his word. When he exhorts, "Let not my love be called idolatry" (105: 1), we should listen. Shakespeare's desire is not, strictly speaking, Petrarchan; it is not, that is to say, structured metonymically. His beloveds, whether fair or dark, leave no trace behind; they do not "show" as idols (105: 2). In place of the reliquaries of traditional Petrarchan verse (those sonnets built like pretty rooms to house a veil here, a golden hair there), Shakespeare gives us a poetry without icon. *My mistress' eyes are nothing like the sun*. . . . Shakespeare's desire thus takes the rhetorical form of abuse – of *abusio*. His love is catachrestic. It is the love of – or, more precisely, love *as* – fetish.

In place of a decisive proof of this claim, or even a full-fledged exposition of it, I will offer a single close reading: an "emblematic" reading, as Nancy Vickers might say. The poem I turn to in closing has been positioned, for well over two hundred years, at the ground-zero of debates over Shakespearean sexuality and gender.[21] All the more remarkable, then, that one of the most obvious readings of the poem has, up until now, escaped notice.

> A woman's face with nature's own hand painted
> Hast thou, the master-mistress of my passion;
> A woman's gentle heart, but not acquainted
> With shifting change as is false women's fashion;
> An eye more bright than theirs, less false in rolling,
> Gilding the object whereupon it gazeth;

A man in hue, all hues in his controlling,
Which steals men's eyes and women's souls amazeth.
And for a woman wert thou first created,
Till nature as she wrought thee fell a-doting,
And by addition me of thee defeated
By adding one thing to my purpose nothing.
　　But since she pricked thee out for women's pleasure,
　　Mine be thy love and thy love's use their treasure.

Sonnet 20, we all know, is a just-so story: the story of how the young man got "pricked." However, in our focus on the story of this "one thing" we have put ourselves in the position of the women in line 14: we've been unable to take our eyes off this treasure. And, accordingly, we've missed the sense in which the sonnet presents a somewhat different creation story. At stake in this poem is not so much the story of the penis, but the story of the *Penisersatz*: of the part that replaces *nothing*.

Understood as an allegory of the fetish, the celebratedly indeterminate volta of the poem now offers a quite pointed reading. "And for a woman wert thou first created": as countless readers have noted, thanks to the ambiguous preposition "for," we can't help but read this line twice. "For" can either denote *intention* ("intended *for*") or *representation* (e.g. "pansies, that's *for* thoughts"). The argument of the octave, however, has set us up for the first denotation: *you've combined the best of both worlds; you're as beautiful as a woman and as constant as a man; you're as alluring as both sexes, and alluring to both sexes. . . . And yet, you were created only for one sex: you were intended for a woman's pleasure.* Of course, no sooner do we reach the next line, than we realize that we've been set up: "Till nature as she wrought thee fell a-doting. . . ." *Oh, I see, Nature wanted you for (denoting 'intention') herself. . . . But at first she created you 'as' a woman: 'for' denoting 'in imitation or representation of'. . . .* And so, the just-so story unfolds.

Most typically readers dismiss the doubleness of "for" as just another of Shakespeare's fatal cleopatras – just another quibble. But the carefully structured sequence of readings here enforces the "double attitude" of the fetish. After all, this is not *The Crying Game*. Instead of being surprised by the phallus, the octave makes us *expect* a phallic woman from the very start. *You have the best of both worlds.* In this context, the quibble on "for" takes us through the castration scenario, taking away what it had appeared to grant. What we discover, as the just-so story unfolds, is not the unsettling presence of a penis, but its far more uncanny absence. This is a story of the castration trauma.

And yet, of course, this poem is not actually traumatic. Instead of the horrified, amnesiac little boy of Freud's 1927 account, we have the infatuated – but also generative – folly of a female figure: Nature. And instead of the "overvalued" fetish object, we find in Sonnet 20 that "one thing to my purpose nothing." Indeed, ultimately, instead of Freud's familiar "double attitude," Sonnet 20 gives us a *triangulated* structure of desire where disappointment is a trap in its own right. The story of the lost object, we learn, is mitigated by the prior recognition of our *own* loss. Just as the young man himself manages to straddle both sexes – managing to be both pricked and unpricked, both created for a woman's pleasure, and created as a woman – so too is the poet simultaneously with and without. For that matter, however, so are we. If the poem tempts us with our own desire for the phallus, thereby aligning us with the women of line 14, it equally aligns us, like the poet, with a *particular* woman: Nature. Like the poet, we are all quite capable of crafting the image of our desire. Like Nature, we *want* the phallus: penis, offspring, Galatea-like beloved. And like Nature, we already have one, wrought from and as our own desire. The penis is already a fetish.

Shakespeare's story of the fetish is not the story of trauma because, as it turns out, we are already fitted with one. Or, to put the same point another way: Shakespeare *is* telling a version of Freud's story, but he does so neither from the credulous standpoint of belief (the little boy *before* he sees) nor from the skeptical standpoint of disillusion (the little boy *after*). Shakespeare tells his story instead from the apex of the triangle: from the position where spirit finally *matters*. This is where the fetishist stands.

Alternatively, it is the position of the analyst.

Notes

Shorter versions of this argument were presented at the Shakespeare Association of America and the American Comparative Literature Association conventions in 2004. I am grateful to my fellow seminarians at both conferences for their incisive feedback. I'd also like to thank John Parker for his generous and helpful comments on fetishism and materialism in his own work, and for sharing with me an advance copy of his essay "What a Piece of Work is Man: Shakespearean Drama as Marxian Fetish, the Fetish as Sacramental Sublime" (*The Journal of Medieval and Renaissance Studies* (Fall 2004 34: 643–72)). Finally, I am indebted to Richard Halpern and, especially, to my colleague Ben Saunders, whose comments and critique at various stages of the project have been invaluable.

1 James Kearney argues the Reformation brings a new element to the centuries-old discourse of Christian iconoclasm: namely, a "demystifying and trivializing discourse [of the religious icon as] trinket" (J. Kearney 2002: 4). For Kearney as for Stallybrass, through its castigations of Roman Catholic and heathen religious forms as paltry "trinkets," Protestantism prefigures "the modern conception of the fetish" (ibid.).

2 For the term "new materialism" see Bruster (2001). Examples of this so-called new materialist criticism abound. Even as I write these words, *The Journal of Medieval and Early Modern Studies* goes to press with a special issue on the "Marxist Premodern" (Fall 2004); the question of material culture was in the air everywhere at the April 2004 convention of the Shakespeare Association of America; and a spate of essays and anthologies have sought to interrogate our field's emphasis on emerging *subjectivities*, arguing instead for the importance of sustained focus on early modern *objects*. The pivotal anthology in this latter regard is the 1996 *Subject and Object in Renaissance Literature*, edited by Margreta de Grazia, Maureen Quilligan and Peter Stallybrass.

3 Would it be too extreme to cite a *Penn Fetish* in this recent publishing trend? Much of the recent fetish-oriented work in early modern studies has been generated by faculty associated with the University of Pennsylvania (e.g. Stallybrass, Jones, de Grazia) and by their former students (e.g. John Parker, James Kearney).

4 See for instance Stallybrass and Jones' (2000) characterizations of the modern "individual" as dematerialized and hence indivisible, because abstracted from a body that has been reduced to mere object, i.e. fetish.

5 The third position – where "simple truth" is suppressed (see Sonnet 138) – corresponds to Manonni's famous "je sais bien, mais quand même": the rhetorical stance of the fetishist. See Manonni 1969. According to Slavoj Žižek, of course, this is the position of all ideological belief. See Žižek 1989. Our relation to the Big Other of ideology is like our relationship to Santa Claus: we all know that he doesn't exist – but we'll keep up appearances "for the kids."

6 "For nothing hold me, so it please thee hold/That nothing me, a something sweet to thee:/Make but my name thy love, and love that still,/And then thou lovest me, for my name is 'Will'" (136: 11–14). – A fuller account of the Shakespearean fetish, and of its relationship both to Luther's triangulated reform, as well as to an emerging discourse of commodity, appears in my forthcoming study: *The Use of Shakespeare*.

7 The crucial essays are Durling 1971, Freccero [1975] 1986 and Mazzotta 1978. See also Durling's "Introduction" to his bilingual edition of Petrarch's poems (1976). All references to and translations of the *Rime sparse* as in this edition.

8 For Augustine – and with him, Petrarch – idol worship is at the heart of all sin as such; it defines the fundamental error of fallen man. The point may seem obvious – and indeed, it passes for self-evident in Freccero's account – but this represents a profound commitment to Platonism. It is precisely this commitment to a rationalist, platonic metaphysics that will be called into question by the sixteenth-century reformers and counter-reformers.

9 Augustine's distinction between *signum* and *res* – the cornerstone of his "Christian doctrine" – is also the linchpin of this orthodox critique of idolatry. See Augustine [397] 1958: 1.2.2ff.

10 Cf. *Rime* 15: "[C]ome posson queste membra/da lo spirito lor viver lontane. . . .'"

11   Non al suo amante più Diana piacque
       quando per tal ventura tutta ignuda
       la vide in mezza de le gelide acque,
       ch'a me la pastorella alpestra et cruda
       posta a bagnar un leggiadretto vel
       ch'a l'aura il vago et biondo capel chiuda;
       tal che mi fece, or quan'egli arde 'l cielo,
       tutto tremar d'un amoroso gielo.

12 It would be useful to explore Petrarch's veil as an example of Lacan's *objet petit a*. Recently Henry Krips (1999) has explicated the relationship between the *objet a* and the logic of fetishism; in a complementary discussion, Richard Halpern (2002) has explored the early modern conception of sodomy in terms of the Lacanian Thing. Both Krips and Halpern offer extraordinary glosses of Lacan, but their readings can be misleading if applied to the early modern fetish. The logic of the *objet a* is in fact the logic of idolatry; missing from the discussion is precisely that "double attitude" that the concept of *disavowal* brings to Freud's 1927 "Fetishism" essay.

13 In particular, Vickers cites the two now-classic analyses of spectatorship, gender and pleasure: Berger 1977 and Mulvey 1975.

14 "Far from representing a continuation of the idea of idolatry, the emergence of the distinct notion of fetish marks a breakdown of the

adequacy of the earlier discourse under quite specific historical conditions and social forces" (Pietz 1985: 6).

15 If time allowed, it would be helpful here to consider *Rime* 16, where another little piece of fabric – St Veronica's handkerchief – reveals in quite literal terms the relationship between religious relic or icon (Veronica as *verum ikon*), and the Petrarchan "fetish."

16 I'm citing Peter Stallybrass' discussion of the medieval relic (2002: 178). For Stallybrass, the great problem with modernity – a problem he sees, as I've already suggested, articulated in the history of the fetish – is the disavowal of materiality. It would seem that the premodern cult of the relic marks one version of what Stallybrass and Jones call elsewhere the "utopian moment of the fetish."

17 The image of a "damming up of libido" (*Libidostauung*) is Freud's, and can connote either a healthy retention/redirection of libidinal energy (e.g. the civilizing effects of sublimation), or the pathogenic frustration of libido that only finds discharge in, for instance, a neurotic symptom.

18 For Freud, what truly horrifies in the castration scenario is not, in other words, the sight of an amputation, but rather the perception that there is *nothing to be amputated*. It is this uncanny sight – the uncanny site of the vagina as absolute void or no thing – that constitutes the trauma per se. The logic here is well known in Hollywood; I'm reminded of the only truly frightening sequence in the Wachowski brothers' *Matrix* films. These films are dense with invaginating images, but only one of these achieves the uncanny pitch of horror. When "Mr Anderson" is first interrogated by Agent Smith, his efforts to resist by screaming are thwarted when his lips melt together and his mouth dissolves into a disgusting, gummy goo. The sight is unpleasant, but the moment only becomes nightmarish when the goo disappears: then, there isn't even the absence of a mouth. What terrifies, finally, is not the gash, but the smooth, impassive blank where the wound *used to be*. The missing mouth is now uncannily missing.

19 See my discussion of catachresis and the young man sonnets in Freinkel 2002.

20 The full thought of the sonnet is, of course, somewhat more complex than I've rendered it: "thy eternal summer shall not fade . . . when in eternal lines to time thou grow'st" (etc.). At first sight, what seems to mitigate the untruth of the "eternal summer" is the vision of future readers who give life and breath to the written word. But since Sonnet 17 has just demonstrated the ways in which literature *itself* is subject to time and decay ("So should my papers, yellowed with their age,/Be scorned. . ." (17: 9–10)), Sonnet 18's concluding image of the book only manages to shift the catachresis slightly. "Eternal lines" is, of course, every bit as much a *figure of abuse* as "eternal summer" was.

21 The lines of this debate have been, from the start, perhaps all too clear: established, as Stallybrass has cogently argued, by the polarized

terms of Shakespeare's eighteenth-century editors. Steevens' famous 1766 protestation ("it is impossible to read this fulsome panegyrick, addressed to a male object, without an equal mixture of disgust and indignation") – along with Malone's 1780 response ("such addresses to men . . . were customary in our author's time, and neither imported criminality, nor were esteemed indecorous") – have, between them, crafted what now seems to be an inescapable critical legacy (see Stallybrass 1999: 86, 84).

6
Bottom's secret . . .
John J. Joughin

I need help in my state of bliss. For I am well practised in the arts of resignation and in the prayer that they provoke. O God, take away this pain, this punishment – prayer in adversity. Yet I have no liturgy for thanksgiving, for praise, for consummation; for my well-being, love-ability, or for a new sensation; a constant awareness of existence, alone or in the company of others, imbued with a silly palpability, a beauty at once tactile and visual – as if on each intake of breath one were immersing one's hands in the deep folds of some fine material saturated with glorious colour. How to give this beauty back? . . . The withdrawal of the abyss, the overwhelming plenitude of every moment leaves me more vulnerable than the busy tumult of distress: I have nothing to clutch, nothing to point to as my burden, nothing from which to beg allevia-tion. My soul is naked: it has lost its scaffolding of regret and remorse or even repentance: it is turned: and the unex-pected result is the sensation and the envelope of invisible and visible beauty. This does not make me ecstatic, unreal, unworldly: it returns me to the vocation of the everyday

... but it needed some response, some way of singing its mystery so that I can concentrate as ever on any fellowship or fickleness which presents itself.

(Rose 1999: 21–2)

In her final work *Paradiso*, the philosopher Gillian Rose faces what she terms 'doxological terror', as, on confronting a terminal illness, amidst new-found bliss and serenity, she contemplates the movement from a state of loss to a state of grace.

Fragments of an unfinished manuscript, Rose's last words on faith and philosophy constitute their own particular form of incomplete completeness; yet at this extreme they also offer the defiance of self-creation, an absolute beginning without preconditions – a lyrical act of *autopoeisis* (cf. Rose 1999: 45, 63). Where, in her previous *Love's Work* (1995), her reader was left in purgatory, emboldened to 'keep your mind in hell and despair not', here, in her *Paradiso*, Rose embraces the sublime in the pedestrian, her ecstasy as ordinary as it is mysterious. Paradoxically, the ultimate gift of death resides in a renewal of the infinite possibilities of the everyday.

In the face of misfortune, spiritual malaise and disenchantment, recent criticism in the Humanities has suffered more from resignation than hope. Ours tends to be a spectral criticism 'companioned by ghosts' and beset by melancholia and loss, which Rose describes in terms of the 'interminable mourning play and lament of postmodernity' (Rose 1996: 64). In Shakespeare studies there is certainly a current tendency to redeploy texts and characters in terms that demand redemption but in forms that simultaneously refuse redress (cf. Joughin 2000a: 14–17).[1] In *Hamlet in Purgatory*, for example, Stephen Greenblatt speaks explicitly of Shakespeare's theatre as 'a cult of the dead' (2001: 258). Indeed, in some sense, as Greenblatt reminds us, our negotiation of old Hamlet's death is an exemplary case in point, insofar as it effectively constitutes the singular act of witness or memorial, which will continue to assure and maintain our literary critical life – 'Thou art a scholar, speak to it, Horatio . . .' (Greenblatt 1997: 481). Questions of how we remember, of disenchantment and re-enchantment, of presence and absence, being and non-being,

visibility and hiddenness, knowing and not knowing, are themselves necessarily linked in intricate ways to the inventive
capacity of what we might term the literary critical 'event'.
Yet in *Specters of Marx* (during another negotiation with old
Hamlet's death) in speaking of and to apparitions, Jacques
Derrida speaks not just of those 'who are no longer there, of
those who are no longer', but also of those 'who are not
yet *present and living*' (Derrida 1994: xix), the ghosts of those
who are not yet born; reminding us that the gift of the apparitional resides in speaking in a relation of absolute singularity
to others:

> Whether he knows it or not, Hamlet is speaking in the
> space opened up by this question – the appeal of the gift,
> singularity, the coming of the event, the excessive or
> exceeded relation to the other – when he declares "The
> time is out of joint." And this question is no longer
> dissociated from all those that Hamlet apprehends as such,
> that of the specter-Thing and of the King, that of the event,
> of present-being, and of what *there is to be, or not*, what there
> is *to do*, which means *to think*, to make do or let do, to make
> or to let come, or to give, even if it be death.
>
> (ibid.: 23)

If, with its own 'scaffolding of regret', our literary life is nothing
more or less than a preoccupation with perpetual mourning
and endless loss – *purgatorio* rather than *paradiso* – then in letting
lost ones go we ought to embrace the gift of death as a precipi-
tation towards the opening up of new relations to others yet
to come. In turn the singularity of literature and its defiance of
extant modes of understanding, also resides in an utopian
or messianic impulse, in the 'coming-to-be of that which is not
yet' and its 'incalculable novelty'.[2]

Littered with dreams, visions and a host of other apparitions
there can be no doubt that the world of Shakespeare's drama
is, as Greenblatt puts it, 'hyperanimated' (Greenblatt 2001). For
his contemporary audience, witnessing the revival of ancient
spirits and the birth of things to come seems to have constituted an everyday occurrence while also remaining a crucial
component of the aesthetic experience of play-going itself. The

relation between the phantasmatic power of the playwright and its reliance on categories that are, or were, religious also seems evident. However, insofar as it constitutes a site of reincarnation and continual renewal, the revelationary capacity of Shakespeare's stage is not just bound to a cult of mourning, but also invites a singular encounter with singularity, a quasi-messianic apprehension of blissful new beginnings – an anticipation of what Rose terms 'the overwhelming plenitude of every moment'. In this chapter, in pushing this relation between the sacred and the secret of the future-to-come, I want to explore the paradoxical novelty of the apparitional as the vocation of the everyday: 'both invisible, hidden' and quite 'ordinarily [rudely?] visible' (cf. Rose 1999: 19).

Bottom's secret, or the visible-invisible of apparitions

> [I]n the temporal world God and I cannot talk together, we have no common language . . .
>
> (Kierkegaard 1985: 64)

> – I have had a most rare vision. I have had a
> dream past the wit of man to say what dream it was. Man
> is but an ass if he go about t'expound this dream. Me-
> thought I was – there is no man can tell what. Methought
> I was, and methought I had – but man is a patched
> fool if he will offer to say what methought I had. The
> eye of man hath not heard, the ear of man hath not seen,
> man's hand is not able to taste, his tongue to conceive,
> nor his heart to report what my dream was. I will get
> Peter Quince to write a ballad of this dream. It shall be
> called 'Bottom's Dream', because it hath no bottom, and
> I will sing it in the latter end of a play, before the Duke.
> Peradventure, to make it the more gracious, I shall sing
> it at her death.
>
> (*A Midsummer Night's Dream*, 4.1.199–211)

Bottom's mystery and the hidden wisdom whereof he speaks threads together the aporia of the embodied and the non-embodied, the visible and the non-visible – does the sanctity of theatrical performance and its communion (its secret) lie in an analogous hidden visibleness?

As several critics have noted, Bottom's account of his 'rare vision' constitutes a deliberately botched re-joining of the Pauline message of spiritual revelation as that which, in being 'past the wit of man', cannot be spoken:

> [W]e speak the wisdom of God in a mystery, *even* the hidden *wisdom* which God ordained before the world unto our glory: Which none of the princes of this world knew: for had they known *it*, they would not have crucified the Lord of glory. But as it is written, Eye hath not seen, nor ear heard, neither have entered into the heart of man, the things which God hath prepared for them that love him. But God has revealed *them* unto us by his Spirit: for the Spirit searcheth all things, yea, the deep things of God.
>
> (1 Cor. 2:7–10)

Yet if Paul's sense of the demonstration of the spirit equates in some respect to the revelationary potential of Shakespearean drama, the kinaesthetic confusion of the senses to which Bottom refers undoubtedly complicates that connection. Bottom's malapropisms of sense aside, it cannot after all be a matter of 'knowing' what Bottom knows, for as Paul adds: '[T]he natural man receiveth not the things of the Spirit of God: for they are foolishness unto him: neither can he know *them* for they are spiritually discerned' (1 Cor. 2:14).

Bottom's initiation into the world of the spirit foregoes the conventional criteria for 'knowing'; it is unrepeatable ('no man can tell what'), absolutely singular. The play reserves the term 'translation' for its interrogation of this form of epistemological and ontological transformation, and once, and only here in *A Midsummer Night's Dream*, the notion of being 'transfigured' (cf. 5.1.24). How then can we translate Bottom's astonishing translation insofar as, as Kierkegaard puts it: '[I]n the temporal world God and I cannot talk together, we have no common language'?

As Peter Brook's remarkable production demonstrated (at Stratford, 1970) there is a sense in which the play's proximity to the visionary is not held in abeyance in some transcendent realm but is already hibernating within the everyday. In a production that deployed ladders, a catwalk and fairies flying on trapezes, Brook hurled himself trustingly into the absurd. Crucially, there was no attempt to conceal the mechanics of flying, so that, as one critic noted, in making the invisible ordinarily visible, Brook had successfully invented: 'an environment for the *Dream* which removes the sense of being earthbound: it is natural here for characters to fly' (Griffiths 1996: 67–9). In this, arguably the most Kierkegaardian of Shakespeare's plays, the sublime and the pedestrian are bound up together, and credulity is unwitting and commonplace, precisely the provenance of Kierkegaard's 'Knight of Faith' who remains open to the 'astonishing nature of what is normally expected' (cf. Rose 1999: 18 and Kierkegaard 1985) – rather than that of Paul's 'princes of this world', for whom knowing is construed as certainty. In turn, one might say that Brook's production was 'Shakespearean' insofar as it understood the apparitional quality of the play as a form of discovering what is 'the very least we need before understanding can be reached' (Brook 1990: 55). As such the play exemplifies what the director terms 'Holy Theatre' or 'The Theatre of the Invisible-Made-Visible' where 'we can try to capture the invisible but we must not lose touch with common sense . . .' (Brook 1990: 69, 47–72). Crucially, and in contrast to what Brook terms the 'deadly theatre', where we rush to give things a prescriptive 'label' (ibid.: 15), the 'Holy Theatre' embraces the potential of a 'Happening':

> A powerful invention. . . . A happening can be anywhere, any time, of any duration: nothing is required, nothing is taboo. The theory of happening is that a spectator can be jolted into new sight, so that he wakes to the life around him . . . this visible-invisible cannot be seen automatically – it can only be seen given certain conditions. The conditions can relate to certain states or to a certain understanding. In any event, to comprehend the visibility of the invisible is a life's work. Holy art is an aid to this, and so we arrive at a definition of a holy theatre. A holy theatre not only presents the invisible but also offers conditions that make its perception possible. The Happening could be related to all of this, but the present inadequacy of the Happening is that it refuses to examine deeply the problem

of perception. Naively it believes that the cry 'Wake up!' is enough: that the call 'Live!' brings life. Of course more is needed. But what?

(Brook 1990: 61–3)

Brook's sense of a 'happening' theatre is a variant of what I have characterised elsewhere as an 'aesthetic attitude' – where one is willing to embrace a form of critical thinking which remains 'eventful' insofar as it refuses to be prescribed by predetermined categories and remains open to: 'imagining the possibility that the world and its objects might be otherwise than they are' (Joughin 2000b; cf. Docherty 2003: 31). Where conventional understandings of the emergence of a 'representational' theatre prescribe a fixed field of vision – a place of the visibly present where that which is secret or hidden is only so in the sense that all remains to be revealed – an aesthetic attitude implies a willingness to remain open to the truth-potential of the particular transformation wrought by aesthetic experience itself, where the distinctive articulation of truth in works of art 'discloses' the world in new ways rather than copying or representing what is known to be already there (cf. Joughin 2000a: 65–7 and Bowie 1997: 5, 301). In contrast, by adhering to a correspondence model of self-evident truths and in failing to see 'more in things than they are', traditionalist critics confuse the apparitional with the merely empirical.[3] This is not quite right, for as Adorno reminds us, in the process of entering the realm of their secular transcendence artworks already 'posit a more as what appears' indeed 'artworks become artworks in the production of this more: they produce their own transcendence' (Adorno 1997: 78). Crucially, as Adorno goes on to suggest, insofar as such artworks become actual, 'in appearing empirically' they are simultaneously 'liberated from the burden of the empirical' (ibid.: 81). In a section of *Aesthetic Theory* dealing with 'Art Beauty' he develops this distinction further by comparing artwork's apparitional potential to fireworks, observing that:

The phenomenon of fireworks is prototypical for artworks, though because of its fleetingness and status as empty entertainment it has scarcely ever been acknowledged by theoretical consideration . . . Fireworks are apparition . . .: They appear empirically yet are liberated from the burden of the empirical, which is the obligation of duration; *they are a sign from heaven yet artifactual,* an ominous warning, a script that flashes up, vanishes, and indeed cannot be read for its meaning. The segregation of the aesthetic sphere by means of the complete afunctionality of what is thoroughly ephemeral is no formal definition of aesthetics. It is not through a higher perfection that artworks separate from the fallibly existent but rather by becoming actual, like fireworks, incandescently in an expressive appearance. They are not only the other of the empirical world: Everything in them becomes other.

(ibid.: 81, my emphasis)

As Isobel Armstrong notes, glossing Adorno:

[Artworks/fireworks] are at once artefactual, actual and other to the empirical world – a magical phenomenon which is not a higher truth but an astonishment and a wonder, intellectual delight and kinaesthetic happening. . . . But ultimately it [the artwork/firework] never transcends empirical reality; it needs the sensuous, the brute physical existence of the material world, and depends on crude mechanism for its very nature as apparition.

(Armstrong 2000: 180–2)

Rather than existing in an ephemeral domain then artworks are fallibly existent. And in reminding us of the sensuous need on which apparition simultaneously relies for its visionary power (for its 'very nature as apparition'), Adorno's theorisation of aesthetic transcendence and disenchantment thus simultaneously draws us back to what he terms an 'art-alien' layer – the material antecedent of all that is 'spiritual' in art, which he proceeds to discuss in terms that are teasingly reminiscent of Brook's sense that the extraordinary is already secreted in the ordinary:

It is not so much that artworks possess ideality as that by virtue of their spiritualization they promise a blocked or denied sensuality. That quality can be comprehended in those phenomena from which artistic experience emancipated itself, in the relics of an art-alien art, as it were, the justly or unjustly so-called lower arts such as the circus. . . . Art becomes an image not directly but by becoming an *apparition* but only through the counter-tendency to it. The preartistic level of art is at the same time the memento of its anticultural character, its suspicion of its antithesis to the empirical world that leaves this world untouched. Important artworks nevertheless seek to incorporate this art-alien layer. When, suspected of being infantile, it is absent from art, when the last trace of the vagrant fiddler disappears from the spiritual chamber musician and the illusionless drama has lost the magic of the stage, art has capitulated. The curtain lifts expectantly even at the beginning of Beckett's *Endgame*; plays and stagings that eliminate the curtain fumble with a shallow trick. The instant the curtain goes up is the expectation of the *apparition*.

(Adorno 1997: 81)

In its becoming apparitional then the artwork retains its common touch. Here again, as Isobel Armstrong notes, Adorno's dialectic begins 'to swing back against itself' as paradoxically 'the very rapture of spirit conjures its antithesis, a blocked corporeal existence. To be outside the empirical world is to leave it untouched, and thus to be physical image, naïve illusion, is art's way of belonging to the world' (Armstrong 2000: 180). When the magic of the circus eventually disappears from drama and it sheds its 'art-alien layer' (Adorno 1997: 81) then 'apparition will be displaced by the dry, transparent artwork which is essentially dead' (cf. Armstrong 2000: 180), or, to coin Brook's term for the same process – theatre will have become deadly.

Adorno's eventual summary of his position on the apparitional quality of art – 'In each genuine artwork something appears that does not exist' (Adorno 1997: 82) – could be extended to a quasi-Cavellian understanding of the ontology of drama. Amidst the dissymmetry of performance, as Cavell reminds us, in occupying the same time as the characters, we effectively 'live through' a sequence of moments with them, even though characters do not exist as things in the world do. This means that while, in one sense, we cannot put ourselves in the 'presence' of characters during performance (where we are absent), in 'another sense', in acknowledging characters specificity as particular individuals: 'we are in, or can put ourselves in, their *present*' (see Cavell 1987, esp. 108, Cavell's emphasis). Here again although 'we do not share the same space' in performance 'we share the same time' (cf. Hammer 2002: 90), the apparitional brings something into our world – something that 'does not exist' and yet is simultaneously tied to its situation and to history. We can't know what the other knows – in that sense making contact with the actors' world is impossible – but in another sense our relation to what takes place on stage cannot be dismissed as a mere illusion.

For Cavell of course the obverse side of detached incredulity and scepticism is the wrong type of credulity. And in his seminal essay on *Othello* he reminds us of the yokel who on attending a performance of the play and in mistaking Othello strangling Desdemona for the real thing, leaps onto the stage and attempts to intervene (cf. Cavell 1976 and Hammer 2002: 89). Curiously of course, the link between these apparent extremes is evoked by the mechanicals' interlude that in dramatising the conditions of the theatre also reminds us that the aloof aristocrats are already cast, by the mechanicals at least, as credulous yokels who might fear the spectacle of a lion roaring. For their part the aristocrats are in turn exposed to the actual danger of confusing kindness with stupidity. In short there is already both more and less to this scene than meets the eye and we will need to return to it later.

Bottom's experience of the visionary 'hath no bottom', which is to say that it is itself without foundation or prior fixity and yet as his pun on 'no bottom' infers it is also bottomless because 'unfathomably profound'.[4] But of course we must not lose touch with common sense. For all that it is 'out of body' Bottom's name is itself a type of 'open secret' – a reminder that the experience of the spiritual secretes the 'promise of a blocked or denied sensuality'. Still, Bottom's experience is no doubt of a singular nature. He is touched. And I mean that not just in the sense of the superlunary madness that pervades the play (though let us not forget that paradise is always on the other side of the moon) but also in the sense that in being touched Bottom is also singled out and blessed. In an analogous fashion one might say that drawing close to the artwork's utopian/ messianic impulse implies another type of contact at a distance – where what touches us (however common) necessarily remains itself untouchable. If, like Bottom's dream, theatre is cast as *tout autre*, wholly other (or 'in another sense'), then here too we are suspended without support, and this encountered otherness ensures that the viewing subject experiences an analogous sense of ungrounding and disorientation – he/she hath no bottom.

Inevitably then, in performance, there is also always a sharing of the secret without sharing it. In this respect, however complex and tangled it becomes, the analogy between a secular theatre and Bottom's experience of an untranslatable *mysterium tremendum* proves sustainable. Each seems to adhere to a logic of a surplus economy (this is true of course, as Walter Benjamin and others remind us, of translation per se) where the true nature of the sharing or the communion in question remains secret. In a sense then 'nothing is untranslatable' (there is always more) but like Bottom's 'more', the 'more' of performance simultaneously remains 'in another sense', where everything is untranslatable.[5] Yet, in coming close, our share of the secret simultaneously raises ethical and political issues concerning the possibility of community and credulity, even credence. How then does one actually apprehend more? More than cool reason ever comprehends? What further 'sense' can be made, in other words, of Bottom's garbled memory of the Pauline text (1 Cor. 2:9), with its messianic expectation of a spirit that transfigures sense? In seeking an answer and in lieu of spiritual discernment it will be necessary to learn to discern spirits, where one apprehends both more and less.

Learning to live with apparitions

> I cannot close my eyes and hurl myself trustingly into the absurd, for me it is impossible, but I do not praise myself on that account. I am convinced that God is love; this thought has for me a pristine lyrical validity. When it is present to me I am unspeakably happy, when it is absent I yearn for it more intensely than the lover for the beloved; but I do not have faith; this courage I lack. God's love is for me, both in a direct and inverse sense, incommensurable with the whole of reality. I am

not coward enough to whimper and moan on that account, but neither am I underhand enough to deny that faith is something far higher.

(Kierkegaard 1985: 63)

It is requir'd/You do awake your faith.

(*The Winter's Tale*, 5.3. 94–5)

A spirit that transfigures sense? Barely discernible? 'Something epiphenomenal'? In our *apprehension* of the visionary or the secret, then as Derrida reminds us:

> We tremble in that strange repetition that ties an irrefutable past (a shock has been felt, a traumatism has already affected us) to a future that cannot be anticipated; anticipated but unpredictable; *apprehended*, but, and this is why there is a future, apprehended precisely *as* unforeseeable, unpredictable; approached *as* unapproachable. Even if one thinks one knows what is going to happen, the new instant of that happening remains untouched, still unaccessible, in fact unlivable. . . . Hence I tremble because I am still afraid of what already makes me afraid, of what I can neither see nor foresee. I tremble at what exceeds my seeing and my knowing [*mon voir et mon savoir*] although it concerns the innermost parts of me, right down to my soul, down to the bone, as we say.
>
> (Derrida 1995b: 54)

These untimely disorientating repetitions that transgress conventions, approached in fear and trembling ('you'll think –/ Which I protest against – I am assisted/By wicked powers' (*The Winter's Tale*, 5.3.89–91)) are a feature (a family trait?) of unlikely scenes of apparition. In the statue scene (5.3) at the end of *The Winter's Tale* (exactly an irrefutable past tied to a future that cannot be anticipated), apprehension is seeing *as*, where, even if one thinks one knows what is going to happen, the 'new instant of that happening remains untouched'. Instead, something comes to be seen *as* something in a new way – something that 'happens' outside an a priori grid of expectations and refuses the foreclosure of traditional attempts to explain it away.[6]

Apprehension, here and elsewhere (in being apprehended as unforeseeable), is a type of blind – but then isn't love, isn't faith, always touchingly so? What exceeds 'my seeing and knowing' produces a longing to touch, or at least to seal (to heal?), touching with a kiss, or even to caress the hand (that organ of touch and healing) with a kiss:

Perdita   Give me that hand of yours to kiss.

(5.3.46)

Leontes   Let no man mock me,
  For I will kiss her.

(5.3.79–80)

Eventually, by Paulina's instruction, that which remains untouched –

Paulina   O patience!
  The statue is but newly fix'd, the colour's
  Not dry.

(5.3.47–9)

Paulina   Good my lord, forbear:
  The ruddiness upon her lip is wet.
  You'll mar it if you kiss it, stain your own
  With oily painting . . .

(5.3.80–83)

– is also, eventually, a re-joining, a leading by the hand:

Paulina   Nay present your hand
  When she was young, you woo'd her. Now, in age,
  Is she beome the suitor?
Leontes   O, she's warm!
  If this be magic, let it be art
  Lawful as eating.

(5.3.107–11)

The extraordinary brings us back to the staple diet of the everyday.
  Touch then, but touch only as *trait*, the remarking of absence and presence. Insofar as they reside in another sense, we cannot

touch the players though they come 'something near' (5.3.23).
In the very instant or event of transfiguration, Leontes' own
'rare vision' or translation, is bound to be untranslatable, his
kinaesthetic confusion wholly akin to rapture:

Paulina   My lord's almost so far transported that
    He'll think anon it lives
Leontes   O sweet Paulina
    Make me to think so twenty years together!
    No settled senses of the world can match
    The pleasure of that madness.

                                        (5.3.68–72)

The tremor repeats itself precisely 'in anticipation of what is to
come' as 'a preliminary and visible agitation' (again cf. Derrida
1995b: 53–4):

Paulina   I have thus far stirr'd you; but
    I could afflict you farther.
Leontes   Do, Paulina,
    For this affliction has a taste as sweet.
    As any cordial comfort. Still methinks
    There is an air comes from her. What fine chisel
    Could ever yet cut breath?

                                        (5.3.74–9)

Barely holding breath (where the body inhales and expires) in
this air of apprehension, a theatre of wonder actually rests on
the appearance of the everyday and of what is already 'being'
(strange but true). As if the vestige of another discourse is
still hibernating (a winter's tail?) within the ordinary. Another
metaphysics then, the very one we need 'in order to cognize
and transform the one we routinely inhabit'.[7] Our experience
of Shakespeare's drollery of the statue is no less wonderful
and commonplace than Autolycus' ballads – the silly songs
of spring to Paulina's winter's tale – 'very true' (4.4.257) yet
overheard and overseen in mocking aloofness (do not mock),
beyond reason, yet still more wonderful, for their all their
'silly palpability' (Rose epigraph), palpable gross silliness, 'the
silliest stuff that ever I heard' (*A Midsummer Night's Dream*,
5.1.207):

Autolycus   My clown, who wants something to be a reasonable
  Man, grew so in love with the wenches' song, that *he*
  would not stir his pettitoes till he had both time and
  words, which so drew the rest of the herd to me that
  all their other senses stuck in ears. You might have
  pinched a placket, it was senseless . . .

  (4.4.592–7; my emphasis)

Paulina   It is requir'd
  You do awake your faith. Then, all stand still . . .
Leon   Proceed.
  No foot shall stir.

  (5.3.94–8; my emphasis)

In stillness and faith and growing in love, the mystery of music,
visibility and their hiddenness.

Yet the moment of reunion and revelation will always remain
a mixed blessing – what's lost as well as found:

Third Gentleman   . . . their joy waded in tears. There was
  casting up of eyes, holding up of hands, with
  countenance of such distraction that they were to be
  known by garment, not by favour. . . . But O, the
  noble combat that 'twixt joy and sorrow was
  fought in Paulina!
  She had one eye declined for the loss of her
  husband, another elevated that the Oracle was
  fulfilled . . .

  (5.2.41–4; 66–9)

Cross-eyed Paulina finds herself positioned between the 'translation' of the secular and the sacred – ('The poet's eye, in a fine
frenzy rolling,/Doth glance from heaven to earth, from earth
to heaven . . .?' (*A Midsummer Night's Dream*, 5.1.12ff.)).

So then how is all this to be divined? In the discrepancy
between seeing and telling? For if by secondhand report 'then
have you lost a sight, which was to be seen, cannot be spoken'
(5.2.38–9). When it eventually arrives the revelation of the secret

lies in learning to live in the instant 'it appears she lives,/Though yet she speak not' (5.3.118–19). Remaining 'unspeakably happy' (Kierkegaard, above) the revelation of the secret resides in 'tongue-tied simplicity' (*A Midsummer Night's Dream*, 5.1.104); it cannot be spoken or divined. In fact, in its unknowability Leontes' 'conversion' secretes an almost Abrahamic paradox of faith.[8] In *Fear and Trembling* Kierkegaard's narrator Johannes *de Silentio* reminds us of Abraham's bewildering silence concerning the sacrifice of his son Issac:

> All along he [Abraham] had faith, he believed that God would not demand Isaac of him, while still he was willing to offer him if that was indeed what was demanded. He believed on the strength of the absurd, for there could be no question of human calculation, and it was indeed absurd that God who demanded this of him should in the next instant withdraw the demand. He climbed the mountain, even in that moment when the knife gleamed he believed – that God would not demand. Certainly he was surprised by the outcome, but by means of a double movement he had come back to his original position and therefore received Isaac more joyfully than the first time. Let us go further. We let Isaac be sacrificed. Abraham had faith. His faith was not that he should be happy sometime in the hereafter but that he should find blessed happiness here in this world. God could give him a new Isaac, bring the sacrificial offer back to life. He believed on the strength of the absurd, for all human calculation had long since been suspended.
>
> (Kierkegaard 1985: 65)

Eventually Leontes' overcoming of self-imposed solitude and perpetual mourning – 'Once a day I'll visit/The chapel where they lie, and tears shed there/Shall be my recreation' (3.2.236–8) – like Abraham's sacrifice resides in undertaking the movement from loss and resignation to a state of grace; so that now, against all probability, he believes that, impossibly, God gives back that which is simultaneously beyond reparation – 'stol'n from the dead!' (5.3.116). Learning to live with wonders means moving beyond erotic disappointment and yearning, as, in embracing the movement of faith, Leontes finally learns how to let go of loss.

Again in any conventional sense there is no sound basis for knowledge here. Like Abraham, like Leontes, we are each led like the blind, so that, as Derrida comments:

> God sees in secret he knows. But it is as if he didn't know what Abraham was going to do, or decide, or decide to do. He gives him back his son after assuring himself that Abraham has trembled, renounced all hope . . .
>
> (Derrida 1995b: 95)

In the interim there is only the voice of another – Paulina, the intermediary who (like the converted Apostle Paul) has herself embraced faith and now 'speaks between', so that, even when she speaks of the non-narratable disclosure of apparition, she understands that it is only in being apart that something still comes something near:

> I like your silence, it the more shows off
> Your wonder. But yet speak; first you, my liege.
> Comes it not something near?
>
> (5. 3. 21–3)

Because it is a shared relation in which we unknowingly share, there is always a sacrificial component in the absolute secret – again, what touches us itself remains untouchable. In unpacking our self-possession, theatre invites us to join (in our dispossession) with the other. Coming close, the proximity of performance takes care, often in not touching – 'Good my lord, forbear./The ruddiness upon her lip is wet./You'll mar it if you kiss it . . .' (5.3.80–2) – to remind us of the capacity for rejoining that which was apart or sundered; if only in wishing and dreaming (as Kierkegaard's 'Knight of Faith' does in *Fear and Trembling*) in unwitting naivety that things could be other than they are. As such, faith is an interior relation beyond the comprehension of an exterior from which those who view it could never know the truth (cf. Derrida 1995b: 63 and 108). It follows then that Leontes too is seen without seeing, for in the economy of the apparitional and in the revelation of the secret, there is, as Derrida reminds us: 'a dissymmetry of looks that cannot be exchanged' (ibid.: 93).[9] Under this gaze we can't 'know' in any conventional sense either what we see or that which is apparently looking at us. It might even be Hermione. . . .

We are in the remove here of a God (albeit now a *deus ex machina*) who sees more – always more than we do. One might say that the theatre itself holds us in regard.

To see in secret

> To see in secret – what can that mean?
>
> (Derrida 1995b: 88)

> I see a voice . . .
>
> (*A Midsummer Night's Dream*, 5.1.190)

For German Romanticism, Shakespeare's translative combination of the visionary and the everyday quickly became a metaphor for the singularity of the playwright's aesthetic achievement and his capacity for poetic invention, so that as Schlegel observes:

> In *The Midsummer Night's Dream* [*sic*], there flows a luxuriant vein of the boldest and most fantastical invention; the most extraordinary combination of the most dissimilar ingredients seems to have been brought about without effort by some ingenious and lucky accident, and the colours are of such clear transparency that we think the whole of the variegated fabric may be blown away with a breath. The fairy world here described resembles those elegant pieces of arabesque, where little genii with butterfly wings rise, half embodied, above the flower-cups.
>
> (Schlegel 1846 cited in Bate 1997: 470)

Schlegel's evocation of a twilight zone of diaphanous folds and 'poetic enchantment' is echoed elsewhere by Keats in several of his poems including 'Ode to Psyche'; evoking a world of liminal states between waking and dreaming – one which offers a non-saturable context for prospective vision, inspiration and further translation: a bower of bliss where the poet presides as Priest pleading pardon 'that thy [Psyche's] secrets should be sung' (Keats 1983). Keats, Schlegel and others hint at a rich kinaesthetic experience that is always already reliant on a material antecedent, a weave of the sensible (albeit one 'blown away with a breath').

Yet even for Romanticism, this sense of the *Dream*'s poetic reverie still tends to occupy a delimited field of vision – where that which is barely concealed will eventually be revealed. For his part, Schlegel goes on to complain that 'the droll wonder of Bottom's translation [as an ass] is merely the translation of a metaphor in its literal sense', while the mechanicals' interlude is another piece of knowing disenchantment, a barely concealed spoof of *Romeo and Juliet* wherein:

> Pyramus and Thisbe is not unmeaningly chosen as the grotesque play within the play; it is exactly like the pathetic part of the piece, a secret meeting of two lovers in the forest, and their separation by an unfortunate accident, and closes the whole with the most amusing parody.
>
> (Schlegel 1846 cited in Bate 1997: 470–1)

In many ways of course amidst claims and counter-claims for the apparitional, the mechanicals' scene quickly situates a crux of interpretation for the play and in a rather different vein, having assimilated the non-illusionary theatre of Artaud, Brecht and Beckett, many critics would now readily agree with Schlegel's sense of Shakespeare's 'not unmeaningful' parody. As such the play within a play is cast as an 'acknowledgement of the limitations of theatrical illusion' which in turn only serves to enhance Shakespeare's powers as a playwright in differentiating him 'from inept attempts to leave nothing to be supplied by the imagination' (cf. Marshall 1982: 545); in other words, as David Young puts it still more succinctly: 'Where the mechanicals fail at dramatic illusion ... *A Midsummer Night's Dream* succeeds.' (Young 1966: 105 also cited in Marshall 1982: 545).

Yet of course these and other distinctions actually sell the play's apparitional potential short. The tendency to read the mechanicals' scene as a knowing form of unknowing, ungenerously misses the point of a visionary theatre where, as Bottom himself puts it, we must first 'look to our eyes' (cf. 1.2.20) – and which in some sense escapes the field of vision altogether, insofar as it proceeds to undo the relation between seeing and knowing.

There are, after all, as Derrida reminds us, 'two ways' in which the invisible can be understood:

There is . . . an invisible of the order of the visible that I can keep in secret by keeping it out of sight. This invisible can be artificially kept from sight while remaining within what one can call exteriority (if I hide a nuclear arsenal in underground silos in a cache, there is a visible surface involved . . . whatever one conceals in this way becomes invisible but remains within the order of visibility, it remains constitutively visible. . . . But there is also absolute invisibility, the absolute non-visible that falls to whatever falls outside of the register of sight, namely, the sonorous, the musical, the vocal or phonic (and hence the phonological or discursive in the strict sense), but also the tactile and odoriferous . . .

(Derrida 1995b: 90)

No doubt each of these two forms of invisibility inform the other, but it is the latter that prevails during the mechanicals' scene – an implicit emphasis on listening, smelling and touching, accessible to senses other than sight, odoriferous and sweet: 'O sweet' (like incense?). Allowing for the absurd within the sensible (listen(ing) to the moon, see(ing) a voice) the mechanicals return us to the untranslatable synaesthesia of Bottom's vision, reminding us insistently of that which is lost from sight.

In fact the kinaesthetic confusion of the mechanicals' scene bears an uncanny resemblance to Peter Brook's exercise for actors as, in his striving for a 'Holy Theatre', the director experiments with an interior beyond exterior relation. The aim, Brook notes, was

to discover what was the very least he [the actor] needed: was it a sound, a movement, a rhythm – and were these interchangeable – or had each its special strengths and limitations?. . . . We worked by imposing drastic conditions. An actor must communicate an idea – the start must always be a thought or a wish that he has to project – but he has only, say, one finger, one tone of voice a cry, or the capacity to whistle at his disposal.

(Brook 1990: 55–6)

At times Brook observes it was 'like crossing an abyss on a tightrope . . .' in their reliance on different wordless languages ('we took an event, a fragment of experience and made exercises that turned them into forms that could be shared . . .' (ibid.: 58)) the actors in Brook's exercise are never allowed to touch, no realistic contact can take place, instead: 'the actor found that to communicate his invisible meanings he needed concentration, he needed will; he needed to summon all his emotional reserves; he needed courage; he needed clear thought' (ibid.: 57). In communicating invisible meanings Brook 'experiments' with silence, or, as he puts it himself: 'we set out to discover the relations between silence and duration . . .' (ibid.: 58).

A faith in the absurd, beyond knowledge in any conventional sense, entails a touching without touching, sharing without sharing, remaining responsive to the irreducible otherness of the other, in an encounter with alterity, a 'dis-figuring' that refuses categorisation and which foregoes philosophical knowing – if that 'knowing' is construed in the narrower sense of mere objectification (see Levinas 1991, *passim* and cf. Bruns 1990, esp. 619–20). In an ethical sense that which joins us in singularity to the absolute singularity of the other is this exposure to 'another sense'. And howsoever immersed they are in their parts actors themselves occupy an analogous 'space of risk or sacrifice' remaining together and open to interchangeability only in their acceptance of being apart (cf. Derrida 1995b, esp. 68). They discover that 'to be an actor' is as David Marshall puts it:

[T]o double and divide oneself, both the part and not the part. The mechanicals feel compelled to acknowledge this on stage: "tell them that I Pyramus am not Pyramus" (III, I, 19) says Bottom the weaver; and so Snout the tinker declares himself Snout and a wall, and the lion insists that he is the lion and Snug the joiner . . .

(Marshall 1982: 563)

Or, as Peter Quince puts it even more succinctly, 'We are not here' (5.1.115). The uncanniness of the ordinary. . . .

Yet curiously of course it is precisely in not knowing who they are, that within a loss of self-possession the mechanicals also rediscover their capacity for 'joining',[10] demonstrating an 'infinite capacity for self-creation and response to [their] fellow self-creators' (Rose 1999: 63). In 'conning' their parts (cf. 1.2.82) they might truly be said to 'learn by heart'. This comes close to the 'learning by heart' of a craft or mystery (and this is the actor's craft too) where 'beyond semantic . . . comprehension one gives without knowing', and where 'to share a secret is not to know or reveal the secret, it is to share we know not what, a secret: nothing that can be determined' (cf. Derrida 1995: 97, 80).[11] In our experience of playing, both as audience and players, we share this condition of being apart together (the same way that 'sharers' in a theatrical company owe every bit to every bit of the other?). Even as they enact a tale of erotic loss and disappointment the mechanicals accept 'the conditions of being sundered and being joined' – a 'union in partition' perhaps best exemplified by the roughcast wall (cf. Marshall 1982): 'Through which the lovers, Pyramus and Thisbe,/Did whisper often, very secretly . . .' (5. 1. 158–9) and which itself, in 'being sensible', also constitutes a literal embodiment of our own remove.

No epilogue, I pray you

In Puck's epilogue this play on 'sundering and joining' (cf. Marshall 1982) is finally recast around another invitation to 'join hands', not by touching, but by accepting disenchantment as a necessary accomplice to dreaming – pardoning the remove and re-joining (or 'mending'), that which in another sense must remain sundered (epilogue). Yet for his part, Bottom's promise of an epilogue (or is it a lament?) in 'the latter end of a play', Peter Quince's 'ballad', is never fulfilled (5.2.390ff); for in Bottom's play there can be no end, only 'true beginning' (5.1.111).

Likewise, in his own brief 'Epilogue' to *Fear and Trembling* Kierkegaard's narrator Johannes *de Silentio* 'begins again' by reminding us that there can be no epilogue and that every generation begins afresh in faith and love:

> However much one generation learns from another, it can never learn from its predecessor the genuinely human factor. In this respect every generation begins afresh, has no task other than that of any previous generation, and comes no further, provided the latter hasn't shirked its task and deceived itself. This authentically human factor is

passion, in which the one generation also fully understands the other understands itself. Thus no generation has learned from another how to love, no generation can begin other than at the beginning, the task of no later generation is shorter than its predecessor's, and if someone, unlike the previous generation, is unwilling to stay with love but wants to go further, then this is simply idle and foolish talk.

(Kierkegaard 1985: 145)

There is no counting on ancestors, rather 'faith must be started over by each generation' (cf. Derrida 1995b: 80). This sentiment of course is all too apparent at the end of *The Winter's Tale* and is also partly echoed in the last lines of *Lear* where in the play's epilogue, in 'coming after' another new generation nevertheless has to learn for itself how to go on and begin again:

> The weight of this sad time we must obey;
> Speak what we feel, not what we ought to say.
> The oldest hath borne most; we that are young
> Shall never see so much, nor live so long.
> *Exeunt with a dead march.*

(5.3.322–5)

Notably, in the closing lines of the play 'feeling' and 'speaking' rather than feeling and seeing, are cast in tantalising proximity. And again this is a form of obligation, a 'speaking' that eventually comes from the heart. If, in the old regime, Goneril and Regan 'spoke dutifully what they *ought to say*' (see Foakes 1997: 392; Foakes' emphasis, and cf. *Lear* 1.1) now there is a duty which exceeds mere public duty and lies beyond the empty rhetoric that attended the official investment of power and authority at the beginning of the play. As a new beginning this outcome is discordant yet it also re-marks a recognition that 'the obligations imposed by the dead *are* the obligations we discover and renegotiate in life'[12] – a form of ethical demand that lives on in ordinary day-to-day commitments and continues to inform our relations with others. A duty beyond duty – a response in part exemplified earlier on in the play by what Rose would call the 'love-ability' of Cordelia's childish 'learning by heart', which, despite its unhappiness, refused to heave its heart into its mouth (1.1.90–1) and offered instead an unjustifiable, yet loving and dutiful silence – and in doing so kept its secret (cf. Joughin 2002: 79–81).

In learning to let go of loss, Shakespearean comedy and tragedy-comedy alike embraces the possibility of 'reinventing tradition' and beginning again. All this happens without precedent and without cause, only by improbable creation. In learning the lesson of love there is no time left for lament or mourning. As such, just as resignation is often the accomplice of maturity, the passion of faith lies in embracing the task in hand anew with childlike credulity, demonstrating a willingness to overcome weariness, for, as Kierkegaard adds:

> So long as the generation only worries about its task, which is the highest it can attain to, it cannot grow weary. That task is always enough for a human lifetime. When children on holiday get through all their games by noon and then ask impatiently, 'Can't anyone think of a new game?', does this show that they are more developed and advanced than children of the same generation who could make the games they already know last the whole day? Or does it not rather show that those children lack what I would call the good-natured seriousness that belongs to play?
>
> (Kierkegaard 1985: 146)

The analogy to 'play' here evokes a precise form of cognitive re-negotiation, in that, as Isobel Armstrong reminds us, children's play itself achieves a special inversion:

> Play achieves an extraordinary reversal, a transformation of the very structure of perception. When one thing begins to stand for another (a stick for a horse) the thing becomes a 'pivot' for severing the idea of a horse from the concrete existence of the horse, [lantern, dog, and bush of thorn presenteth Moonshine?] and the rule-bound game is determined by ideas, not by objects. Play liberates the child into ideas, into an understanding of categories and their *relation* to objects . . . play is liberating through its capacity to be interactive: because the child can create an alienated meaning within the constraints of a specific, concrete situation, play occupies 'the realm of spontaneity and freedom'.
>
> (Armstrong 2000: 38)

Tied to actuality, in ways that cannot be reduced to the empirical or verifiable, the experience of 'play' allows instead for the creation of new possible worlds. In its interactivity it encourages us to explore, to respect and to learn to live together, exploring the boundaries of blissful boundless love. Open to new perceptions, immersed in childlike, silly palpability . . .

In contrast, within our own loss-laden philosophical and political maturity, the infinite movement of faith has never been harder to accomplish. Or more wearisome. In no small part of course, this is because (amid 'state of the art' surveillance) politicians wilfully misconstrue the nature of the secret. The original lack of faith that now finds Tony Blair conceding that weapons of mass destruction (WOMD) may never be found in Iraq – 'I do not know is the answer . . . I believe that we will [find WOMD] but I agree there were many people who thought we were going to find this [*sic*] in the course of the actual operation' – betrays a 'wait and see' policy that itself remains constitutively visible, and finally, in the name of 'justice', can only ever claim its alibi in the form of an 'open' 'objective' verification:

> I can assure you I have no intention of hiding away from this at all . . . On the contrary, I am enthusiastic about being at long last able to debate these issues on the basis of an objective, independent judgment by a judge, rather than speculation.[13]

In failing to understand that acts of faith lie 'beyond the economy of the terrestrial visible or sensible' Blair (who himself professes Christianity) would 'take possession of the secret' (Derrida 1995b: 87, 98). But his disingenuous admission that he no longer believes confirms a betrayal of faith that is both ancient and modern. Whether or not Bush and Blair pray together, their vision for the future congregates alongside all the other mad monotheisms within the current crisis of faith. As such it constitutes a dogmatic and totalising response to the 'emergency' – a crusading faith that stakes its claim for certainty around 'homeland security'. In the wake of these destructive alliances with God, Derrida calls instead for general messianic end to the 'determinate faiths . . . that divide humanity into warring parties' and make 'war on the other' (see Caputo 1997a: 195) calling instead for a 'nondogmatic doublet of dogma . . . a thinking that "repeats" the possibility of religion without religion . . . *at bottom* [Derrida suggests] this list has no limit'.[14]

In its infinite capacity for constant renewal and absolute beginnings, Shakespeare's drama (which itself could not openly speak of God) offers us an analogous taste of, and for, the invention of the wholly other. As such, its open secret resides in joining and sundering and learning to live together apart, sharing (we know not what) in the sacramental relation of the visible-invisible of apparitions. Partaking in the good-natured seriousness that belongs to play. Resisting the maturity of generational conflict and embracing love-ability.

Enjoining us to begin again . . .

Notes

1 Constituting a notable exception to the rule, Kiernan Ryan, a fellow contributor to this volume, urges us instead to embrace the future, asking:

> What if the changing meaning of the most valuable [Shake-spearean] works is not held in the gravitational grip of the past or the present, but is printed into their form and texture by the pressure of futurity, by the secret contract with a dispensation that might do justice to our dreams?
>
> (Ryan 2002: 175–6)

2 See Derek Attridge (2004), *The Singularity of Literature* (*passim*) and cf. esp. p. 151 where he cites Badiou 2001.

3 For the time being it is worth noting that in attempting to discriminate between reality and illusion in these terms critics necessarily remain complicit with a claim for universal validity that as Derrida and others remind us 'inspires philosophy and ethics in their most powerful and coercive forms'. Bound as it is to a schema of identity thinking empirical-idealist variants of lit-crit reinstall a request for truth, where as Derrida comments 'the manifest is given priority over the hidden or secret' and where 'there are finally no secrets for philosophy, ethics or politics' (cf. Derrida 1995b: 63).

4 See Brooks 2001: cxvii. I owe this reference to Geza Kallay.

5 Again compare Derrida, this time on translation: 'In a sense, nothing is untranslatable; but *in another sense*, everything is untranslatable; translation is another name for the impossible' (Derrida, 1998: 56–7).

6 For more on 'seeing *as*' and a discussion of the revelationary potential of aesthetic disclosure during the statue scene see Joughin 2000b.

7 Again, see Joughin 2000b and also compare Bernstein 1992: 9.

8 Did God originally impart a secret to Leontes? – we will never know.

9 Cf. Derrida 1995b: 'It is dissymmetrical: this gaze that sees me without my seeing it looking at me . . . a gaze that sees me without my seeing it' (91, 93).

10 As Marshall notes, the mechanicals are all concerned with 'some form or manner of joining. Carpenter, joiner, weaver, bellows mender, tinker, tailor' as such he adds 'their occupations enact the preoccupations of *A Midsummer Night's Dream*. . . . All join together what is apart or mend what has been rent, broken, or sundered' (Marshall 1982: 562).

11 In speaking of the secret Derrida reminds us:

> It is a matter of learning 'by heart' beyond any semantic comprehension. In fact God asks that one give without knowing, without calculating, reckoning, or hoping, for one must give without counting, and that is what takes it outside of sense.
>
> (Derrida 1995b: 97)

12 I owe this formulation to Wendy Wheeler (1999: 78) though I should note that both Wheeler and I are indebted in turn to Gillian Rose, cf. esp. Rose 1996.

13 These soundbites from Blair are taken from *The Guardian*, 12 January 2004.

14 Derrida 1995b: 49 my emphasis, though I owe the translation and the illumination to Caputo 1997a: 195.

7

Spectres of *Hamlet*

Richard Kearney

Before religious dread comes 'daemonic dread' with its queer
perversion, a sort of abortive offshoot, the 'dread of ghosts'. It
first begins to stir in the feeling of 'something uncanny', 'eerie',
or 'weird'. It is this feeling which, emerging in the mind of
primeval man, forms the starting point for the entire religious
development in history.

(Otto 1958: 14)

Shakespeare's *Hamlet* is a play about spirits. But how should
this be read – theologically, aesthetically, psychoanalytically?
This is a question that has preoccupied many thinkers from
Kierkegaard and Lacan to Girard and Derrida. In what follows
I propose to revisit some of the most significant philosophical
interpretations of Hamlet's phantoms from a contemporary
perspective. I will begin with a brief presentation of *Hamlet* as
a play about a *crisis of narrative memory*, before then going on to
review how several theorists have sought to interrogate its role
as a drama of holy and unholy ghosts. I will look at four main
readings: (1) the psychoanalytic paradigm of phantom-as-
unconscious; (2) the existential paradigm of phantom-as-failure;

(3) the deconstructive paradigm of phantom-as-erasure; and (4) the theological paradigm of phantom-as-conscience.

Hamlet is a play that opens with a spectre enjoining the protagonist to remember something that cannot be remembered. From the opening scene we find ourselves embroiled in a play about the terrible impossibility – yet inescapability – of memory. 'Remember me', says the ghost of King Hamlet to his son (1.5.91). Tell my tale and transmit my memory to future generations so that my role in history – abruptly cut off – can be restored. It is common in Shakespearean plays to find kings bidding their children to inherit their secret story, blessing or birthright. And was not young Hamlet born for this? To tell his father's story to the people of the Union: the Union of two nations, Denmark and Norway, sealed with the pearl won by his father in the famous duel with Fortinbras the Elder. (A duel fought, as is later recalled by the gravedigger, the *same day* that young Prince Hamlet entered this world.) Was not Prince Hamlet born, then, to respond to the summons of his father's spirit – namely, to carry on his father's history and avenge his murder?

But there's a rub. First, we cannot be sure *who* speaks when the spectre speaks. There is a profound ambivalence about the origin and character of the ghost. Hamlet's friend Horatio says 'tis but our fantasy' (1.1.21). Or worse 'a guilty thing' (1.2.129). At best a 'spirit' (1.2.135), one moment there, one moment gone, there and not there, present and absent, the past-as-present. And when the sepulchral phantasm finally talks, after much equivocation, he claims he is a creature come, not back from Heaven (as we would expect for such a noble father), but from Hell or Purgatory: from 'sulphrous and tormenting flames' (1.5.3). He is indeed a 'questionable shape' (1.4.24). So, from the very outset of the play, it would appear that religious questions of guilt, sin, repentance, redemption and the afterlife deeply inform Hamlet's dilemma.

But there's another rub. If we can't be sure *who* the ghost is, neither can we be sure of *what* he is trying to say. He bids his son, 'remember!' Yes. *But what is he to remember?* His father's glories as illustrious monarch, faithful to his people, spouse and son? Or the exact hidden details of his untimely murder? No. The irony is that the first thing father tells son is *what he cannot tell him*. Recall the actual words spoken in Act 1, scene 5:

I am thy father's spirit,
Doomed for a certain term to walk the night,
And for the days confined to fast in fires
Till the foul crimes done in my days of nature
Are burnt and purged away. But that I am forbid
To tell the secrets of my prison house,
I could a tale unfold whose lightest word
Would harrow up thy soul . . .

$$(1.5.9-16)$$

In other words, the very secret that the father is bidding his son to *remember* is a 'tale' that the father is actually *forbidden* to tell! No wonder the young Prince is going to experience – like most other characters in the play – a crisis of narrative memory.

But there are further problems. King Hamlet's ghost proceeds to command his son to prevent the 'royal bed of Denmark' from being 'a couch . . . of damned incest' (1.5.82–3). Here again the Prince is thrown into disarray, for his father's spirit immediately adds: 'nor let thy soul contrive against thy mother aught' (1.5.85–6). In other words, Hamlet is confronted with another contradictory injunction. First: Remember me/remember me not. Second: intervene/don't intervene. The paralysis of narrative memory is thus doubled as a paralysis of moral action.

In this light, the spectre's opening injunction – 'Remember me!' – can be reread as a double command: (1) to commemorate the ghost's memory by honouring his summons to avenge; and (2) to recall what 'foul crimes' the Ghost-King actually committed in his own youth, if he could only recount them (which alas he is 'forbid'). This self-contradicting summons represents what we might best describe as a *tragedy of narrative memory*. Hamlet has a history to express, and to vindicate in action, but cannot express it; and he cannot express it because he is not permitted to remember it.

Hamlet, then, is a play (an enacted story) about the simultaneous necessity and impossibility of stories. And without stories, there are no histories. For histories too are narrated memories. Ophelia cannot tell her story until she goes mad (when she tells everything but is no longer herself: 'There's rosemary, that's for remembrance' (4.5.173)). Claudius cannot tell his story, even in the confessional, and so it has to be acted out for him by the play-within-the-play. Gertrude cannot tell her story because she is ignorant of it (she does not know that Claudius killed the King). Polonius and his fellow courtiers – Rosencrantz, Guildenstern, Osric – cannot tell their stories either since they contrive only to serve others' versions of events. But most dramatically, of course, Prince Hamlet cannot tell *his* story for as long as conscience makes a coward of him. Not, that is, until dying of a fatal rapier wound he begs his friend Horatio: '[a]bsent thee from felicity awhile . . . [t]o tell my story' (5.2.289–91). All of which means that this is a play where no one actually tells their story, where no one truly remembers. Until Prince Fortinbras arrives too late on the scene, and announces: 'I have some rights of *memory* in this kingdom/ Which now to claim my vantage doth invite me' (5.2.333–4; my emphasis).

What exactly these rights of 'memory' *are*, Shakespeare never tells us. And if he could have told us the play would probably not have survived the first act. In other words, the play is about a cover-up, the concealment of a crime (but which? whose? King Hamlet's or Claudius's?) that the hero is trying to uncover – and ultimately recover from. And the way in which Hamlet seeks to do this is by having his story told, even if it is after his demise. Only thus, it seems, may the disjunction of time, signalled by the anachronistic return of the Ghost, be finally addressed. For the telling of the tale is an attempt to respond to the time being 'out of joint' (2.1.189), to bring concordance back, to synthesise the heterogeneous. But the matter is not simple. The Ghost is not about to yield his secret easily. Hamlet will have to pay a tragic price for the recovery of this deeply buried 'crime'.

In short, the task of remembrance, staged here by Shakespeare, is deeply paradoxical. Indeed, were it *less* so one wonders if Shakespeare would have succeeded in turning a standard revenge play into a spiritual masterpiece. It's true 'the play's the thing/Wherein [we'll] catch the conscience of the king' (2.2.581–2). But *which* king are we speaking of? King Hamlet, King Claudius or King Fortinbras? Who is the *rightful* king in this whole sorry history of poison and betrayal? Who *truly* possesses the legitimate 'rights of memory'? And *who* speaks when the Ghost speaks? Indeed, is the real *crisis of memory* –

with which the play opens and closes – not itself a *crisis of legitimacy* that in turn expresses itself as a *crisis of identity*: the famous '[t]o be, or not to be' (3.1.58)? It is because there's no quick solution to these interlocking puzzles that *Hamlet* the play survives to this day and Hamlet the prince is the most written about person in Western culture after Jesus and Napoleon.

Psychoanalytic reading

Freud, as we know from his famous comment on the play in the *Interpretation of Dreams*, reads these paradoxes as symptomatic betrayals of Hamlet's Oedipus Complex. Memory is playing tricks, he argues, because of Hamlet's repressed desire to destroy his father and possess his mother (Freud 1983: 365–8, 575–6). Certain followers of Freud go much further and deeper than their mentor, however, in describing Hamlet's double injunctions as deep symptoms of loss and melancholy. But all agree that the ghosts of *Hamlet* have less to do with a theology of spirit than with a psychology of trauma.

Jacques Lacan, for example, declares that *Hamlet* is, from first to last, a play about *mourning*.[1] And he relates this in turn to the fact that the play should be read, at an ontological level, as a 'tragedy of desire' – expressing the protagonist's excessive sense of his 'lack of being' (*manque-à-être*). Although Lacan does not focus explicitly on the crisis of narrative provoked by the breakdown of the father–son relation, with its attendant crises of identity and legitimation, he does offer some fascinating observations on the play's obsession with doubles, ghosts and the un-mourned dead.

Lacan writes, 'I know of no commentator who has ever taken the trouble to make this remark, however hard it is to overlook once it has been formulated: from one end of *Hamlet* to the other, all anyone talks about is mourning' (Lacan 1982: 38–9). He cites as prime evidence (1) Hamlet's return to find his father already buried without proper funeral rites; and (2) Gertrude's remark that the cause of Hamlet's 'distemper' is '[h]is father's death and our o'erhasty marriage' (2.2.55, 7). The entire play, on this reading, revolves around the 'relationship of the drama of desire to mourning'. The recurrence of the Ghost is attributed to the insufficiency of mourning (played out again in Hamlet's hiding of Polonius' dead body in the castle thereby preventing a proper funeral rite). And this explains, furthermore, the intimate link between 'the lack, skipping or refusal of something in the satisfaction of the dead' and 'the appearance of ghosts and spectres in the gap left by the omission of the significant rite' (Lacan 1982: 39). This insufficiency of mourning is exacerbated by the fact that for Hamlet, as for Oedipus – the two dramatic heroes who captivate the imagination of psychoanalysis – there is an uncanny secret behind the crisis of mourning.

Lacan, and several of his followers, interpret the play accordingly as a process of successive detachments from fetish-objects of lure and illusion: what Lacan calls the 'little a objects' (*objets petit a*) that stand in for the missing phallus. This process eventually leads to the moment of truth when Hamlet confronts the 'real' by meeting his own death – the ultimate act of detachment – and so finally succeeds in mourning. It is only with the decline of the Oedipus Complex, argues Lacan, that the phallus (as stand-in for the original lost object) can be mourned. In other words, it is only when 'Hamlet's hour' finally comes at the moment of death, that he can act and accept the 'hole in being' – the uncanny abyss of the Real anticipated by the empty grave of Act 4. Until then, Hamlet is unable to act, a paralysis most evident in his incapacity to avenge his father by striking at the phallic substitute, Claudius. 'It's a question of the phallus', says Lacan, 'and that's why he (Hamlet) will never be able to strike it, until the moment when he has made the complete sacrifice . . . of all narcissistic attachments, i.e., when he is mortally wounded and knows it' (ibid.: 51). In this light, Lacan construes the entire drama as a critique of the power of the phallus – and its passage towards 'symbolic castration' via a progressive disillusionment with the various *objets petit a* supplements. In other words, the play interrogates the phallic compulsion to draw agents into imaginary identifications with the phallic to the point of psychotic splitting and doubling – a point epitomised by the upsurge of spectral visitations and voices.

Prince Hamlet's arduous journey through the 'guts of a beggar' (4.3.31) is interpreted thus as a progressive disenchantment with the claims of the illusory fetish-phallus: (1) the Ghost's appeal to a fallacious paternal authority and vengeance; (2) Claudius' link to a 'divinity [that] doth hedge a king' (4.5.100) (reinforced by the erotic desire of Gertrude); (3) Ophelia's incarnation of phallic substitution; (4) Laertes' rival phallic passion that represents the 'desire of the other' and sets the phallic signifier in motion.

Only when Hamlet finally undergoes symbolic castration in the hour of death, liberated at last from the desire of the other and its endless fetishistic signifiers, can Hamlet become his own subject and accept the 'real': namely, the truth that the phallus is 'nothing' and that the 'readiness [to accept this] is all' (5.2.100). Hamlet may well be a melancholic neurotic for most of the play; but when he dies, he dies 'cured'. It is then he realises that the phallus does not exist – or, in Hamlet's own words, that 'the King is a thing – ... of nothing' (4.3.26–8). In short, it is only when Hamlet faces the true strangeness of death, and sees through the paralysing estrangement of the Ghost (his father's returned double), that he is freed from illusory attachments to the phallus, qua spectral phantom, and from the mimetic cycles that hold him in thrall. But, sadly, Hamlet only comes into his own desire posthumously, when it is too late. His desire dawns in the moment of dying, which is why his desire is tragic.

In an essay entitled the 'The Phantom of Hamlet', Nicolas Abraham takes this psychoanalytic line of argument in a somewhat different direction when he claims that what haunts Hamlet is an 'unspeakable' event that has been buried and entombed. Abraham reads the whole crisis of narrative memory as a symptom of the *gap* left in Hamlet by the untold secrets of those who came before him. What the 'phantom' objectifies is the cavity carved within the unconscious 'by the concealment of some part of a love object's life' (Abraham 1988a: 171). Abraham advances the following bold hypothesis:

> The appearance of the Father's ghost at the start of the play objectifies the son's awareness-unawareness. Awareness-unawareness of what? Of his own uneasiness due to a circumstance not to be doubted: the late King must have taken a secret with him to the grave. Does the ghost appear in order to lift the state of unawareness? If that were the case, the ghost's objectification would have no more object than Hamlet's own dubious 'madness of doubt'. A ghost returns

to haunt with the intent of lying: its would-be 'revelations'
are false by nature.

(Abraham 1988b: 188)

Abraham concludes that what audiences and critics have generally ignored for over four centuries is that the so-called 'secret'
revealed by the ghost – that he has been murdered and so
must be avenged – is itself but a subterfuge for another *more
secret* secret: 'this one genuine and truthful, but resulting from
an infamy which the father, unbenown to his son, has on his
conscience' (ibid.: 189). Read in this manner, Hamlet provokes
the *phantom effect* of a repressed generational secret encrypted
in the 'spirit' of Hamlet's father. The Ghost is a symptom of
blocked memory. A phantasmatic past repeating itself as present
through its absence. In sum, a phantom.

Abraham argues that the aim of Shakespeare's play 'is to
cancel the secret buried in the unconscious and to display it
in its initial openness' (ibid.: 189). But how can such a secret
be exposed given that the shame and guilt attached to it persist?
Their exorcism, suggests Abraham, leads not to the punishment, real or imagined, of the other, but rather to a 'higher
wisdom about oneself and the world of humans at large' (ibid.).
But to exorcise the phantom, to lay the ghost, is to 'reduce the
sin attached to someone else's secret and state it in acceptable
terms so as to defy, circumvent, or domesticate the phantom's
(and our) resistances, its (and our) refusals, gaining acceptance
for a higher degree of "truth"' (ibid.).

Abraham proceeds, accordingly and rather brazenly, to write
a fictional sixth act to the play in which Hamlet and Fortinbras
become reconciled. In this supplementary act, the two enemy
sons acknowledge their respective fathers' secrets and 'restore
to Poland the kingdom which their fathers had stolen from it
. . . even returning the usurped Pole, Polonius, to his native
Poland for proper burial!' (ibid.).

A related psychoanalytic perspective on spectral representation in *Hamlet* is offered by André Green in his pioneering
book, *Hamlet et Hamlet* (1982), where he claims that the whole
play is a theatrical uncovering of the buried, covered-up
memory of murder. For Green, it is precisely the play as form
(rather than content) that functions as disclosure. *Theatrical representation itself* becomes, in Shakespeare's ingenious experiment

with dramatic fantasy, an operation of proto-psychoanalytic 'showing' of the unshowable primal scene. And this, in turn, serves a therapeutic-cathartic role for audiences. This of course gives extra weight to Hamlet's throwaway line after his staging of the play-within-the-play – 'The play's the thing/Wherein I'll catch the conscience of the king'. In sum, Green's basic hypothesis is that Shakespeare's drama actually succeeds in staging the unconscious and enables us to show/say what cannot otherwise by shown/said at a purely conscious, and therefore censored, level.[2]

What Lacan's reading fails to sufficiently appreciate, it seems, is that Hamlet's tragedy also comprises narrative catharsis. If the phantom has the first word, it does not have the last. The spirit as haunting spectre is finally overcome by another kind of spirit, the spirit of surrender to a 'divinity that shapes our ends/Rough-hew them how we will' (5.2.10–11). In the terminal scene, after all, Denmark is saved from its 'rotten-ness', and the memory of Hamlet's successful (if tragic) overcoming of phantoms lives on, thanks to the testimony of Horatio who absents himself from felicity to tell his story. And thanks also, we should not forget, to Hamlet's supposed rival, Fortinbras-the-son, who, himself ultimately liberated from the cycle of mimetic desire and revenge, ensures that Hamlet-the-son has the proper mourning and burial that Hamlet the father never received.

It appears that Shakespeare is aware of a healing power that escapes Lacan and his apocalyptic apostles of 'nothing': namely, the power of narrative memory and imagination. *Hamlet*, I would argue, can teach contemporary culture – crippled as it is with phantasmatic crises of desire, identification and legitimation – that spirits can be holy or unholy, allies or adversaries, and that some sons *can* truthfully acknowledge the secrets of their fathers. In sum, that certain stories heal. When one considers the vast number of contemporary tales – literary, cybernetic and cine-matic – dealing with the collapse of the father–son relation (*Ulysses, Magnolia, American Beauty, Star Wars* etc.), one appreci-ates that if the *Hamlet* narrative is indeed perennial it is especially pertinent to our postmodern predicament of paralysis, simula-tion and psychosis. Wherever the logic of doubling rules, phantoms proliferate; and where phantoms proliferate, the story of Hamlet needs to be re-told and re-enacted, again and again.

Existential reading: Kierkegaard

While psychoanalytic readings construe the paradoxical injunctions of the 'spirit/spectre' in terms of repressed memory or blocked desire, Søren Kierkegaard signals a more existential and dialectical interpretation. In an appendix to *Stages on Life's Way*, entitled 'A Side-Glance at Shakespeare's *Hamlet*', Kierkegaard raises the question of *Hamlet* as a religious play. The pseudonymous narrator, Father Taciturnus, confesses that he is 'engrossed' by the claim that '*Hamlet* is a Christian drama' (Kierkegaard 1988: 453).[3] This claim is attributed to a certain Borne who shares the determination, in common with two of his contemporaries, Heine and Feuerbach, to have nothing to do with the 'religious'. But precisely because of this, says Taciturnus, such thinkers can often offer us a unique insight into the religious. Just as a jealous lover can know as much about the erotic as a happy one, so those offended by the religious can be just as insightful about it as believers. And in an age where great believers are few and far between, we should be grateful that we have at least 'a few really clever people who are offended (by religion)' (ibid.: 452).

After this mischievous preparatory remark, the author comes to his main statement on the matter: 'Borne says of *Hamlet*: "It is a Christian drama". To my mind this is a most excellent comment. I substitute only the word a "religious" drama, and then declare its fault to be not that it is that but that it did not become that or, rather, that it ought not to be drama at all' (ibid.). Once unpacked, this dense formulation seems to be saying that *Hamlet* should be really considered a *failed religious drama*. Or to be more precise, *Hamlet* is a work that should have been properly religious, and therefore not an aesthetic drama at all. Or else, it should have been properly aesthetic and therefore not a religious work at all. The fact is, however, that it is neither. It falls between the religious and aesthetic stools and so, as T.S. Eliot would famously pronounce a half century later, *Hamlet* is a *dramatic failure* (Eliot 1951). This is not, of course, to deny that it is the most fascinating drama ever written. Hamlet, as both Kierkegaard and Eliot were aware, is the literary character who most fascinates modern minds.

Kierkegaard's pseudonym spells out his evaluation of *Hamlet* as a failed religious play as follows. If Shakespeare deprives

Prince Hamlet of religious presuppositions and doubts that conspire against him and prevent him from acting, then he is merely a 'vacillator' in a comedy. In other words, if Hamlet is not paralysed with genuinely religious visions and moral-spiritual misgivings there is no good reason for him not to proceed with the summons to avenge his father's murder and restore Denmark to its former state. But Kierkegaard does not think that Shakespeare does make Hamlet religious in this manner. And the play fails to be the great religious drama it could have been.

So how should Shakespeare have written this play according to the author of the 'Side-glance'? Well, first, Hamlet's grand-iose plan to become the avenger to whom vengeance belongs should have been confronted from the start with the religious prohibition on revenge killing. But since one does not see Hamlet sink religiously under his revenge plan, his conscience stricken by biblical prohibitions, one expects quick action as in a normal revenge tragedy where one deals only with 'external' obstacles. Alas, however, in the case of Hamlet there seem to be neither internal subjective religious doubts nor external objective obstacles to action – yet Hamlet fails to act. And as a result the whole vacillating, procrastinating drama becomes one huge introspective psychodrama where Hamlet's misgivings take on a purely psychological form of 'dialectical repentance' – a non-religious and ultimately unfounded repentance that, in Taciturnus' reckoning, 'comes too early'. As a result, Hamlet comes across as simply 'morbidly reflective'. In short, for Kierkegaard, Hamlet is not a genuinely religious drama because the genuine act of 'repentance' is lacking.

Returning to the guiding idea of a Revenge Plan that Hamlet sets himself but fails to realise, Taciturnus argues as follows:

> If the plan remains fixed, then Hamlet is a kind of loiterer who does not know how to act; if the plan does not remain fixed, he is a kind of self-torturer who torments himself for and with wanting to be something great. Neither of these involves the tragic.
>
> (Kierkegaard 1988: 453)

In short, without the presence of the religious, Hamlet simply degenerates into (1) a revenge hero who cannot live up to his purpose; or (2) a reflective melancholic with no real purpose at all who analyses himself to death in the name of some empty (i.e. areligious, amoral) imago. Taciturnus then goes on to repeat his argument, for a second time, that Hamlet is *neither properly aesthetic nor properly religious*. (Anticipations of Derrida's concepts of 'aporia' and 'undecidability' perhaps?)

> If Hamlet is kept in purely esthetic categories, then what one wants to see is that he has the demonic power to carry out such a resolution. His misgivings have no interest whatsoever; his procrastination and temporizing, his postponing and his self-deluding enjoyment in the renewed intention at the same time as there is no outside hindrance merely diminish him, so that he does not become an esthetic hero, and then he becomes a nonentity.
>
> (ibid.)

On the other hand, says the author, 'if he is religiously oriented, his misgivings are extremely interesting, because they give assurance that he is a religious hero'. But this, were it the case, would not lead to good drama either because it would belong to the order of the 'interior being' where alone such religious misgivings could have their 'essential significance' (ibid.: 454). In sum, trying to make a good drama out of the religious struggles of subjective inwardness is like trying to make a silk purse from a sow's ear. It simply cannot be done. If it could be done, Kierkegaard seems to be saying (via his pseudonym) that he, SK, might well have tried his hand at religious drama himself! But religious drama is, according to the above logic, a contradiction in terms – at least for our modern age of Reformed Christianity where the religious gravitates inwards toward subjective solitude and away from external action. Father Taciturnus contrasts this to Medieval Catholicism where a zealous believer could become a tragic hero for the sake of the Church. In other words, for pre-modern Roman Catholics the idea of being a militant actor on behalf of a religious messianic politics – i.e. a saintly agitator, crusader, missionary or martyr – was still a possibility. Were Shakespeare a religious author in the Medieval Catholic Church, attuned to Aristotelian poetics and missionary militancy, he might indeed have written a genuinely religious-aesthetic drama. But he was not; and, for Kierkegaard, those days are gone.

Yet Taciturnus has not totally given up. In the same 'Side-Glance' appendix, he tries a third tack. What, he asks, if Shakespeare had allowed Hamlet to carry out his plan of action – in keeping with the dramatic demands of the aesthetic model – and then, having murdered Claudius (and perhaps Gertrude too), realised his sin and collapsed back into an attitude of genuine religious repentance after the event? First the evil action, then the good reaction. First the aesthetic (imitation of an action), then the religious (pardon and peace). It could thus be argued that Hamlet exposes the folly of mimetic desire and sacrificial revenge in favour of a true Christian revelation: No to revenge, yes to providence! This is how Kierkegaard has his pseudonym, Taciturnus, tease out his final, yet still self-defeating attempt to save *Hamlet* as religious drama:

> If Hamlet is to be interpreted religiously, one must either allow him to have conceived the plan, and then the religious doubts divest him of it, or do what to my mind better illuminates the religious (for in the first case there could possibly be some doubt as to whether he was capable of carrying out his plan) – and give him the demonic power resolutely and masterfully to carry out his plan and then let him collapse into himself and into the religious until he finds peace there. A drama, of course, can never come from this; a poet cannot use this subject, which should begin with the last and let the first shine out through it.
>
> (ibid.: 454)

Thus this third scenario is also impossible, for no matter how subtly and dialectically one might try to manage such a move, it would ultimately make for a moralising-sermonising tract where the aesthetic action of revenge is used merely to make a religious point. In that instance, the drama would be no more than a means towards an end, a pretext for a pre-established doctrine, the moral of the story having been set from the start – rendering the action of the drama entirely redundant. In short, the only way such a scenario could work would be as religious propaganda. And this prospect is unpalatable for Kierkegaard.

So it would seem that, for Kierkegaard, Hamlet is neither a religious activist nor an aesthetic (tragic) actor but something in between. Neither fish nor fowl. A hybrid creature. In short an aesthetic-religious mess. Perhaps not unlike Kierkegaard himself.

In the piece immediately following the 'Side-Glance', Taciturnus makes a supplementary and useful distinction between the two kinds of hero. By way of trying to get a final fix (if that were possible) on what Kierkegaard is really getting at, I think it might be worthwhile bearing with Taciturnus on this ostensibly laboured point. So let's take one last spin of the dialectical wheel. The tragic-aesthetic hero is, we are now told, great by suffering in such a way that he conquers in the external – which is what 'uplifts the spectator while he weeps for the dying one' (ibid.: 455). As such the suffering of the tragic hero 'must arouse fear and cleanse the passions', provoking the spectator's sympathies, which differ within the various views of the world (ibid.: 454, 636). No surprises here, standard Aristotelian poetics. Now, by contrast, the religious hero is great by suffering without conquering in the external, and therefore without inviting the spectator to be purified (as Aristotle put it) through pity and fear. The religious hero, in other words, is someone 'emancipated from externals' and from the tragic world of actions and passions. But precisely because of this, he is uniquely capable of that 'qualitative qualification that is reserved for the religious, where a farthing is worth just as much as kingdoms and countries' (ibid.: 455). One thinks here not only of the Gospel allusions to the widow and her farthing or the kingdom of heaven as a mustard seed, but also of the passages in *Hamlet* itself where the hero observes how important it is 'to find quarrel in a straw' (4.4.9.45), or to realise 'when our deep plots do pall(fail)' that 'there's a divinity that shapes our ends,/Rough-hew them how we will' (5.2.9–11). But, Kierkegaard insists, Hamlet does not ultimately pass muster when it comes to the religious category. Why? Because as we learn from a journal entry of 1844 (deleted from the 'Side-Glance' appendix to *Stages on Life's Way*): 'The mistake in Shakespeare is precisely that Hamlet does not have religious doubts. If he does not have them, then it is sheer nonsense and indecision if he does not settle the matter straight away' (Kierkegaard 1967: journal entry 1561).

Since (according to Kierkegaard) Hamlet does not have religious doubts, he does not qualify as a religious hero; and because he does not settle the matter straight away in a dramatic act, he does not qualify as a tragic hero. So what, we might ask at this point, is Hamlet to Kierkegaard that he should weep for him? Apart from the fact that both are morbidly reflective Danes – enough perhaps in itself to justify the connection – there would seem to be other, less avowed, reasons.

First, it would seem obvious that Kierkegaard himself had keen concerns during the writing of *Stages on Life's Way* in 1844–5 about his own vocation as a religious individual. Indeed, his view of himself is probably not much different from that of Hamlet: namely, that he is (1) too interior, subjective, shut-up and inactive to be properly tragic, provoking sympathy and fear in his readers; and (2) too full of morbid reflection ever to be able to make a proper leap of faith! In short, Kierkegaard sees in his compatriot Hamlet a symptomatic embodiment of the in-between condition he once confessed to – namely, being too religious to fit into the aesthetic category of Climacus but not religious enough to meet the religious category of Anti-Climacus (Kierkegaard 1967: journal entries 6431, 6433).

Second, Kierkegaard appears to identify with Goethe's remark about Hamlet that in 'relation to his body his soul was an acorn planted in a flower pot which at last breaks the container' (quoted in Kierkegaard 1959: 209). The Dane of Copenhagen seems to have shared with the Dane of Elsinore a deep sense not only of being ill-fitted for his task in life, incapable of heroic action or passionate love, but also of being shackled with a summons to amend a wrong that cannot be atoned for. (I am thinking here of Kierkegaard's father's cursing of God and misbehaviour with his maid; and of Hamlet's father's 'foul deed done in his days of nature' and his mother's incestuous relations with Claudius.) Indeed, Kierkegaard must have been fascinated by the way in which Hamlet is caught in the paralysing bind of his father's double injunction: remember me/I cannot tell you what to remember.

It could be said that this is not entirely dissimilar to Kierkegaard's own personal sense of paralysis and paradox following his famous Easter conversion experience of 1848: he initially believed he had received a direct summons from God to 'speak out' – only to revert subsequently to the aesthetic and pseudonymous ploys of 'indirect communication' once again. Reflecting upon the event afterwards, Kierkegaard was horrified by his own demonic hubris at supposing himself to be a chosen martyr of God – like the medieval hero-martyrs he considers so anachronistic in 'Side-Glance'. This critical reflection was later to be corroborated by his disapproval of the self-proclamation of Pastor Adler as chosen advocate of divine mission, recorded at length in the pages of Kierkegaard's *Authority and Revelation* (1848). Kierkegaard's ultimate sentiment seems to have been that of the spectator of tragic aberration: 'there but for the grace of God go I . . .'

The fact, moreover, that for both Kierkegaard and Hamlet the legacies of their heavenly father and their ghostly father were at times so diabolically intermixed, made their language, and their lives, a process of inevitable and ineluctable vacillation.

Third, and finally, it is almost certain that Kierkegaard saw in Hamlet's relationship to Ophelia a mirror-image of his own relationship to Regina Olsen. The vehemence of Kierkegaard's criticism of Hamlet in this regard – as failing to live up to his 'secret' religious mission by distracting himself with Ophelia and loving her almost by default – surely betrays a veiled criticism of his own behaviour. The analogy between Kierkegaard–Regina and Hamlet–Ophelia is not explicitly mentioned in *Stages on Life's Way* but it surfaces in the following entry to his journal. Let us read the passage deliberately in light of our above hypothesis:

> Hamlet and Ophelia. Hamlet cannot be regarded as really being in love with Ophelia. It must not be interpreted in this way, even though psychologically it is quite true that a person who is going about hatching a great plan is the very one who needs momentary relaxation and therefore can well use a love affair. Yet I do not believe that Hamlet is to be interpreted this way. No, what is indefensible in Hamlet is that, intriguing in grand style as he is, he uses a relationship to Ophelia to take the attention away from what he actually is keeping hidden. He misuses Ophelia.

This is how it should be interpreted, and one can also add that precisely because he is so overstrained he almost goes so far that momentarily he actually is in love.

(Kierkegaard 1967: journal entry 1562 entitled 'Hamlet')

And yet in spite of all, and especially in spite of Kierkegaard's complaint about how 'incredible' he finds it that 'Goethe has taken such great pains to uphold *Hamlet*' (Kierkegaard 1988: 635), Kierkegaard himself feels compelled to conclude with this admission:

> On a specific point, one may have a doubt ... and yet agree on the one opinion that has been the opinion of one and two and three centuries – that Shakespeare stands unrivalled, despite the progress the world will make, that one can always learn from him, and the more one reads him, the more one learns.
>
> (ibid.: 454)

That this final admission is ostensibly inconsistent with all the criticisms of *Hamlet* that precede it, is typical of a point of view so deeply contradictory that it begins to look like a deconstructive aporia.

Deconstructive reading

No analysis of philosophical readings of Hamlet's ghosts should ignore Derrida's allusions to this theme in *Spectres of Marx*. For Hamlet, the spectre in question was his own father. For Derrida, it is the less personal surrogate father figure of Marx (as well as Shakespeare himself). In spite of this obvious difference, the logic of posthumous influence is, Derrida suggests, similar in both cases. It is, as he says in the Exordium, the 'non-contemporaneity with itself of the living present' (Derrida 1994: xix). One is prompted, in the light of our analysis of Kierkegaard's 'Side-Glance', to think here of what the latter had to say about the out-of-kilter temporality of Shakespeare's failed attempt at a religious drama (where the end informs the beginning); or again, of his comments about 'ventriloquism' as the eruption of non-continuous time.

But before teasing out such matters, let's see what Derrida himself has to say about this spectral temporality – or what he calls 'spectropoetics'. The context is that of trying to do justice to those who are no longer – or not yet – part of the 'living present'; and the passage in question culminates, tellingly for our purposes, with a reflection on *Hamlet*: 'To be just: beyond the living present in general – and beyond its simple negative reversal. A spectral moment, a moment that no longer belongs to time, if one understands by this word the linking of modalised presents (past, present, actual present: "now", future present). We are questioning in this instant, we are asking ourselves about this instant that is not docile to time, at least to what we call time. Furtive and untimely, the apparition of the spectre does not belong to that time, it does not give time, not that one: "Enter the ghost, exit the ghost, re-enter the ghost" (*Hamlet*)' (Derrida 1994: xx).

Derrida's first chapter, entitled 'Injunctions of Marx', opens with an explicit citation from Act I, scene V of *Hamlet*. The passage in question concerns the episode where Hamlet and his companions are sworn to silence by the Ghost; yet we know, since it is the opening act of the play, that the matter will not rest there. Though Hamlet does indeed admonish his guards, 'And still your fingers on your lips, I pray' (2.1.188), he goes on immediately to state his deep unease at the fact that while he is not responsible for what has occurred, he is obliged nonetheless to 'set it right'. The voice from the past is summoning him to his future. 'The time is out of joint: Oh cursed spite,/That ever I was born to set it right' (2.1.189–91). Derrida then proceeds to invoke the opening reference to another ghost, this time in Marx's *Communist Manifesto* – 'A spectre is haunting Europe – the spectre of communism'. He suggests the following analogy between the two kinds of ghost:

As in Hamlet, the Prince of a rotten State, everything begins by the apparition of a spectre. More precisely by the waiting for this apparition. The anticipation is at once impatient, anxious, and fascinated: this, the thing ('this thing') will end up coming. The revenant is going to come. It won't be long. But how long it is taking. Still more precisely, everything begins in the imminence of a

reapparition, but a reapparition of the specter as apparition for the first time in the play.

(Derrida 1994: 4)

Derrida does not hesitate to suggest that 'in the shadow of
a filial memory, Shakespeare will have often inspired Marxian
theatricalization' (ibid.: 5). A strange use of the future anterior
tense here! Or as he puts it, invoking Valéry's famous text on
the 'European Hamlet', 'Shakespeare qui genuit Marx . . . (and
a few others)' (ibid.). (We are inclined to include Kierkegaard
and Derrida himself, of course, among these other few, but
more of that anon.) What the spectre represents for Hamlet,
as later for Marx and others, is a 'Thing that is not a thing'.
Or as Derrida says: 'One does not know what it is' (ibid.: 6).
One does not know if it corresponds to a name or an essence
or any specific identity; and yet this invisible thing looks at us
even though we cannot look at it. 'The Thing meanwhile looks
at us and sees us not see it even when it is there. A spectral
asymmetry interrupts here all specularity. It de-synchronizes,
it recalls us to anachrony' (ibid.: 6–7). Derrida calls this the
'visor effect', namely, the impression that 'we do not see who
looks at us'. Or more specifically in the case of Hamlet's father,
'Even though in his ghost the King looks like himself ('As thou
art to thy selfe', says Horatio), that does not prevent him from
looking without being seen: his apparition makes him appear
still invisible beneath his armor' (ibid.). Derrida claims that this
definition of the visor effect will be presupposed by everything
he, Derrida, has to say on the subject of the spectre in general.
And as will become more obvious later in the book, what is
at issue is not just Marx and Marxism but the whole 'spectropoetics' of messianicity in general. This is the very religious
structure of existence as what Derrida calls 'religion without
religion', which, broadly speaking, is the form of religion
without any predetermined, dogmatic content: an openness to
whatever is beyond.

Now replace the spectres of Hamlet or Marx with the Holy
Ghost of messianic Christianity, and we are no longer a million
miles away from Kierkegaard. Indeed, if we compare (1) what
Kierkegaard has to say about Hamlet not being sufficiently
'religious' in his doubts, with (2) Kierkegaard's contrasting
analysis of his true religious hero, Abraham, in *Fear and*

Trembling, we can read the entire analysis of spectral logic in a more evidently Kierkegaardian light. The following description by Derrida of Hamlet's response to his ghostly father could, I submit, as easily have been written about Abraham's response to the voice of the angel in *Fear and Trembling* (or, for that matter, about Levinas' religious response to the summons of the infinite Other): 'This spectral someone other looks at us, we feel ourselves being looked at by it, outside of any synchrony, even before and beyond any look on our part, according to an absolute anteriority . . . and asymmetry, according to an absolutely unmasterable disproportion' (ibid.). More specifically, we might consider the relevance of this analysis for the notion of messianic commitment or summons – the very thing which, according to Kierkegaard, Hamlet would have had to be more struck by if he were to be a properly religious character:

> Here anachrony makes the law. To feel ourselves seen by a look which it will always be impossible to cross, that is the visor effect on the basis of which we inherited from the law. Since we do not see the one who sees us, and who makes the law, who delivers the injunction (which is, moreover, a contradictory injunction), since we do not see the one who orders 'swear', we cannot identify it in all certainty, we must fall back on its voice. The one who says 'I am thy Father's Spirit' can only be taken at his word. An essentially blind submission to his secret, to the secret of his origin: this is a first obedience to the injunction. It will condition all the others. It may always be a case of still someone else. Another can always lie, he can disguise himself as a ghost, another ghost may also be passing himself off for this one . . .
>
> (ibid.: 8–9)

In short, how can we ever be sure which kind of ghost, holy or unholy, is here before us? Especially if, as Derrida often says: 'every other is every (bit) other' (*tout autre est tout autre*)? And the simple answer is: we can't be sure.

Moreover, this question of the undecidability of the spectral injunction is in turn related, for Derrida, to the dilemma of *mourning*. Here we find curious echoes of the psychoanalytic reading. Nothing is worse for the work of mourning, notes

Derrida, than confusion about the identity of the one dead and gone. 'One has to know who is buried where – and it is necessary (to know – to make certain) that, in what remains of him, he remain there. Let him stay there and move no more' (Derrida 1994: 9). Or as the prayer for those finally buried goes: *requiescat in pace*. May they rest in peace! Now Hamlet, as we know, is notorious as someone who cannot properly mourn his dead father precisely because he cannot properly identify his father's nature or his past (e.g. 'those foul deeds committed in [his] days of nature whose very tale would harrow up [his, Hamlet's] soul' etc. (1.5.12 ff.)). It is, of course, natural for anyone who has lost a loved one at sea or in some natural disaster to want to recover and identify the body so that the work of mourning can take place. But this is experienced as an even deeper anxiety by Hamlet. For not only has he missed his father's burial (he returned too late from Wittenburg), but he can't even be sure that the paternal spectre who is summoning him to murder his uncle is really his father at all – or at least the father he thought he knew! Hamlet, like the Ghost who confronts him, is riven with undecidability – and so he is unable to mourn (his father), to love (his mother), to desire (Ophelia) or to act (by taking revenge on Claudius). But, in Kierkegaard's reading, this undecidability is even more accentuated. For we recall Taciturnus's view that Hamlet is not only confused by the undecidable vision of an invisible ghost – a thing that is nothing; he is doubly confused in that he has no real religious experience of a God who forbids revenge (e.g. 'Vengeance is mine says the Lord!' (Rom. 12:19)).

In short, Kierkegaard's Hamlet is deprived of both an earthly father and a divine one. And the same might – who knows? – have been true of Kierkegaard himself in certain 'non-religious' moments of vacillation, inaction or faithlessness – moments almost too disturbing to be acknowledged. For remember, not only did Kierkegaard have a most troubled relation with his own father (who cursed God and crushed his own son), he also experienced moments of deep hesitation and confusion, especially prior to his Easter conversion. (An experience during which he felt summoned by God to speak out and write directly in his own name and voice. And why one might legitimately ask, was it a 'conversion', if he was already converted?)

But there is, I think, another key point at which the Kierke-gaardian and Derridean readings of Hamlet overlap. Derrida concludes the second chapter of his Marx book by stating that the 'deconstructive procedure' he practices attempts to put into question our inherited 'onto-theological' notions of historical time by way of thinking another kind of temporality or 'historicity'. This, says Derrida, would allow us to think 'another opening of event-ness as historicity that permitted one not to renounce, but on the contrary to open up access to an affirm-ative thinking of the messianic and emancipatory promise as promise' (1994: 74–5). As promise, insists Derrida, and 'not as onto-theological or teleo-eschatological program or design' (ibid.). Derrida's deconstructive thinking seeks to preserve this very promise by inscribing the 'possibility of the reference to the other, and thus of radical alterity and heterogeneity (i.e. of differance)'. And this in turn signals the impossibility of the present ever being fully contemporaneous or identical with itself (ibid.). Deconstruction maintains the indestructability of 'emancipatory desire', which is, Derrida concludes, the very condition of 're-politicisation', or perhaps even of 'another concept of the political' (ibid.). In light of this rather 'up-beat' deconstructive reading of Hamlet's undecidability, we can, I submit, reinterpret Kierkegaard's verdict on *Hamlet* in a variety of ways. Let me outline at least three.

First hypothesis: Kierkegaard was incapable of moving from a traditional Christian understanding of the religious to a deconstructive understanding of religion-without-religion as 'messianicity' – and so he was unable to appreciate the positive implications of Hamlet's failure as a 'religious hero' (in the traditional sense). In other words, the problem with Kierkegaard, on this score, would be that he hadn't read Derrida. Or to put it more plainly, he wasn't deconstructive enough – that is, sufficiently to realise that Hamlet's undecid-able reflectiveness is actually a very good and profoundly religious thing, once one accepts the notion of 'religion without religion'.

Second hypothesis: Kierkegaard failed to move beyond the old alternatives of the aesthetic versus the religious to embrace a new category of the *political*. There is not one mention of the political in all of Kierkegaard's references to Hamlet. While, contrariwise, one might note that there is not one of Derrida's references to *Hamlet* in *Specters of Marx* that is not political. Had Kierkegaard espoused such a new concept of the political he might have been able to escape the paralysing either/or of aesthetic versus religious options to which he condemns Hamlet.

Third hypothesis: Kierkegaard is prefiguring, in his 'Side-Glance at *Hamlet*' and other texts, Derrida's rethinking of the religious and the political. Read in this manner, in tune with commentators like John Caputo, Kierkegaard may be construed as a 'radical hermeneut' whose deconstructive reading of Hamlet as neither aesthetic nor religious *in strictu sensu* is already opening up a new sense of that very 'event-ness as historicity' that Derrida sees as the precondition of emancipatory desire.[4] By this account, *Works of Love* and other signed works, may be seen as anticipating the possibility of just such a new politics.

Such a deconstructive politics might, I suggest, signal the following six features: (1) a commitment to action in fear and trembling – that is, in tolerance and vigilance; (2) a way of acting and suffering in the world so that the inwardly subjective and reflective is never sacrificed to the dictates of the purely 'objective' and impersonal imperatives of the global techno-capitalist network; (3) a way of reflecting and acting 'religiously' – that is, 'messianically' in Derrida's terms, or 'in light of the Kingdom' in Kierkergaard's terms – so that the impossible tasks of justice, pardon and hospitality (the three great works of love) become more and more possible in each instant of decision and commitment; (4) a deconstructive-existential hermeneutic that tempers our instinctive rush to judgement and condemnation in favour of more refined deliberation; (5) a new political practice based on Hamlet's insight that 'memory' is indispensable and that amnesty can never be founded upon amnesia: for the 'story' of the father needs to be told, the adversary's 'rights of memory' needs to be honoured, so that the repetitive cycles of mimetic desire and revenge may be overcome; (7) an acknowledgement, finally, that the best kind of politics is one open to both endless responsibility and the surprise of the unexpected – the possibility of the impossible.

Read in this proto-deconstructive way, Kierkegaard may be conceived as a kind of Derrida *avant la lettre*. Maybe. It's possible. But I'm not certain. The ghost of Hamlet that migrated into Kierkegaard's reading of Hamlet is not, I think, identical to the one that migrated into Derrida's – however similar on questions of non-synchronous time, undecidability and the logic of the spectral. For when it comes to spectres and spirits, as Derrida reminds us, 'there is more than one of them and they are heterogenous' (Derrida 1994: 75). This irreducible heterogeneity of ghosts is perhaps itself a guarantee of the heterogeneity of Kierkegaardian and Derridean readings. That question remains open. But one thing is sure: new concepts of the 'religious' and the 'political' urgently need to be opened up and thought through in our postmodern age of growing indifference and indifferentiation. And if either Kierkegaard (as read through Derrida) or Derrida (as read through Kierkegaard) can help us in this task, which I suspect they can, we must be grateful.

Theological reading

While Kierkegaard and Derrida argue that *Hamlet* is neither aesthetic nor religious but something undecidable between the two, there are other thinkers who claim that *Hamlet* is in fact a deeply theological play – and that when Shakespeare talks about spirits, he sometimes means just that: '*spiritual* spirits'! In his bold reading in *A Theater of Envy* (1991), René Girard argues that *Hamlet* is nothing less than a profoundly religious rewriting of a revenge play (Kyd's *Spanish Tragedy*), converting it into a drama of eschatological wisdom and peace.[5] The ambiguities and ambivalences of the psychoanalytic, existential and deconstructive readings here give way to a theological solution.

Everyone in the play, notes Girard, is 'to double business bound' (3.3.41). All are symptoms of an original forgetfulness that has blighted the kingdom. No character escapes the mimetic cycle of compulsive repetition and revenge, epitomised by the return of the ghostly phantom and covered over with a rhetoric of 'seems' and ceremony. Until, that is, reality is confronted at the end of the play and young Fortinbras enters the scene to reclaim his 'rights of memory' to the kingdom. Thus while Girard's diagnosis of the play as a pathological tragedy of desire confirms in some measure the psychoanalytic perspective, his conclusion is radically different: he moves from a hermeneutic of suspicion to one of eschatological affirmation.

Girard begins with a critical reading of Hamlet's imprison-
ment in the doubling mechanism of mimetic desire. He interprets the play as a literary attempt to go beyond the stifling
logic of rivalry and sexual betrayal – a logic that he attributes
to Shakespeare's 'originary traumatism' of the 'cuckold bawd'
experience (Ann Hathaway's betrayal with Shakespeare's
brother alleged by Joyce). *Hamlet* is a parody of a revenge play,
says Girard, pointing to the disclosure at the play's outset that
the one to be avenged – King Hamlet – is no innocent victim
but someone who is now purging his own 'foul crimes' in
Purgatory. In short, the fact that the assassinated victim (King
Hamlet) was himself an assassin undermines the whole revenge-
sacrifice mechanism. The exposure of this inner mechanism,
argues Girard, reveals Claudius's crime to be just one more
loop in a chain of revenge-murders which the young Hamlet
will simply continue if he kills Claudius in turn, as he is
commanded to do by his father's ghost.

Shakespeare's play dramatises the way in which the mimetic
cycle of desire, imitation and revenge has led to a 'crisis of
indifferentiation' where each character loses his identity and
becomes the mirror-image of the other. This inability to distinguish one murderer from the next is powerfully expressed in
the boudoir scene where Hamlet presents his mother with
two portraits – one of his father, the other of Claudius – only
to show, in spite of himself, that there is more of a symmetry
between the two brothers than he wishes to admit. The
alarming symmetry (non-difference) is further revealed by
Gertrude's inability to distinguish between the two. It is not
the Lady that doth protest too much, however, but the Prince
himself who is becoming increasingly aware of how 'undiffer-
entiated' his father and his uncle actually were. The
interchangeability of those caught in the revenge cycle – the
'crisis of indifferentiation' – is also evident in the scene by the
graveside where Hamlet and Laertes are presented as twin-
images of each other.

For Girard, *Hamlet* is a play that re-enacts and subverts the
sacrificial logic of mimetic violence at the heart not only of
society but, at a more symbolic and originary level, of theatrical
culture itself. It serves as a dramatisation of drama exposing
the hidden structures of theatrical pretence and cover-up. Like
The Mousetrap play-within-the-play, Hamlet too tries to 'catch

the conscience of the king' – and of the rest of us as well. In this respect, concludes Girard, *Hamlet* should be read as a quintessentially moral and Christian play that endeavours to expose the long repressed truth of the repetitive sacrificial logic upon which most human societies, and not just Denmark, are founded. The only way to answer the spirit of pathological doubling and return, signalled by the demonic Ghost, is by invoking a Holy Ghost that redeems us from mimetic revenge and emancipates us into pardon and letting-go – a spiritual 'divinity that shapes our ends'. This is finally the difference between the two Hamlets: (1) a ghostly father caught in the reiterative cycles of the past; and (2) an ultimately, if tragically, enlightened son who opens up a future of forgiveness.

For any theological reading of the play, the graveyard scene is of course pivotal. The moral recovery of the original cover-up is already prepared for in the graveyard scene where Hamlet, who was unable to properly mourn his own father, comes to mourn his surrogate father, Yorick. A skull is thrown up by the gravediggers – 'as if 'twere Cain's jawbone, that did the *first murder*' (5.1.71–2; my emphasis). But of course, Yorick is a foster-father who has managed, through play-acting and humour, to escape the mark of Cain, which condemns most other characters in the play to a cycle of fratricide. And in so doing he, the King's jester, has proved capable of genuine paternity towards Hamlet – 'here hung those lips that I have kissed/I know not how oft' (5.1.174–5). Now he can be mourned as a father after the event *(nachträglich)*.

In the grave scene, Hamlet confronts the *real*. He comes to acknowledge death. This acceptance of separation and loss amounts, as noted earlier, to what Lacan and other psychoanalytic readers of the play call 'symbolic castration'. This exposure of the 'real' is symbolised not only in the exhuming of dead skulls – in particular that of Yorick – but also in a whole metaphorics of vanity and ashes running through the exchanges between Hamlet and the gravediggers. These include jokes about how such mighty figures as Alexander and Caesar were finally 'turned to clay' (5.1.196); and perhaps most pointedly, Hamlet's command to the skull that it go to the 'lady's chamber and, tell her, let her paint an inch thick/To this favour she must come' (5.2.178–9). The grave episode teaches

Hamlet that no matter how much we cover over our earthly origins we must all undergo the 'fine revolution' that returns us to the 'base uses' of a 'sexton's spade' (5.1.82–3, 187). Ornamental pomp and make-up count for nought.

But arguably the most telling disclosure of the graveyard scene is that Hamlet was born on the very day his father fought the duel with King Fortinbras thirty years previously. This fact is recalled by the gravedigger since he, coincidentally, became a gravedigger that *same* day. So, the message seems to be that this gravedigger's uncovering of skulls reminds Hamlet of two forgotten facts of paternity: (1) the crucial role played by his foster-father Yorick (whom he now belatedly mourns); and (2) the dispatching of King Fortinbras by his actual father on the day of his birth. So we may reasonably suppose, may we not, that the body the gravedigger committed to the ground on that first day of his employment, coinciding with Hamlet's birthday, was the corpse of King Fortinbras? And we may surmise, by extension, that it is to the *recovery* of his father's body that Fortinbras the younger refers in his closing allusion to his 'rights of memory in this kingdom'?

The 'primal secret' (or 'sin' in Girard's reading) is what King Hamlet did to King Fortinbras – and what Claudius does to both Hamlets: namely, poison them to secure the rights of kingship. The 'rights of memory' restored by young Fortinbras in the last act would refer therefore to the final righting of the wrong committed against Fortinbras' own father by Hamlet's father. And the fact that King Hamlet's 'foul crime' occurred on Hamlet's birthday becomes central to the un-concealing plot: a crucial revelation confirming the Prince's opening invocation of the 'dram of evil' – that 'vicious mole of nature in (particular men),/as in their birth, wherein they are not guilty,/since nature cannot chose his origin . . .'(1.4.18.8–10). Only by passing through the guts of a beggar can Hamlet come to his own self. By mourning his surrogate father (Yorick), and then embracing his own death in Act V, Hamlet ultimately undergoes – after the passage of much time – the spiritual mourning and letting-go of his ghostly father. A letting-go that sets him free. Hamlet gives up the ghost in every sense.

Such religious surrender itself coincides, finally, with the young Fortinbras' claim to realise his own right/rite of commemoration at his father's grave. Some four thousand lines after the ghost of King Hamlet bids his son to 'remember', we find another son remembering his deceased father with cathartic mourning. Young Fortinbras, Hamlet's princely double, completes the latter's insufficient mourning. And by mourning Hamlet in turn – instead of gloating at his demise – Fortinbras brings an eschatological end to the bitter cycle of repetition and revenge.

Conclusion

In *Hamlet* Shakespeare transforms a revenge tragedy into a play of cathartic remembering. He stages the *working through of the immemorial* until it yields peace. This transfiguring of melancholy – or what I call 'impossible memory' – into epiphanic mourning is powerfully expressed in Hamlet's final acceptance of the reality of mortality. So much so that one has good reason to suspect that if the Ghost were to return in the last act, he would be given short shrift by his son. Indeed, were this to happen, the mature and illusion-less Prince would, logically, neither hear nor see the spectre. Why? Because his mourning would have been activated. Moreover, I would claim that it is Hamlet's final passage from melancholy to mourning that not only enables him to face death but to preserve life. And if not his own life (since he must literally lose it to regain it) then at least that of others after him. This is why Hamlet's parting words to Horatio are so crucial. He begs him to renounce suicide in order to heal his (Hamlet's) 'wounded name' by living on to serve as his memorialist. 'Absent thee from felicity awhile', pleads the dying Prince, '[t]o tell my story' (5.2.286, 289–91).

Against the standard view that *Hamlet* marks the 'majesty of melancholy', I prefer to read the play accordingly as a metamorphosis of melancholy into a miracle of mourning. Shakespeare moves beyond a play of compulsive rivalry and revenge to one of deep spiritual enlightenment by staging one of the finest dramas of narrative memory in Western literature.

Notes

For an earlier formulation of the opening section of this chapter, see R. Kearney 2002.

1 See Lacan 1982. For an elaboration of this psychoanalytic thesis see the entry on 'Hamlet' in *Dictionnaire de la Psychanalyse* (Chemama 1993: 60–2).
2 See Green 1982.
3 For a more extensive treatment of this subject see Kearney 2003.
4 See Caputo 1987.
5 See Girard 1991: 271–89.

8

The last act
Presentism, spirituality and the politics of *Hamlet*
Ewan Fernie

In recent Shakespeare studies, 'presentism', a deliberate strategy of interpreting texts in relation to current affairs, has emerged to challenge the dominant fashion of reading Shakespeare historically.[1] Presentism relinquishes the fantasy of restoring 'Shakespeare's artistry to the earliest conditions of its realisation' in favour of embracing its true historicity as something irreversibly changing in time.[2] As Terence Hawkes writes in *Shakespeare in the Present* (2002), 'none of us can step beyond time. It can't be drained out of our experience'. Hawkes recommends presentism as the form of criticism whose 'centre of gravity is accordingly "now", rather than "then"' (Hawkes 2002: 3, 22). In this temporally specific sense, presentism presents Shakespeare *as he is*. The reception of presentism, to date, has been mixed. According to Helen Moore writing in the *Times Literary Supplement*, 'Presentism is the new kid on the Shakespearean block' (Moore 2003). But although presentism has 'arrived', it is often criticised, at conferences and in print, for eliding or dissolving historical difference.[3]

David Scott Kastan asserts that we must begin with Shakespeare's 'difference from us' (Kastan 1999: 16). This matters to the extent that we have a moral responsibility to the past. Moreover, the difference of history offers a standpoint from which to challenge the present. But, as this latter point concedes, our primary and most urgent responsibility is to the present not the past. And backward-looking historicism is in no position fully to exploit what difference the past can make *now*. I have argued elsewhere for a form of presentism more deliberately attuned to the challenging strangeness of literature – which I characterised in terms not just of historical alterity but also of the extra, unforeseeable difference literature makes to history.[4] This chapter analyses the strange spirituality of the last act of *Hamlet* as a striking epitome of literary difference that speaks powerfully and provocatively in favour of a complete commitment to the present.

The present isn't a closed and coherent structure. Shakespeare's presence in the present is itself an excellent example of this. I will begin by exploring the surprising scope for reading Shakespeare spiritually in the present in Stephen Greenblatt's *Hamlet in Purgatory* (2001) and Jacques Derrida's *Hamlet*-inspired *Specters of Marx* (1994). But I also take off from the fact that, for Greenblatt and especially for Derrida, spirituality breaches the present from beyond. Derrida writes, 'Hegemony still organizes the repression and thus the confirmation of a certain haunting' (Derrida 1994: 37). Greenblatt spiritualised historicism when he famously cast it as speaking to the dead (Greenblatt 1988: 1ff.). If this first formulation seemed whimsical, *Hamlet in Purgatory* lends it more weight. There Greenblatt analyses Purgatory as the institution that kept the living in touch with the departed.[5] He sees *Hamlet* as the inheritor of that cultural function. It's easy to share Hawkes's objection to Greenblatt that criticism should speak not to the dead but to the living; but the danger for presentist criticism is that, unless it's exposed to difference, it will tell the living what they already know.[6] Derrida interprets the eruption of Old Hamlet's spirit as a revelation of 'the non-contemporanaeity with itself of the living present' (Derrida 1994: xix): a disclosure of the difference of the past that intimates the difference of the future and even the pure idea of difference itself. The time, for Derrida, is always out of joint, the present thoroughly ruptured by all kinds of difference. A presentist criticism that wishes to avoid historical complacency will nourish itself and thrive on such differences.

After *Specters of Marx*, spirituality recommends itself to critical attention as a particularly direct and rich experience of otherness, alterity, etc. But ghosts fall short of fully manifesting spirituality as what is not just other but also ultimately significant and valuable. In *Specters of Marx*, Derrida finally develops out of *Hamlet* a novel spirituality of the absolute difference that never appears in history. This operates like a metaphysical magnet, drawing humanity towards a different future. It's as if postmodernism had discovered its own repressed belief and truth; so much for the end of 'grand narratives'. And yet, in the startling fifth act of *Hamlet* what is spiritually other and ultimate is not beyond but *immanent* in events (such as 'the fall of a sparrow' (5.2.157–8)) and action or 'rashness' (5.2.7). Shakespeare's most famous play ultimately dramatises a kind of eschatological presentism that suggests that our present is the place – the only and, therefore, the absolute place – of agency and decision where all time may and perhaps must be consummated.

Greenblatt in Purgatory

As well as confessing that he 'began with a desire to speak with the dead', the Greenblatt of *Shakespearean Negotiations* wrote that 'literature professors are salaried middle-class shamans' (Greenblatt 1988: 1). Though the spiritual colouring is less exotic, *Hamlet in Purgatory* brings him full circle. Greenblatt is frankly drawn to *Hamlet*, and the traditions of Purgatory, as a way of saying *kaddish* for and laying to rest the 'ghost' of his own father. *Kaddish* is a Jewish prayer of thanksgiving and praise, part of the daily life of the Synagogue but specially recited by orphaned mourners. Greenblatt observes that the Jewish ritual 'originated precisely at the time that Christianity in the West formalized the practice of praying for the dead in order to alleviate their sufferings in Purgatory' and suspects it was derived from the Christian tradition (Greenblatt 2001: 9). It seems clear he identifies with Hamlet as the son of a dead father, and even envies the tragic hero his chance of a supernatural encounter with Old Hamlet's spirit:

> Anyone who has experienced the death of a close friend or relative knows the feeling: not only the pain of irrevocable

loss but also the strange, irrational expectation of recovery. The telephone rings, and you are suddenly certain that your dead friend is on the other end of the line; the elevator door opens, and you expect your father to step out into the hallway, brushing the snow from the shoulders of his coat.

(Greenblatt 2001: 102)

Greenblatt's desire to contact the dead has become urgently personal. The historical alterity of Shakespeare's drama of death is certainly not erased (much of the book offers an extended cultural history of Purgatory) but it is charged with Greenblatt's particular, twenty-first-century, Jewish-American experience. The father expected in the elevator has come in from the battlements. The 'cultural poetics' of death of the late medieval and early modern periods assuage the pains of death in the present.[7] Greenblatt's bereavement, and the filial intensities it evokes, probably carry over into his recent Shakespeare biography. *Will in the World*'s attempt to capture Shakespeare's ghost is largely staked on a new reading of *Hamlet* in terms of Shakespeare's grief for his son, Hamnet, and anticipation of his father's death.[8]

The last chapter of *Hamlet in Purgatory* ends as follows:

With the doctrine of Purgatory and the elaborate practices that grew up around it, the church had provided a powerful method of negotiating with the dead, or, rather, with those who were at once dead and yet, since they could still speak, appeal, and appall, not completely dead. The Protestant attack on 'the middle state of souls' and the middle place those souls inhabited destroyed this method for most people in England, but it did not destroy the longings and fears that Catholic doctrine had exploited. Instead . . . the space of Purgatory becomes the space of the stage where old Hamlet's ghost is doomed for a certain term to walk the night. That term has now lasted some four hundred years and it has brought with it a cult of the dead that I and the readers of this book have been serving.

(Greenblatt 2001: 256–7)

Typically for Greenblatt, *Hamlet in Purgatory* is a richly unsystematic book but this crystallises its essential thesis: a 'structure of feeling' – 'a powerful method of negotiating with the dead' – is embodied in Purgatory and survives in the continuing life of Shakespeare's play.[9] *Hamlet* supplies an important spiritual supplement, a secret 'cult of the dead', to mainstream English Protestant culture and the later Western secular culture of our own time.

In Marlowe's most celebrated play, Faustus tells Mephistopheles that Hell's a fable. It's a pretty silly thing to say to a devil, and Mephistopheles responds, 'Ay, think so still, till experience change thy mind' (*Doctor Faustus* (1616 text), Marlowe 1999: 2.1.132). In respect of Purgatory, Greenblatt manages to take up both Faustian and Mephistophelean positions at the same time. That is, the middle station of souls is an invented place – as, by implication, are the upper and lower chambers of the afterlife. And yet, to the extent that it shaped the life and the selves of Christendom, Purgatory was very real indeed. Greenblatt presents the disestablishment of Purgatory as an historical trauma involving a massive deportation of spirits and a second bereavement for the living, as their dead kin passed utterly beyond the scope of their indulgent love – as well as their more negative emotions of guilt and anger. This evocation of exile is doubtless influenced by Greenblatt's earlier reflections on Jewish and postcolonial themes.[10] Purgatory also provided an imagined buffer zone before the finality of death for the living. But, most importantly for this bereaved son, by institutionalising the felt proximity of the dear departed, Purgatory met what is understood in *Hamlet in Purgatory* as a transhistorical, fundamental human need to relate to and make peace with them.[11]

Greenblatt's new reading of *Hamlet* unfolds from a recognition of the plain but routinely overlooked fact that the ghost asks not so much to be revenged as *remembered*. The spirit of Hamlet's father is seen in relation to the old supplicating spirits of Catholic England. Noting John Shakespeare's supposed recusancy, Greenblatt even imagines the Bard subjected to the purgatorial pleadings of his deceased parent. This resonates with his own felt duty to say *kaddish*. Greenblatt presents Shakespeare's tragedy as dramatising the progressive forgetting of the father, thus particularising and allegorising the cultural forgetting of Purgatory that he has narrated already and perhaps exorcising his own ghost.

The spiritual content of *Hamlet in Purgatory* thus essentially falls under the rubric of what Derrida (after Freud) calls 'the work of mourning'. The aim of such labour for Greenblatt is 'organizing, articulating and making sense of a tangle of intense, intimate feelings in the wake of a loved one's death: longing, regret, guilt, fear, anger, and grief' (Greenblatt 2001: 132). For the mourner or mourners, this is more important than the physical burial of the corpse, for only this will liberate them from overwhelming grief and the chains of memory and restore them to the living present. From such a perspective, speaking to the dead must come to an end, which seems to admit the limitations of historicism and our primary responsibility for what is happening now. Greenblatt's book shows how Purgatory provided institutional conventions and a cosmic station for the work of mourning, a kind of waiting-room where the dead are polite enough to linger until those they have bereaved are ready to dispatch them and resume their own obstructed lives. Greenblatt opposes 'cold memory' to 'warm memory' or what Shakespeare calls 'green' memory. He writes of the 'fading of remembrance' in *Hamlet* (Greenblatt 2001: 143, 218ff.). In his account, Shakespeare's play as much as Purgatory addresses the process of bereavement. Both keep lines of communication with the dead open for a certain time in order to allow for a more complete leave-taking. At the same time, each takes the edge off the fear of death by making it more gradual, less absolute.

Spirituality in *Hamlet in Purgatory* thus serves a remarkably presentist function. It takes the specific form of an ancestor cult: a common territory for mourners and historians that brings together Greenblatt's personal and professional concerns. It serves a purpose in the ordinary world by enabling the living to come to terms with the past and face their own deaths more bravely. It is, in a word, therapeutic, more self-centred than ethical or political. As the harbour of dead souls in the experience of the living, the spiritual experience that Greenblatt evokes constitutes an experience of ultimacy but not of ultimate values. It intimates a wider human community, but it doesn't really entail any vision of an alternative society such as Christ expresses in the Gospel of John: 'My kingdom is not of this world' (John 18.36). Greenblatt is sensitive to the sufferings of the dead and recognizes their traditional origins in sin, but Purgatory's crucial position in the theatre of judgement and salvation – to which Shakespeare's ghost clearly and frighteningly testifies (1.5.9ff.) – is eclipsed by the main theme of bereavement and remembrance.[12]

There is something insinuatingly unsatisfying about Greenblatt's title. *Who* is in Purgatory? Not Hamlet. Presumably Greenblatt means to refer to Hamlet's father, but it would be customary to call him Old Hamlet to distinguish him from the tragic hero. Another implication might be that *Hamlet*-the-play is in Purgatory, but Greenblatt's argument is more that Purgatory's in the play. In a sense, it is true to say that Greenblatt's in Purgatory. Suspended between this world and the next, Purgatory facilitates but also defers final judgement. In its comparable deferral of the ethics and politics of spirituality, *Hamlet in Purgatory* affords a troubling image of our own seminal Shakespeare critic himself languishing there.

Paradise postponed

Before *Hamlet in Purgatory*, and outside mainstream Shakespeare studies, Jacques Derrida's engagement with Shakespeare's tragedy had already conjured up a spiritual Shakespeare with an urgent message on his lips. *Specters of Marx* (1994) is considered in Richard Kearney's essay in this volume; its insights are diffused throughout the book. My purpose with it is to show how Derrida opens the ethical and political dimension of spirituality in *Hamlet* that remains obscure in Greenblatt.[13] I will then argue that both Greenblatt and Derrida neglect the last act of the play, with crucial critical and theoretical consequences.

Derrida is more in tune with Shakespeare's play than the father of new historicism in one crucial respect. In his humane responsiveness to his father's spirit, Greenblatt is identifiable with a more pragmatic Hamlet always aware of the necessity of coming to terms with grief. By contrast, Derrida is like the Hamlet, who, according to Claudius's worldly measure of mourning (1.2.87ff.), exhibits an *exorbitant* responsiveness and accountability. Derrida suggests:

> It is necessary to speak *of the ghost*, indeed *to the* ghost and *with* it, from the moment that no ethics, no politics,

whether revolutionary or not, seems possible and thinkable and *just* that does not recognize in its principle the respect for others who are no longer or for those others who are not yet *there*, presently living, whether they are already dead or not born.

(Derrida 1994: xix)

This puts intercourse with the dead at the centre of human life and recalls, even more than *Hamlet in Purgatory*, the shamanic Greenblatt of *Shakespearean Negotiations*. It's tempting to say that *Specters of Marx* provides a belated rationale for the new historicist project in terms of responsibility for the absent historical Other. To the extent that the Greenblatt in *Hamlet in Purgatory* wants to speak with the dead to complete the work of mourning, he is moving through history in the direction of presentism. But Derrida contends we cannot, should not lay our ghosts to rest.

Shakespeare's ghost is in being but also beyond. The purely spiritual, Derrida implies, is that which is not at all present, whereas the spectral hovers uncannily between presence and absence as embodied spirit. Hamlet's encounter with the ghost is a primal scene of ethics: an experience of the irreducible alterity of the other. As Derrida plainly puts it, 'One does not know what it is' (Derrida 1994: 7). *All* others are ultimately beyond knowledge. Moreover, because identities are determined by the free play of difference, nothing has more than a flickering and passing presence: 'the phenomenal form of the world itself is spectral', 'the phenomenal *ego* (Me, You, and so forth) is a specter' (Derrida 1994: 135). It is a question not of 'to be' and 'not to be', then, but of *being-in-between*, as *Hamlet* powerfully dramatises. In encountering the ghost, Derrida suggests, Hamlet comes face to face with *the ghastliness of his own self*, which affords one reason for what Greenblatt calls the 'magical intensity' of the tragedy and partly elucidates the Prince's strange and repeated utterance that draws Greenblatt's attention, 'I am dead' (Greenblatt 2001: 4, 229). The ghost is an avatar of the Other that additionally reveals the fleetingness and dependency of human being as such. In exemplifying our own 'lack-in-being', mortality and difference, it encourages solidarity not just with the living but equally with the dead and unborn.

Reading *Hamlet* therefore opens up a spiritual horizon for deconstruction in terms of the Prince of Denmark's traumatic reorientation towards otherness, but Derrida pushes beyond the only partial absence and otherness of the ghost towards a strange new notion of 'the messianic'. Whereas the ghost arrives and is recognised, Derrida's Messiah is absolutely, unimaginably other because it is always absent or 'to come'. The ghost summons Hamlet into specific engagement with itself, but the messianic is an opening towards unpredictable difference – because we simply can't know who or what the coming Messiah will be. Openness to the unforeseeable difference of this shadowy figure is openness to difference as such and it generates an openness to all particular differences: out of Derrida's novel spiritual conception a political vision of 'a universalizable culture of singularities' unfurls (Derrida 2002: 57). Unlike Marx's utopia, Derrida's is not the communist fruition of teleological history but the 'messianic promise' of a perfect democracy, a state of perfect responsibility to all that will never be realised.[14] But, far from being hopeless, this unrealisable dream – 'life beyond life, life against life, but always in life and for life' – elevates human beings above mere biology, supplying the ecstatic, aspirational energy of human history (Derrida 2002: 289).

For Derrida, nothing is present in the present – not even the present itself, which is defined by its difference from other times. Derrida's present is where we respond to difference. He portrays a Hamlet who is dutifully responsive to the other that is the ghost, but whose responsibility to *others in general* prevents him from committing revenge. This Hamlet protests in the name of (other-directed) responsibility against the (self-centred) law of right, looking towards a day outside time when justice would no longer be embroiled in the partisanship and fatality of vengeance. His eyes are locked on an alien 'messianic extremity', an 'eskhaton' of purified justice that ruptures historical complacency and ushers us towards a different future (Derrida 1994: 37). It is an astonishing response to Shakespeare's tragedy. But at the end of *Hamlet* 'divinity' (5.2.10) is immanently present in the present, which is charged with 'a special providence' (5.2.157–8). The Prince is called not to relate fastidiously to the beyond but to the 'rashness' of a spontaneous intervention.

There are more things in heaven and earth than are dreamt of in your philosophy

Greenblatt and Derrida's responses to *Hamlet* are in tune with the Prince's remark to Horatio. In the context of prevailingly materialist criticism, *Hamlet in Purgatory* plugs back into the power of Shakespeare's tragedy to move and even heal us by exploring themes that most post-Enlightenment thought has completely neglected. Derrida, too, reads Shakespeare against materialism, finding in the seemingly archaic and superstitious figure of the ghost a revelation of the primal scene of ethics. Moreover, the ghost provokes a new poststructuralist spirituality that is also 'another concept of the political' (Derrida 1994: 44). And yet, what Hamlet says to Horatio seems equally to critique Greenblatt and Derrida, who both quickly tame the sublime content they identify in *Hamlet* with interpretation. In Shakespeare's tragedy, the ghost speaks and, such is the magnificent horror of his presence, Hamlet listens. For all their disarming eagerness to relate, Greenblatt and Derrida don't listen to the ghost so much as place it at the centre of their own respective systems of significance: for Greenblatt, the historical loss of Purgatory itself as a way of experiencing and coming to terms with death; for Derrida, his whole philosophy of *différance*.[15] The terrifying strangeness of the ghost is thus at least partly dissipated. Remember it 'harrows' Horatio 'with fear and wonder' (1.1.42), and poor Marcellus and Barnardo it 'distill[s]/Almost to jelly with the act of fear' (1.2.204–5). It is said to have been vomited up from the grave:

> Making night hideous, and we fools of nature
> So horridly to shake our disposition
> With thoughts beyond the reaches of our souls . . .
>
> (1.4.33–5)

Later it tells the Prince that it 'could a tale unfold' whose 'lightest word' would induce a number of startling physical convulsions except that 'this eternal blazon must not be/To ears of flesh and blood' (1.5.15–22).

Derrida has said something genuinely new about *Hamlet*, ethics and spirituality, but Shakespeare has things to say back to him. The French philosopher admits that thinking 'continues

to do battle against ghosts', that 'formulation throws up barri-
cades, or digs trenches, surrounds itself with barriers, increases
the fortifications' (Derrida 1994: 165). By making the ghost an
avatar of difference, he has allegorised it, crucially stripping
it of the uncanny *sameness* that is a main source of its terrifying power. Hamlet says of his father, 'I shall not look upon
his like again' (1.2.187): shockingly, he does. What 'harrows'
Horatio is that the ghost is 'most like' Old Hamlet (1.1.42).
Barnardo sees it coming '[i]n the same figure like the king
that's dead' (1.1.39). With its strugglingly ponderous expression, this evokes a mind-bending prospect of death-defying
sameness. Marcellus asks, 'Is it not like the king?', to which
Horatio answers, 'As thou art to thyself' (1.1.57–8), which at
once reduces difference to sameness *and* alienates self from self.
The following description perhaps best expresses the ghost's
disruptive, questionable identity with the dead monarch: 'These
hands are not more like' (1.2.212).[16]

Of course, the ghost is crucially different from ordinary
mortals. But if encountering it reveals the primal scene of ethics,
then sameness should figure in that scenario too. The sameness of the other is what encroaches on and threatens the
autonomy of the self, particularly in the case of a father and
son both called simply 'Hamlet': Hamlet's identity is disestab-
lished and imperilled by the unlooked for return of the other,
previous Hamlet. And Old Hamlet has come to claim, indeed
to possess his son because his identity, throne and queen have
been usurped by the next male family member, his brother
Claudius. But if the sameness of the other provokes unethical
self-assertion and revenge, identification and solidarity enables
Hamlet's responsibility towards his father. A natural, familial
ethics of sameness is generalised in his experience of the
undoing of differences in death in the graveyard scene. That
difference is the essence of ethics, as Emmanuel Levinas as
much as Derrida suggests, isn't beyond dispute:[17] indeed, Alain
Badiou has scandalously announced, 'the whole ethical predi-
cation based on recognition of the Other should be purely and
simply abandoned' (Badiou 2001: 25). This is because,
according to Badiou, the status quo is defined by differences
– of race, gender and class, etc. What would really change
things is the advent of a universal truth that deposed or even
abolished such differences.

But the chief limitation of Greenblatt and Derrida on the spirituality of *Hamlet* is not so much that they idealise the ghost as that they each begin and end with it. Greenblatt recognises that the trajectory of the play describes the Prince's gradual forgetting of the ghost, but it does so as he proceeds towards an apprehension in the fifth act of 'a divinity that shapes our ends' (5.2.10) and 'a special providence in the fall of a sparrow' (5.2.157–8). Kearney (this volume) and Girard (1991; discussed by Kearney) also pass over this, although they remark on the transcendence of mourning. The relevant speeches occur in the graveyard scene. In the first case, Hamlet is telling Horatio that, when his ship for England was assailed by pirates, he replaced Claudius's warrant for his death with a similar warrant for Rozencrantz and Guildenstern. '[L]et us know', he goes on,

> Our indiscretion sometimes serves us well
> When our deep plots do pall, and that should teach us
> There's a divinity that shapes our ends,
> Rough hew them how we will –
>
> (5.2.7–12)

It's an aside but its very offhand casualness serves only to heighten the shocking access of metaphysical confidence and security in this erstwhile prince of doubters: 'let us know', 'and that should teach us'. Hamlet declares that 'divinity' perfects spontaneous, awkward human action. He locates this divine force specifically in the killing of his erstwhile friends; he perceives 'heaven's ordinance' in having to hand his father's royal signet ring with which to seal their deaths (5.2.49). We should put this together with his retroactively casting himself as heaven's 'scourge and minister' after slaying Polonius (3.4.159). '[P]raised be rashness for it' (5.2.7): within the famously overwhelming atmosphere of mortality in the grave-yard scene as a whole, Hamlet invokes a god of 'casual slaughter' (see 5.2.326).

He subsequently associates 'a special providence' with a dubious prospect. Osric has brought him the King's challenge to duel with Laertes. Hamlet accepts this, despite being invaded with a malaise evidently intended as a premonition of his own death. A troubled Horatio says he will catch up with Osric and cancel the bout. Hamlet responds as follows:

> Not a whit. We defy augury. There's a special providence
> in the fall of a sparrow. If it be now, 'tis not to come. If
> it be not to come, it will be now. If it be not now, yet it
> will come. The readiness is all. Since no man knows aught
> of what he leaves, what is't to leave betimes? Let be.
>
> $(5.2.157–61)^{18}$

Again, in what is said, as well as in the short, declarative
sentences in which Hamlet says it, there is the same surprising
note of absolute assurance. But it is matched here by the
sheer inscrutability of the statement. The fall of a sparrow?
Does this imply Hamlet's own death? Or, since sparrows were
associated with lechery, Claudius's? *What* will be now or to
come or not? And what would it mean to be ready for it? By
the penultimate sentence, Hamlet seems to be contemplating
death as valediction. To what 'Let be' refers is less clear. The
central focus of the speech brings together the humble, random
specificity of a tumbling sparrow with the entire generality of
'it'. Both are vehicles for 'a special providence', suggesting each
and every event is inhabited by some kind of divine excess and
that history is ultimately beyond human ken. Hamlet submits
to history and the coming event in a strange spirit of passive
readiness. As Roger Starling suggests, it is as if he is opening
up to the Derridean 'messianic' (Starling 1997/8: 207–8). But
what is to come in *Hamlet* makes way for an actual tragic climax
now, which encompasses a number of deaths, including
Hamlet's own.

Hamlet's god of 'rashness' is certainly more 'other' than
Shakespeare's patriarchal ghost which, for all its uncanniness,
is very much an emanation of the social status quo – indeed,
responsibility to such a ghostly father could as easily be cast
in terms of conservative ideology as progressive politics. At
this juncture in the play, A. C. Bradley, still one of the most
subtly responsive critics of the spirituality of *Hamlet*, identifies
an intense 'feeling of a supreme power or destiny' and 'a particular tone which may be called, in a sense, religious'. But Bradley
admits 'I cannot make my meaning clear without using
language too definite to describe truly the imaginative impression produced' (Bradley 1971: 140). The irreducible opacity
of Hamlet's god suggests its inexpressible otherness: for Søren
Kierkegaard, the 'Knight of Faith' speaks not in any human

language but 'in tongues'.[19] Yet, as Bradley recognises, Hamlet says enough to distinguish his 'divinity' from the Christian God. Where St Paul is visited by a suffering Jesus (Acts 9.4), Hamlet bears witness to a divine force more active and less personal. As a god not of being and the beyond but of becoming and history, Hamlet's 'divinity' evokes the theology of the incarnation.[20] As a 'special providence', it recalls the specifically Calvinist theology of 'predestination': Alan Sinfield points to parallels between Hamlet's phrasing here and Calvin's in the *Institutes* (Sinfield 1992: 226).[21] According to Sinfield, Hamlet's indifference to his 'special providence' fatally undermines and weakens it: I will return to indifference later.

In fact, much more subversive of Christian orthodoxy is the pure violence of a 'divinity' that Hamlet speaks of only in contexts of hoisting friends with their own petard and agreeing to take part in a suspicious sword-fight that turns into something like an orgy of death. The violence of 'rashness' is the Kierkegaardian violence of seemingly unwarranted action, of spontaneous, reckless choice, of pure historical agency – 'I just did it' – which bursts beyond custom and expectation into an incalculable future. Hamlet 'defies augury': knowing he is likely to lose, intuiting that – like the sparrow – he will die, he goes ahead anyway. His sudden metaphysics of rashness goes further (or madder) than Kierkegaard, who proposed that 'rashness' might in special cases be justified by a 'special providence' beyond ordinary ethics, by finding 'divinity' *solely* in 'rashness'[22]. '[P]raised be rashness': in that shocking utterance, rashness seems to be the very name of Hamlet's god.

Greenblatt is convinced that 'nothing comes of nothing, even in Shakespeare' (Greenblatt 2001: 4) but no context – certainly not Purgatory's cultural history – is totally adequate to *Hamlet*'s last act. Kierkegaard is right that *Hamlet* is not a religious play in any conventional sense (see Kearney, this volume). Hamlet's faith in a 'divinity' or 'providence' that expresses itself through worldly events and actions in time is suggestive, to a certain extent, of 'the hour' in which time is divinely fulfilled in the Gospel of John: 'The hour is come that the Son of Man should be glorified' (12:23); 'for this cause came I unto this hour' (12:27); 'his hour was come that he should depart out of this world unto the father' (13:1), etc. But, strange though it is to say, Hamlet's sudden spiritual confidence in rashness resonates more powerfully with the Hindu text, the *Bhagavad Gita*. In the *Gita*, Arjuna is hesitating to fight in an agony of compassion when the god Krishna addresses him as follows:

> Simply because it ought to be done, when action
> That is religiously required is performed, Arjuna,
> Abandoning attachment and fruit,
> That abandonment is held to be of goodness.

> He loathes not disagreeable action,
> Nor does he cling to agreeable (action),
> The man of abandonment who is filled with goodness,
> Wise, whose doubts are destroyed.
>
> (Bhagavad Gita 1944: 2.47, 18.9–10)

Arjuna responds, 'I stand firm, with doubts dispersed;/I shall do thy word' (ibid.: 73); and he joins the fray. Against the run of the play, Hamlet shares Arjuna's enabling assurance. A breath of metaphysical irony returns via the biblical resonances of 'a fall of a sparrow' in Matthew 10:28–32 and Luke 12:4–7. These parallel texts are disturbingly ambiguous. They cultivate religious comfort. Matthew's version reads:

> Are not two sparrows sold for a farthing? and one of them shall not fall on the ground without your Father. But the very hairs of your head are all numbered. Fear ye not therefore, ye are of more value than many sparrows.
>
> (Matt. 10:30–2)

But at the same time they provoke anxiety. Matthew again:

> [F]ear not them which kill the body, but are not able to kill the soul: but rather fear him which is able to destroy both soul and body in hell.
>
> (Matt. 10:28)

The prospect of Hell is a reminder that rashness may be demonically inspired, as Hamlet feared in relation to the promptings of the ghost from the first ('Be thou a spirit of health or goblin damned . . .' (1.4.21)). For Kierkegaard, nothing – nothing humanly discernible – separates the saint from the psychopath:

rashness is a terrible wager.[23] But, apart from the unsettling biblical reverberation, irony and anxiety do not undermine Hamlet's rashness, not so much because he has dispersed his doubts, like Krishna disperses Arjuna's, as because he has engrossed them into himself and his deed in advance – by means of his 'antic disposition' (2.1.173) and his obsessive mental rehearsal of action. As a result of this anticipation of irony, Hamlet's rashness is actually *more* convincing than that of confirmed Shakespearean action-men like Pyrrhus, Laertes and Fortinbras, even Coriolanus.[24]

Where does this leave us in relation to Derrida on *Hamlet*? Too often criticism is theory's latecomer and parasite when, as a less systematic, more phenomenological and responsive form of thinking, it is in a position to make a creative contribution to theory. Richard Halpern has provided an engaging materialist critique of Derrida's reading of *Hamlet* already, pitting the gravedigger and Yorick's skull against Derridean 'spectropoetics'. He concludes, 'If Derrida really wants to play the Gravedigger in *Hamlet*, as he claims, it is necessary to put off his princely fastidiousness, curtail his project of endless "filtering" and purgation, and delve in the sometimes unpleasant muck of real history' (Halpern 2001: 51). By contrast with Halpern, I develop in what follows a materialist critique of Derrida paradoxically grounded in the novel spirituality of immanence that *Hamlet* develops in its last act. Such spirituality is not only compatible with the graveyard where it is revealed, it is a spirituality *of* the graveyard – of time, mortality and the event. I propose that the graveyard scene, and the confrontation with human finitude it represents, snuffs out the ghost, but that at the same time spirituality is transfused into material life, being absorbed into becoming.

Hamlet's god of 'rashness' challenges Derrida in at least three ways. First, the manifestation to the Prince of a 'divinity' immanently involved in experience and action contravenes Derrida's structure of messianic deferral. Slavoj Žižek has written that the

> fundamental lesson of postmodernist politics is that *there is no Event*, that 'nothing really happens', that the Truth-Event is a passing, illusory short-circuit, a false identification to be dispelled sooner or later by the reassertion of difference

or, at best, the fleeting promise of the Redemption-to-come, towards which we have to maintain a proper distance in order to avoid the catastrophic 'totalitarian' consequences.

(Žižek 2000a: 135)

But Žižek opposes this 'structural scepticism', insisting, after Jacques Lacan and Badiou, that *'miracles do happen'* (Žižek 2000a: 135). According to Hamlet, they happen through the very meanness and contingency of life – criminal confusion at sea, a dodgy sword-fight, and so on. This manifestation of the absolute through dubious means precipitates, within the play, the overthrow of a corrupt regime. To this extent, in place of Derrida's Marx of messianic expectation, *Hamlet* seems to give us back the Marx of material intervention. In an exact reversal of what we might expect, Hamlet's mystical experience turns him from a kind of conscientious objector into an activist who says, 'The readiness is all' (5.2.169). Joyce saw this when he wrote, 'Khaki Hamlets don't hesitate to shoot' (Joyce 1992: 239–40). What Hamlet achieves is what Michael Witmore calls 'a form of quasi-agency', 'a cooperation with divine providence which, paradoxically, allows him to fulfil the ghost's charge for revenge' (Witmore 2001: 109). And yet, I would add, because Hamlet's act is inspired by the absolute rather than his affronted father, it transcends revenge in the direction of justice.

The existential dimension of this immersion of divinity in the messy human element entails a more substantial human spirituality than either Greenblatt or Derrida describe. Hamlet has been pained by the degrading contradiction between the transcendent qualities of human being and what Greenblatt calls 'the material leftover' (Greenblatt 2001: 242): 'What a piece of work is a man! how noble in reason, how infinite in faculty. . . . And yet, to me, what is this quintessence of dust' (2.2.293–8).[25] But, as Greenblatt does not recognise, Hamlet's recognition that 'there's a divinity that shapes our ends' now teaches him that mere physical life is *already* caught up into divine life. This, as it were, reverses Hamlet's earlier thought: 'What a quintessence of dust is a man. . . . And yet, to me, how noble in reason, how infinite in faculty, etc.' As Žižek writes, '[h]uman life is never just life, it is always sustained by an excess of life' (Žižek 2001: 104–5). For Derrida and his disciples, this 'excess' is the messianic expectation – but that defers and displaces life into the future. Hamlet's revelation and theology suggests instead that 'divinity' irradiates and operates through the very imperfections of existence. This enables him to act in favour of the absolute even as a compromised agent in a compromised world.

If Hamlet's avowal of a politically enabling 'immanentization of spirit' (see Badiou 2003: 69) defies Derrida's messianic structure of expectation and possibility, then his commitment to his god of 'rashness' also contravenes Derrida's ethical spirituality of a universal responsiveness to difference. Perhaps partly because of his thesis that '[t]he tragic hero remains within the ethical', partly because he was suffering from Bloomian 'anxiety of influence', Kierkegaard explicitly missed the Shakespearean transcendence of ethics in *Hamlet*. He writes in suspiciously bardolatrous tones, 'Thanks be to thee, great Shakespeare, who art able to express everything, absolutely everything, precisely as it is – and yet why didst thou never pronounce this pang?' (Kierkegaard 1955: 69, 72). But, in his religiously inspired violence, Hamlet achieves the very 'teleological suspension of the ethical' that Kierkegaard discovered in the biblical story of the sacrifice of Isaac. In his consideration of Kierkegaard's *Fear and Trembling*, Derrida observes, 'Abraham is faithful to God only in his absolute treachery, in the betrayal of his own and the uniqueness of each one of them, exemplified in his beloved son'. This means in general terms: 'I cannot respond to the call, the request, the obligation, or even the love of another without sacrificing the other other, the other others' (Derrida 1995b: 68). In *Specters of Marx*, Derrida had already written in relation to Shakespeare:

> How to distinguish between two disadjustments, between the disjuncture of the unjust [i.e. the betrayal of others in favour of some one] and the [disjuncture] that opens up the infinite asymmetry of the relation to the other [i.e. of ultimate responsibility to the one in spite of everything and all others]. Whether one knows it or not, Hamlet is speaking in the space opened up by this question.
>
> (Derrida 1994: 22)

But, like much literary criticism, *Specters of Marx* is stuck with the impotent Hamlet who is prevented by ethical scruples from committing revenge. Once Hamlet has committed himself to 'divinity' rather than the furious spirit of a murdered father, the play dramatises the enabling power of a complete commitment. After his mystical experience, Hamlet, like Abraham, is willing to do whatever is required, and without Abraham's 'pang' – which suggests Shakespeare went further than Kierkegaard beyond ordinary good and evil.[26] As if to stress the historical potential of spirituality, Hamlet's mystical commitment to a 'special providence' is inseparable from a commitment to intervening in time. His god of 'rashness' plunges ethical idealism into the flux and chance of history, abolishing a separate sphere of ethics.

Only a pledge to the absolute can combine the violence of a specific commitment with the assurance of doing right. The other side of Hamlet's unconditional engagement is his achievement of what seems to be a kind of inspired, militant indifference. This too challenges Derrida's ethics of difference and is the third count in which the play offers grounds for critiquing poststructuralism. In *Hamlet*, justice is *not* achieved by exposure to difference as in Derrida's prescription for it. Hamlet is devoted to difference before Act Five: he wants to be different from the world; he wants 'man' to be different from 'woman' and his own mortality; he desperately asserts the distinction of his father. But this just gets him more stuck in the system of differences (of individuality, of gender, of class) that constitutes social life. It is Hamlet's engagement with the absolute that decidedly lifts him out of this system of differences and enables him to see and, more crucially, to act disinterestedly.

No one to my knowledge has placed Hamlet's crucial transition from 'To be, or not to be' (3.1.58) to 'Let be' in the context of the rich history of indifference and letting-be in the history of ideas in the Western tradition. The medieval German mystic Meister Eckhardt (1270–1327) characterised true religion as the relinquishing of self-centred being in order to let God be.[27] As Hans Urs von Balthasar points out, the Thomist tradition in theology explains the spiritual worth of indifference by saying that the 'part' should love the 'whole' more than itself, while Augustinian, Anselmian and Franciscan thoughts hold that the right should be desired for its rightness regardless of subjective considerations. Balthasar himself writes of a 'new and deeper' virtue of 'indifference' able to let the Good be without trying to acquire it (Balthasar 1988: 212–13). In philosophy, the later Heidegger appropriated this theological tradition in his own crucial notion of *Gelassenheit* (Heidegger 1966). This is thinking as the renouncing of willing, especially of that utilitarian instrumentality which drives the advance of technology; it is pure contemplation, free from desire to master the world. All these accounts present indifference as the subjective path to ethical truth. Most recently, Badiou has approached the matter from the other side, stressing that truth is indifferent to subjective differences (Badiou 2001). Indifference, letting-be, *Gelassenheit*: all these correspond to the 'mysterious and beautiful disinterestedness' Harold Bloom attributes to the fifth-act Hamlet (Bloom 1989: 57).

Hamlet cannot do justice in his own behalf, especially as he is the son of the victim. As Kant saw, justice must be performed in the name of transcendental objectivity.[28] 'If it be now, 'tis not to come. If it be not to come it will be now' is illuminated by unselfish indifference: whether 'it' is Hamlet's or Claudius's death or any other event, it's all one to Hamlet. In this context, the confusing generality of the Prince's 'Let be' begins to look more like gracious largesse. It suggests resignation to 'a special providence' and acceptance of his own imperfection. It seems to make peace with the world, bearing fruit in courtesy to Gertrude, solidarity with Laertes and communion in death with both – and even with Claudius, whom Hamlet forces to drink from the poisoned cup with the strange words suggestive of the Eucharist, 'Is thy union here?' (5.2.268). But far from preventing him from passing violent judgement on the world, such peaceful resignation enables Hamlet to channel 'a special providence' purely and knowingly, with a self-transcending, missionary conviction that he is acting in favour of the absolute. As it turns out, this involves not just killing but suicidally surrendering himself to the judgement he recognises in chance and death as well. Such is his defiance of 'augury' and his own best interests. It might still be hard to see how Hamlet's distant and strange serenity facilitates decisive action but, in *Welcome to the Desert of the Real*, Žižek quotes G. K. Chesterton to bring out the militant potential of indifference: 'A soldier surrounded by enemies, if he is to cut his way out. . . . must seek his life in a spirit of curious indifference to it; he must desire life like water and yet drink death like wine' (Chesterton 1995: 9; quoted in Žižek 2002: 89–90). As any athlete or actor knows, you've got to be sufficiently relaxed to spring powerfully into action.

From his sudden indifference to life, Hamlet gets life back: 'He that loveth his life shall lose it; and he that hateth his life in this world shall keep it unto life eternal' (John 12.25). He receives the power to act not from his father but from elsewhere. And yet his sudden faith that 'divinity' is absorbed in the mess and chance of history enables him to live and die confidently and unanxiously. His indifference and belated enactment of his heroic role are intimately related.

Indifference in *Hamlet* involves what Žižek describes as 'unplugging' from the symbolic order (Žižek 2000b: 123ff.). Hamlet's 'unplugging' extends to his removal from the Danish succession. Hamlet doesn't succeed Hamlet, and never looks like doing so: he certainly doesn't kill Claudius in order to gain the Danish throne. Hamlet is also removed from marriage and even sexual relations. Is he a virgin? It would intensify the pity and fear. That the thought is somehow unbearable is suggested by Kenneth Branagh's flashback in his 1996 film of the play placing Hamlet in Ophelia's bed. Manly Old Hamlet is more appropriately succeeded by the straightforwardly potent Fortinbras. Lapsed as a lover, passed over for Fortinbras, Hamlet is effectively emasculated by the play. More positively, he seems to move beyond cultural conditioning and more or less arrive on the *other side* of social and sexual difference, thereby furnishing an important counter-example to criticism that sees character as wholly culturally determined.

Perhaps most importantly in the context of current criticism, Hamlet's deed suggests the possibility of an authentic act *not* determined by prevailing conventions, in this case of revenge. The deterministic historicism of contemporary intellectual life has weakened the credit and perhaps even the scope for individual agency and resistance.[29] But Hamlet's divinely inspired act breaks the deadlock of the prevailing situation. Through it, in the most unlikely circumstances, an extraneous justice takes the place of partisan revenge, not in the name of Hamlet's father but as it is disposed by 'divinity' and a 'special providence'.

But what sort of justice is achieved at the end of *Hamlet*? Rough justice, certainly. The fratricidal usurper, Claudius, is

dead. As is his (previously the murder victim's) queen. The
degree of Gertrude's guilt is disputed.[30] She recognises some
(3.4.78–81) and is surely involved in Claudius's, but does she
deserve to die? Laertes, who has conspired with Claudius to
kill Hamlet, is dead. Polonius is dead already: he schemed with
the wrongful king and (to the detriment of especially his
daughter) was superficial and a tedious talker. Hamlet, who
killed Polonius, is dead. By his own morally strenuous account,
he is guilty of more offences than we have words to put them
in (3.1.125ff.) – among them must be numbered vacillating
with bloody consequences, as well as mistreating Ophelia
and killing her father, which causes her death. And Hamlet
was supposedly the best person in the play: 'O what a noble
mind is here o'erthrown!/The courtier's, soldier's, scholar's
eye, tongue, sword' etc. (3.1.149ff.). According to the Prince,
all are guilty – all of the above, and all others as well – which
would validate universal punishment.

The justice of the last act remains finally undecidable.
Hamlet, as Sinfield writes, 'plays with Osric (this scene seems
purposefully desultory), competes recklessly with Laertes, makes
no plan against the king. The final killing occurs in a burst of
passionate inspiration' (Sinfield 1992: 228). And yet, Hamlet
has prepared us for rough justice beyond human scope by
testifying that 'a special providence' operates through exactly
such 'rashness' and seemingly random contingency. Bradley
suggests that

> in all that happens or is done we seem to apprehend some
> vaster power. We do not define it, or even name it, or
> perhaps even say to ourselves that it is there; but our
> imagination is haunted by the sense of it, as it works its
> way through the deeds or the delays of men to its inevit-
> able end.
>
> (Bradley 1971: 139)

I have said that Hamlet engrosses irony into his long-awaited
action to the effect that, when finally he performs it, it is less
susceptible to deconstruction. But so obscure is the last act
of the play, so wide is the gap between its 'accidental judge-
ments' and 'casual slaughters' (5.2.326) and the significance
Hamlet claims for accidents, that it's even more than usually

true to say that interpretation cannot be definitive. As in Kierkegaard, we ultimately don't know. Hamlet proclaims we must act without knowing. Of course, it is possible that his indifference is a screen for his interest. Perhaps *Hamlet* exposes action as a form of passivity, and we should take the equation between action and letting-be at face value? Perhaps Hamlet really achieves agency in the *refusal* to act that he sadly relinquishes at the end? Again, Bradley seems most apt because he is most sensitive to the ambiguities. He writes, 'the Hamlet of the Fifth Act shows a kind of sad or indifferent self-abandonment, as if he secretly despaired of forcing himself to action, and were ready to leave his duty to some other power than his own'. But Bradley immediately havers in this interpretation, confessing there is '[s]omething noble in [Hamlet's] carelessness', and then reverting to bemused wonder at the strange power he insists is moving through the action (Bradley 1971: 116–17, 141).

I maintain that the spirituality of rashness discussed earlier is a major, intellectually and politically provocative implication of the immanent operation of the ultimate in the play. It is inherent in the structure of *Hamlet* and of drama itself. A theatrical pun is at work in that Hamlet's act ends the last act of the play, and with the specific act expected with increasing intensity from the beginning. Hamlet's act is a last or ultimate, an eschatological act, because it's performed in the name of the absolute, because it's the last thing he does and because it entails his own death. Action is the distinguishing feature of dramatic art. Rashness is action denuded of reason, action that surges ahead of words and thinking in a shameless overstepping of 'the modesty of nature' (3.2.17–18) – in other words, pure action: action itself. Hamlet's god of rashness is therefore the god of drama even more than it's a god of history, and it enables a simultaneously aesthetic and spiritual resolution. Witmore suggests that *Hamlet* is a 'trial' challenging its audience to recognise theatre's 'reigning provisional deity' (Witmore 2001: 109). After all the Prince's sustained recoil from action and, as a result, from the very medium of theatre in which he finds himself stranded, Shakespeare's play improvises a new ontology of being-in-action, an ontology that doesn't so much drag the present into the artifice of eternity as it drags eternity into the mess and artifice of the present.

What are we to make of this in our present? At Riverside Studios in London 2004, Sulayman Al-bassam's award-winning *The Al-Hamlet Summit* (2004) cast Hamlet as a diffident, Europeanised Arabic playboy. Its most stunning moment was the Prince's reappearance in the robes of Islamic fundamentalism.[31] Perhaps we should recall here that in our contemporary world, after the collapse of Soviet communism, the dominant and representative form of political resistance to Western capitalism is religious. As the subject of an ambiguous otherworldly act, Hamlet seems disturbingly like a contemporary terrorist. Does Shakespeare's play propose that invoking the absolute in order to act might facilitate good as well as evil? The unfocused 'War on Terror' sometimes seems like a neurotic, itself terroristically pre-emptive clampdown on any resistance to conventional Anglo-American culture. Can we imagine a peaceful revolution? With Fortinbras waiting in the wings, few commentators would be optimistic about the political future suggested by Shakespeare's tragedy. But, in the vivid present of its own event, Shakespeare's play epitomises a metaphysics of rashness – an absolute now – wherein everything is gathered and staked upon a deed.

Notes

1 Presentism's most important exponents are Hugh Grady and Terence Hawkes. See especially Grady 1991, 1996 and 2002 and Hawkes 2002.
2 See Kastan 1999: 17.
3 This, for example, was the basis of Margreta de Grazia's critique of presentism in a 2004 Shakespeare Association of America session in New Orleans titled 'Missing Links: Historicism, Presentism, and the Limits of the Modern'. Kastan writes against presentism in similar terms (Kastan 1999: 17). For a more detailed critique, see Wells 2000a and 2000b. See also Pechter 2003, especially pp. 521–2. For a more positive account, see Fernie 2005. For overviews, see Moore 2003 and Brown 2004.
4 See Fernie 2005.
5 According to a review article by David Schalkwyk, *Hamlet in Purgatory* 'strikes at the heart of the most fundamental of Materialist dogmas' – 'the primacy of the material' – by showing how an imagined spiritual space produced an immense material apparatus (Schalkwyk 2002).

6 See Hawkes 2002: 4.

7 For a sophisticated and illuminating discussion of how new historicism, and especially *Hamlet in Purgatory*, meet 'present needs and interests', see Schalkwyk 2004.

8 See Greenblatt 2004.

9 Gallagher and Greenblatt 2000 assert that the unsystematic empiricism of new historicist thought is a distinct advantage.

10 Gallagher and Greenblatt 2000 includes reflections on Jewishness. Greenblatt 2000 addresses the subject autobiographically. On postcolonial themes, see especially Greenblatt 1992.

11 It may be that Greenblatt's concern with death and bereavement is focused and sharpened by the thought of the Holocaust. In the prologue to *Hamlet in Purgatory*, Greenblatt recalls that the book was partly written at Wissenschaftskolleg zu Berlin and that 'the fact that Berlin is haunted by ghosts was itself a powerful inducement to reflect on the claims of the dead and the obligations of the living' (Greenblatt 2001: xi). Greenblatt 2000 evokes a visit with his younger son to his ancestral homeland where he contemplated the massacre of the Vilna Jews.

12 For an astute historical and theological perspective on the narrowness of Greenblatt's treatments of Purgatory and *Hamlet*, see Sarah Beckwith 2003. Beckwith details Greenblatt's exclusion of 'justice, judgement and reconciliation' and 'the incarnation of performance' in terms of his failure to consider the medieval sacrament of penance. In the same volume, David Aers critiques Greenblatt's handling of the Eucharist in *Practicing New Historicism* (Aers 2003).

13 For a positive account of Derrida's reading of Shakespeare's play, see Starling 1997/8. For a more sceptical treatment, see Halpern 2001.

14 See Derrida 1997 for much discussion of the place of this notion in Derrida's thought.

15 The verbal clue here is that Greenblatt desires to speak *to* the dead; and although Derrida says it is needful to speak *to*, *of* and *with* the ghost and ghosts, that still isn't exactly listening.

16 Greenblatt can productively be read against Derrida here. He too reflects on the uncanny likeness that the text stresses (Greenblatt 2001: 210ff.).

17 For an introduction to Levinas's thought, see Levinas 1985 and 1989.

18 I follow the Oxford editor (and most others) here in including 'Let be' which is not in the Folio text. See Shakespeare 1987.

19 See Kierkegaard 1955.

20 See Swinburne 1994 for a recent consideration of the doctrine of incarnation.

21 For a more subtle treatment of *Hamlet* in terms of Protestant providentialism and theatrical aesthetics, see Witmore 2001. My argument below intersects with Witmore's in a number of ways but, to my

mind, Witmore underplays the extent to which *Hamlet*'s theology of 'accident' is also a theology of 'rashness'. Witmore's emphasis is metatheatrical. He suggests that through Hamlet's avowals of 'providence' Shakespeare is prompting recognition of his own authorship. I focus instead on the existential and metaphysical implications of a spirituality of accident and rashness for Hamlet himself and for agency in general.

22 See Kierkegaard 1955.

23 Ibid.

24 In Shakespeare's play, this more resolute and heroic Hamlet forcefully supplants the wan and fainting figure of critical tradition from Goethe onwards (Goethe 1989: 146).

25 See also Gallagher and Greenblatt 2000: 141.

26 For more on Kierkegaard and *Hamlet*, see Kearney's essay, this volume.

27 See Eckhardt 1941: 127.

28 Kant writes, 'I ought never to act except in such a way that I could also will that my maxim should become a universal law' (Kant 1997: 402).

29 Greenblatt's avowal that subversion is always contained is the *locus classicus* of such hopelessness (Greenblatt 1988: 65). The history of politically ambitious cultural materialism can be cast in terms of a struggle with the pessimistic determinism suggested by its own name. As Claire Colebrook observes, 'Because of the problematisation of the humanist subject and the Marxist economic base, post-Marxist criticism has struggled to find a legitimating ground from which its political critique can be launched' (Colebrook 1997: 194).

30 See, for instance, Ouditt 1996 and Smith 1980.

31 This reworking of *Hamlet* produced by Zaoum Theatre from an Arabic viewpoint and in a non-specific Arabic setting won a Fringe First Award at Edinburgh in 2002 before coming to London.

Afterword
Jonathan Dollimore

There is, of course, feel-good spirituality, as in the advice once given me by a Californian new-ager: 'choose the kind of spirituality you feel most comfortable with'. And then there is its opposite, spirituality of the anguished kind wherein consciousness is tormented by loss, lack, guilt, conflict and finitude, and always and restlessly searching for something other.

It is to their credit that the contributors to this volume eschew feel-good spirituality while at the same time avoiding the histrionic gestures of its agonised opposite. Readers will find here an engagement with both Shakespeare and spirituality that is intelligent, original, and challengingly optimistic, one that surely succeeds in its wish to 'reinvigorate and strengthen politically progressive materialist criticism' (Introduction: 3). Haunting is just one of its intriguing themes, and I want to suggest that a collection such as this, precisely because of its intelligence and commitment, must be haunted by that darker, agonised spirituality that was a driving force of early modern culture, and indeed of Western culture more generally, right up to and including the present.

Tragedy, and especially Renaissance tragedy, presupposes anguished spirituality even or especially when it is irreligious.

The famous *Chorus Sacerdotum* from Fulke Greville's *Mustapha* suggests how the agonised spirituality of the West is potentially also politically dangerous:

> Oh wearisome condition of humanity!
> Born under one law, to another bound:
> Vainly begot yet forbidden vanity,
> Created sick, commanded to be sound:
> What meaneth nature by these diverse laws?
> Passion and reason self-division cause:
> Is it the mark or majesty of power
> To make offences that it may forgive?[1]

Shakespeare's sonnet (129) 'The expense of spirit in a waste of shame' is perhaps the most famous dramatisation of the 'self-division' consequent on the conflict between 'passion and reason', but there are many more from this period. And the fact that 'spirit' here links semen and soul via the notion of vital energy is a reminder of how inclusive the early modern spiritual sensibility could be.

The editor of this volume is surely right in saying that historical/materialist approaches to Shakespearean drama have been unable to handle its spiritual dimensions. Consider something obsessively central to both spirituality and tragedy, namely death. The historical approach to death insists that it is not some essential thing, but a socio-historical construct; it tells us that to look for the transhistorical continuities in the human experience of death is fundamentally misguided; on the contrary, we must understand death as something that changes across time within any one culture and that fundamentally differs between cultures (and religions). So, in the latter case there will be, e.g. a Buddhist conception of death, and a Christian one; in the former, there will be a medieval way of dying and a Victorian one, and so on. Difference is all.

This is true, as far as it goes. But as is often the case, the agreeable truth (diversity and difference) is used to evade the less agreeable (the anguish of mortality). Historicism performs this evasion not just with respect to specific topics such as death, but in its very methodology, and especially in its assumption that anything in the past can be explained if its full history can be retrieved. Of course, historicism knows that full history is rarely if ever retrievable, but the assumption that all would be revealed if it were, is the ideal to which the historian aspires. In other words, nothing of itself, and in relation to us, is inexplicable in principle, only in practice. Nothing more than inadequate historical data stands between us and a full understanding of the past. To the extent that this assumption pervades historicism of all kinds, it entails a certain irony: this most empirical of procedures has at its methodological heart something of the a priori. By contrast, a spiritual perspective might (for example) accept in principle that the object of its understanding may be ultimately incomprehensible, or comprehended fully only at the cost of undermining what currently counts as understanding.

Not surprisingly, then, the contemporary encounter with spirituality proceeds via deconstruction and postmodernism. To the extent that this entails finding spirituality where it might least be expected, it is encouraging: the most interesting forms of the spirit are always the unexpected ones. But the urbane complexities that characterise both deconstruction and postmodernism, at least in their academic forms, are as likely as historicism to obscure the less palatable truth with the more agreeable one.

Why are the most interesting forms of spirit the unexpected ones? Partly because spirituality survives most interestingly via a kind of radical continuity – that is, a continuity arising from negation. Something is negated but survives by mutating into the form of its opposite; so, for example, spirituality survives in and as unbelief (only the sacrilegious truly understand the sacred).

Thus Freud, who professed himself the unbelieving scientist, redramatised human interiority – the very space of spirituality – by enlarging its domain, elaborating its complexity and intensifying its conflicts. Psychoanalysis became a new religion, or at least was embraced by those who might otherwise have been religious, or for whom unbelief made religion proper untenable. Not for nothing does Anthony Burgess in *Earthly Powers* have a prospective Pope remark in 1938 that Freud could still be a good Jewish theologian if only he would stop inventing words like 'id' (Burgess 1981: 394).

But it is Nietzsche who is most significant here. He who pronounces the death of God is the greatest of spiritual modernists, and never more so than when he is castigating all religion and especially Christianity; his anguished consciousness, his desperate quest for intellectual truth and an authenticity of self, his sense of supreme effort (will to power) born of lack, and, above all, his acute sense of conflict as the very condition of being, make him the heir of Western spirituality. And like Renaissance writers before him, Nietzsche realised that tragedy at its most challenging derives from spiritual dissatisfaction – specifically the convergence of forbidden knowledge and dissident desire.

Milton's Adam and Eve are told: 'know to know no more' (*Paradise Lost* 4. 775).[2] They disobey, and their transgressive desire for forbidden knowledge brings death into the world, into desire. In other words, transgressive desire is inseparable from forbidden knowledge and together they kick-start history and become the stuff of tragedy.

For those like Milton this produces a state of spiritual alienation as terrible as it is deplorable. But for Nietzsche we are most ourselves when in this destructive and suffering state of knowing and desiring more than we should. This is one aspect of his transvaluation of values (continuity through negation), the upshot of which is a survival in him of a specifically Christian sense of free will: we retain the capacity to violate the restraints of the history that has produced us, even if at a terrible cost. This was also a view that Nietzsche attributed to Shakespeare. The rationalist typically regards the accumulation of knowledge as a progressive and irreversible consolidation of civilisation. But Nietzsche affirms another kind of knowledge, one that does not consolidate civilisation, but threatens it. It is the knowledge that civilisation itself is at heart illusory. 'Illusory' here refers not to some residual superstitions, soon to be swept away by the march of rational progress, but to the very structure of 'rational' civilisation; anticipating Freud, Nietzsche believes that human civilisation requires illusion in order to be what it is. (Later Freud would elaborate this idea in terms of repression, disavowal and sublimation.) To know that this is so makes one a spiritual outcast from society, understanding too much from a spiritual position 'beyond good and evil'.

This is Nietzsche's reading of Hamlet – he has 'seen through' the illusions by which his culture maintains itself; inaction derives not from confusion and doubt, but from too much knowledge. Likewise with Macbeth, but with him it is also about affirming what has been repressed – of desublimating the life force itself, turning it against civilised morality, and celebrating its destructive power. So it's a mistake, says Nietzsche, to think that Shakespeare's theatre was aiming for a moral effect. In this regard *Macbeth* does not warn against hubris and ambition; on the contrary it affirms their attraction. And the fact that Macbeth 'perishes by his passions' is part of his 'daemonic attraction'. By 'daemonic' (*dämonisch*) Nietzsche means 'in defiance *against* life and advantage for the sake of a drive and idea' (*Gedankens und Triebes*). He adds:

> Do you suppose that Tristan and Isolde are preaching *against* adultery when they both perish by it? This would be to stand the poets on their head: they, and especially Shakespeare, are enamoured of the passions as such and not least of their *death-welcoming* moods.

Shakespeare, like other tragic poets, 'speaks . . . out of a restless, vigorous age which is half-drunk and stupefied by its excess of blood and energy – out of a wickeder age than ours is'. But the guardians of high culture in our own day disavow this: they seek to '*adjust* and *justify* the goal of a Shakespearean drama' precisely in order that they (and we) 'not understand it' (Nietzsche 1982: 140–1).

Thus Shakespeare and his guardians fall on opposite sides of Nietzsche's great divide between, on the one hand, those who affirm the life force, and on the other those who turn away from it – between, in other words, the daemonic and the humanitarian. In *The Gay Science* this distinction is expressed in terms of two distinct kinds of sufferer – those who suffer from a superabundance of life and those who suffer from an impoverishment of life. The former live with a spiritual intensity, wanting 'a Dionysian art as well as a tragic outlook and insight into life', and willingly confront 'the terrible and questionable . . . every luxury of destruction, decomposition, negation'; while the latter avoid that same intensity, choosing instead 'mildness, peacefulness, goodness in thought and in deed . . . a certain warm, fear-averting confinement and enclosure within optimistic horizons' (Nietzsche 2001: 234).

All this is to the point, although Nietzsche wilfully miscon-
strues *Macbeth*. This play is indeed a profound exploration of
the daemonic, but its *tragedy* is the recalcitrant conflict between
the daemonic and the humane, between the Macbeths' 'black
and deep desires' and the 'milk of human kindness' (1.4.51,
1.5.15). And if this type of conflict is the focus of many of the
most memorable tragedies, it is also embedded in the history
of human civilisation, and one reason why tragedy is widely
regarded as the most profound of all literary genres. But
Nietzsche's view of the artist and philosopher as knowing too
much, of seeing through, demystifying and maybe undermining
the ideological, religious and cultural 'fictions' of society, and
thereby 'de-repressing' subversive desires – all this is clearly
relevant to Shakespeare, whose own heroes, anti-heroes, lovers
and malcontents are already doing something similar. Similar
but perhaps with even darker implications: if Nietzsche revels
in the idea that Macbeth 'perishes by his passions', these plays
dramatise the agony, the violence and the psychological conflict
generated by the destructive and illicit desires that the Macbeths
entertain. On the one side is the world of humane values,
expressed most vividly in the imagery of nurturing the depen-
dent infant, and whose condition is repression, suppression,
exclusion and disavowal, these being the preconditions for civilisation itself. On the other, the dangerous knowledge that
understands the price being paid for the humane, and the transgressive desire that knowledge permits and incites, and that
will not pay the price even if the consequence is a terrible
inhumanity: courage screwed to the sticking place in a will to
power (spirit as 'undaunted mettle' (1.1.73)) that would willingly dash out the brains of the sucking infant rather than fail.
Black and deep desires can only be free of the humane in and
through its deepest violation, which means of course that they
can never be free. *Macbeth* shows how the threat of the daemonic
derives not from a pure, pre-social nature or instinct, clearly
distinct from the culture it threatens, but from the return of
repressed desire so inextricably bound up with culture it is
impossible anymore to distinguish between the two. This is
why only the highly civilised can become truly daemonic. Early
modern writers knew well that 'corrupted' reason was capable
of an intensity of evil unknown to the non- or irrational; lilies
that fester smell far worse than weeds. Thus the return of the

repressed has a virulence that is not the opposite of civilisation but its inversion; not unfettered pre-social libido indifferent to the civilising restraint it has escaped, but, on the contrary, desire returning via the 'civilising' mechanisms of its repression, mechanisms it is still inseparable from, even as it violates them. Thus Lady Macbeth's image of herself dashing out the brains of her own child.

Is Nietzsche right about the 'death-welcoming' moods of artists such as Shakespeare? His was a religious culture whose more extreme forms were death-obsessed; thus Richard Crashaw, writing in the seventeenth century about St Teresa and martyrdom: 'Such thirsts to die, as dares drink up/A thousand cold deaths in one cup' ('A Hymn to the Name and Honor of the Admirable Sainte Teresa', 37–8).[3] Truly, a thirst for annihilation. And Shakespeare's is a theatre in which those who desire most illicitly not only die, but also seem to embrace death. One reason is to be found in that early modern (spiritual) sensibility for which death was at once the enemy of desire (it destroys what we love) but also that which guarantees the end of desire; both cause of and release from pain. A diligent researcher (ungraciously I have forgotten who – such diligence deserves better) once counted more than two hundred suicides in around one hundred plays between 1580 and 1640; apparently Shakespeare has no less than fifty-two – remarkable indeed for a society in which suicide was severely demonised. If in real life suicide is most often a desperate escape from wretched suffering, in literature it is most often a profoundly spiritual expression of the suffering born of dangerous knowledge and/or dissident desire.

Nietzsche paid with his sanity for trying to live just such a spirituality, at once austerely severe and romantically excessive. I suspect that had he remained sane, he would have killed himself.

Notes

1   Greville 1973.
2   Milton 1971.
3   Crashaw 1968: 318.

Bibliography

Abraham, N. (1988a) 'Notes on the Phantom: A Complement to Freud's Metapsychology', *Diacritics* 18: 171–6.

Abraham, N. (1988b) 'The Phantom of Hamlet or the Sixth Act', *Diacritics* 18: 187–205.

Adorno, T. W. (1997) *Aesthetic Theory*, trans. R. Hullot-Kentor, London: Athlone Press.

Aers, D. (2003) 'New Historicism and the Eucharist', *Journal of Medieval and Early Modern Studies* 33: 241–59.

Ali, T. (2002) *The Clash of Fundamentalisms: Crusades, Jihads and Modernity*, London and New York: Verso.

Amirthanayagam, D. P. (1999) '"I Know Thee Not Old Man": The Renunciation of Falstaff', in *Literary Imagination, Ancient and Modern: Essays in Honor of David Grene*, ed. T. Breyfogle, Chicago: University of Chicago Press.

Armstrong, I. (2000) *The Radical Aesthetic*, Oxford: Blackwell.

Attridge, D. (2004) *The Singularity of Literature*, London: Routledge.

Augustine ([397] 1958) *On Christian Doctrine*, trans. D. W. Robertson Jr, New York: Macmillan.

Badiou, A. (2001) *Ethics: An Essay on the Understanding of Evil*, trans. P. Hallward, London and New York: Verso.

—— (2003) *Saint Paul: The Foundation of Universalism*, trans. R. Brassier, Stanford: Stanford University Press.

Balthasar, H. U. von (1988) *Theo-Drama: Theological Dramatic Theory*, vol. 1: *Prolegomena*, trans. G. Harrison, San Francisco: Ignatius Press.

Bate, J. (ed.) (1997) *The Romantics on Shakespeare*, Harmondsworth: Penguin.

Baudrillard, J. (1995) *The Gulf War Never Happened*, Oxford: Polity Press.

Bauman, Z. (1992) *Intimations of Postmodernity*, London and New York: Routledge.

Beckwith, S. (2003) 'Stephen Greenblatt's *Hamlet* and the Forms of Oblivion', *Journal of Medieval and Early Modern Studies* 33: 261–80.

Benjamin, A. (1993) *The Plural Event: Descartes, Hegel, Heidegger*, London and New York: Routledge.

Benjamin, W. (1968) *Illuminations*, ed. H. Arendt, trans. H. Zohn, New York: Schocken.

Berger, J. (1977) *Ways of Seeing*, Harmondsworth: Penguin.

Berger, P. L. (ed.) (1970) *A Rumor of Angels: Modern Society and the Rediscovery of the Supernatural*, New York: Doubleday Anchor Books.

—— (2000) *The Desecularization of the World: Resurgent Religion and World Politics*, Grand Rapids, MI: Eerdmans.

Bernstein, J. M. (1992) *The Fate of Art: Aesthetic Alienation from Kant to Derrida and Adorno*, Oxford: Polity Press.

Berry, P. (1999) *Shakespeare's Feminine Endings: Disfiguring Death in the Tragedies*, London and New York: Routledge.

—— (2004) 'Nomadic Eros: Remapping Knowledge in *A Midummer Night's Dream*', in *Forgetting in Early Modern English Literature and Culture: Lethe's Legacies*, ed. C. Ivic and G. Williams, London and New York: Routledge.

—— and A. Wernick (eds) (1992) *Shadow of Spirit: Postmodernism and Religion*, London and New York: Routledge.

Bhagavad Gita (1944) trans. F. Edgerton, New York: Harper & Row.

Bishop, T. G. (1996) *Shakespeare and the Theatre of Wonder*, Cambridge: Cambridge University Press.

Bloom, H. (1989) *Ruin the Sacred Truths*, Cambridge, MA: Harvard University Press.

—— (1998) *Shakespeare: The Invention of the Human*, New York: Riverhead Books.

Bowers, F. (1975–6) 'Hal and Francis in *King Henry IV, Part I*', *McNeese Review* 22: 62–9.

Bowie, A. (1997) *From Romanticism to Critical Theory*, London: Routledge.

Bradley, A. C. (1909) 'The Rejection of Falstaff', in *Oxford Lectures on Poetry*, London: Macmillan.

—— (1971) *Shakespearean Tragedy*, 2nd edn, London: Macmillan.

Brook, D. (1994) *The Shifting Point: 1946–1987*, New York: Theatre Communications Group.

Brook, P. (1990) *The Empty Space*, London: Penguin.

Brooks, H. F. (2001) 'Introduction', in W. Shakespeare, *A Midsummer Night's Dream*, ed. H. F. Brooks, Walton-on-Thames: Thomas Nelson & Sons.

Brown, M. (2004) 'Literature in Time', *Modern Language Quarterly* 65: 1–5.

Bruns, G. (1990) 'Stanley Cavell's Shakespeare', *Critical Inquiry* 16: 612–32.

Bruster, D. (2001) 'The New Materialism in Renaissance Studies', in *Material Culture and Cultural Materialisms in the Middle Ages and Renaissance*, ed. C. Perry, Turnhout, Belgium: Brepols.

Buber, M. (1970) *I and Thou*, trans. W. Kaufman, New York: Touchstone.

Burgess, A. (1981) *Earthly Powers*, Harmondsworth: Penguin.

Callaghan, D. (2001) 'Body Problems', *Shakespeare Studies* 29: 70–1.

Calvin, J. (1961) *Institutes of the Christian Religion*, vol. 1, ed. J. T. McNeill, trans. F. L. Battles, London: SCM Press.

Caputo, J. D. (1987) 'Repetition and Kinesis: Kierkegaard on the Foundering of Metaphysics', in *Radical Hermeneutics*, ed. John Caputo, Bloomington, IN: Indiana University Press.

—— (1997a) *The Prayers and Tears of Jacques Derrida: Religion without Religion*, Bloomington, IN: Indiana University Press.

—— (ed.) (1997b) *Deconstruction in a Nutshell: A Conversation with Jacques Derrida*, New York: Fordham University Press.

—— (2000) 'For the Love of the Things Themselves: Derrida's Phenomenology of the Hyper-Real', *Journal of Cultural and Religious Theory* 1, www.jcrt.org.

—— (2001) *On Religion*, London and New York: Routledge.

—— (ed.) (2002) *The Religious*, Oxford: Blackwell.

—— and M. J. Scanlon (eds) (1999) *God, the Gift, and Postmodernism*, Bloomington, IN: Indiana University Press.

Cavell, S. (1976) *Must We Mean What We Say? A Book of Essays*, Cambridge: Cambridge University Press.

—— (1987) *Disowning Knowledge in Six Plays of Shakespeare*, Cambridge: Cambridge University Press.

Chemama, R. (ed.) (1993) *Dictionnaire de la Psychanalyse*, Paris: Larousse.

Chesterton, G. K. (1995) *Orthodoxy*, San Francisco: Ignatius Press.

Coakley, S. (1996) 'Kenōsis and Subversion: On the Repression of "Vulnerability" in Christian Feminist Writing', in Hampson 1996.

Cohen, W. (1982) '*The Merchant of Venice* and the Possibilities of Historical Criticism', reprinted in Coyle 1998.

Colebrook, C. (1997) *New Literary Histories: New Historicism and Contemporary Criticism*, Manchester and New York: Manchester University Press.

Coleridge, S. T. (1930) *Coleridge's Shakespearean Criticism*, vol. 1, ed. T. M. Raysor, London: Constable.

Coyle, M. (ed.) (1998) *New Casebooks: The Merchant of Venice*, New York: St Martin's.

Crashaw, R. (1968) *The Poems English, Latin and Greek of Richard Crashaw*, ed. L. C. Martin, 2nd edn, Oxford: Oxford University Press.

Dean, P. (1997) 'Shakespeare's Historical Imagination', *Renaissance Studies* 11: 27–40.

de Grazia, M., M. Quilligan and P. Stallybrass (1996) 'Introduction', in *Subject and Object in Renaissance Culture*, ed. P. Stallybrass, M. de Grazia and M. Quilligan, Cambridge: Cambridge University Press.

Derrida, J. (1972) *Positions*, trans. A. Bass, Chicago: University of Chicago Press.

—— (1992) *Given Time: 1. Counterfeit Money*, trans. P. Kamuf, Chicago: University of Chicago Press.

—— (1994) *Specters of Marx: the State of the Debt, the Work of Mourning, and the New International*, trans. P. Kamuf, London and New York: Routledge.

—— (1995a) *On the Name*, ed. T. Dutoit, trans. D. Wood, J. P. Leavey Jr. and I. McLeod, Stanford, CA: Stanford University Press.

—— (1995b) *The Gift of Death*, trans. D. Wills, Chicago and London: University of Chicago Press.

—— (1997) *Deconstruction in a Nutshell: A Conversation with Jacques Derrida*, ed. J. D. Caputo, New York: Fordham University Press.

—— (1998) *Monolingualism of the Other; or, The Prosthesis of Origin*, trans. P. Mensah, Stanford, CA: Stanford University Press.

—— (2002) *Acts of Religion*, ed. G. Andijar, London: Routledge.

de Vries, H. (2002) *Philosophy and the Turn to Religion*, Baltimore: Johns Hopkins University Press.

Diehl, H. (1997) *Staging Reform, Reforming the Stage: Protestantism and Popular Theater in Early Modern England*, Ithaca, NY and London: Cornell University Press.

Docherty, T. (2003) 'Aesthetic Education and the Demise of Experience', in Joughin and Malpas 2003.

Dolan, F. (1999) *Whores of Babylon: Catholicism, Gender and Seventeenth-century Print Culture*, Ithaca, NY and London: Cornell University Press.

—— (2002) 'Gender and the "Lost" Spaces of Catholicism', *Journal of Interdisciplinary Study* 32: 641–65.

Duffy, E. (1992) *The Stripping of the Altars: Traditional Religion in England 1400–1580*, New Haven and London: Yale University Press.

Durling, R. M. (1971) 'Petrarch's "Giovene donna sotto un verde lauro"', *Modern Language Notes* 86: 1–20.

—— (1976) 'Introduction', *Petrarch's Lyric Poems: The Rime sparse and Other Lyrics*, trans. and ed. R. M. Durling, Cambridge, MA: Harvard University Press.

Dutton, R., A. G. Findlay and R. Wilson (eds) (2004a) *Theater and Religion: Lancastrian Shakespeare*, Manchester: Manchester University Press.

—— (2004b) *Region, Religion and Patronage: Lancastrian Shakespeare*, Manchester: Manchester University Press.

Eagleton, T. (1990) *The Ideology of the Aesthetic*, Oxford: Blackwell.

—— (2003) *Sweet Violence: The Idea of the Tragic*, Oxford: Blackwell.

Eckhardt, Meister (1941) *Meister Eckhardt*, ed. R. Blakney, New York: Harper & Row.

Eco, E. (1989) *The Aesthetics of Chaosmos: The Middle Ages of James Joyce*, trans. E. Esrock, Cambridge, MA: Harvard University Press.

Eliot, T. S. (1951) '*Hamlet*', in *Selected Essays*, London: Faber & Faber.

Ellis-Fermor, U. (1946) *The Frontiers of Drama*, New York: Oxford University Press.

Felperin, H. (1995) 'Political Criticism at the Crossroads: The Utopian Historicism of *The Tempest*', in *The Tempest: Theory in Practice*, ed. N. Wood, Buckingham: Open University Press.

Fernie, E. (2002) *Shame in Shakespeare*, London and New York: Routledge.

—— (2005) 'Shakespeare and the Prospect of Presentism', *Shakespeare Survey* 58: 169–84.

Finlayson, M. G. (1983) *Historians, Puritanism, and the English Revolution: The Religious Factor in English Politics before and after the Interregnum*, Toronto, Buffalo, London: University of Toronto Press.

Foakes, R. A. (1997) 'Introduction', in W. Shakespeare, *King Lear*, ed. R. A. Foakes, Walton-on-Thames: Thomas Nelson & Sons.

Foucault, M. (1991) *The Order of Things: An Archaeology of the Human Sciences*, London and New York: Routledge.

Frascati-Lochhead, M. (1998) *Kenosis and Feminist Theology: The Challenge of Gianni Vattimo*, New York: SUNY Press.

Freccero, J. ([1975] 1986) 'The Fig Tree and the Laurel: Petrarch's Poetics', in *Literary Theory/Renaissance Texts*, ed. P. Parker and D. Quint, Baltimore, MD: Johns Hopkins Press.

Freinkel, L. (2002) *Reading Shakespeare's Will: A Theology of Figure From Augustine to the Sonnets*, New York: Columbia University Press.

Freud, S. ([1927] 1957) 'Fetishism', *The Standard Edition of the Complete Psychological Works of Sigmund Freud*, vol. 5, London: Hogarth Press.

—— ([1905] 1975) *Three Essays on the Theory of Sexuality*, trans. James Strachey, New York: Basic Books.

—— (1983) *The Interpretation of Dreams*, New York: Pelican.

Friedman, M. S. (1955) *Martin Buber: The Life of Dialogue*, Chicago: University of Chicago Press.

Fukuyama, F. (1992) *The End of History and the Last Man*, London: Hamish Hamilton.

Gallagher, C. and S. Greenblatt (2000) *Practicing New Historicism*, Chicago and London: University of Chicago Press.

Gallagher, L. (1991) *Medusa's Gaze: Casuistry and Conscience in the Renaissance*, Stanford, CA: Stanford University Press.

Gardner, L., D. Moss, B. Quash and G. Ward (eds) (1999) *Balthasar at the End of Modernity*, Edinburgh: T. and T. Clark.

Geneva Bible, A Facsimile of the 1560 Edition (1969) Madison, WI: University of Wisconsin Press.

Girard, R. (1991) *A Theater of Envy*, Oxford: Oxford University Press.

Goethe, J. W. von (1989) *Wilhelm Meister's Apprenticeship*, trans. E. Blackall, Princeton, NJ: Princeton University Press.

Grady, H. (1991) *The Modernist Shakespeare: Critical Texts in a Material World*, Oxford: Clarendon Press.

—— (1996) *Shakespeare's Universal Wolf: Studies in Early Modern Reification*, Oxford: Clarendon Press.

—— (2000) 'Shakespeare's Links to Machiavelli and Montaigne: Constructing Intellectual Modernity in Early Modern Europe', *Comparative Literature* 52: 119–42.

—— (2002) *Shakespeare, Machiavelli and Montaigne: Power and Subjectivity from Richard II to Hamlet*, Oxford: Oxford University Press.

Green, A. (1982) *Hamlet et Hamlet: Une Interprétation Psychoanalytique de la Représentation*, Paris: Balland.

Greenblatt, S. (1985) 'Invisible Bullets: Renaissance Authority and Its Subversion', in *Shakespeare's 'Rough Magic': Essays in Honor of C. L. Barber*, ed. P. Erickson and C. Kahn, Newark: University of Delaware Press.

—— (1988) *Shakespearean Negotiations*, Oxford: Clarendon Press.

—— (1992) *Marvelous Possessions: The Wonder of the New World*, Chicago: University of Chicago Press.

—— (1997) 'What is the History of Literature?', *Critical Inquiry* 23: 460–81.

—— (2000) 'The Inevitable Pit: On Becoming American', *London Review of Books* 21 November: 8–13.

—— (2001) *Hamlet in Purgatory*, Princeton, NJ: Princeton University Press.

—— (2004) *Will in the World: How Shakespeare Became Shakespeare*, London: Cape.

Gregerson, L. (1995) *The Reformation of the Subject: Spenser, Milton, and the English Protestant Epic*, Cambridge: Cambridge University Press.

Greville, F. (1973) 'Mustapha', in *Selected Writings*, ed. J. Rees, London: Athlone.

Griffiths, T. R. (1996) *Shakespeare in Production: A Midsummer Night's Dream*, Cambridge: Cambridge University Press.

Habermas, J. (1992) *Postmetaphysical Thinking: Philosophical Essays*, trans. W. M. Hohengarten, Cambridge: Polity.

Hall, K. (1992) 'Guess Who's Coming to Dinner? Colonisation and Miscegenation in *The Merchant of Venice*', reprinted in Coyle 1998.

Halpern, R. (2001) 'An Impure History of Ghosts: Derrida, Marx, Shakespeare', in *Marxist Shakespeares*, ed. J. E. Howard and S. Cutler Shershow, London and New York: Routledge.

—— (2002) *Shakespeare's Perfume: Sodomy and Sublimity in the Sonnets, Wilde, Freud, and Lacan*, Philadelphia, PA: University of Pennsylvania Press.

Hamilton, G. (2003) 'Mocking Oldcastle: Notes Towards Exploring a Catholic Presence in Shakespeare's Henriad', in *Shakespeare and the Culture of Christianity in Early Modern England*, ed. D. Taylor and D. Beauregard, New York: Fordham University Press.

Hammer, E. (2002) *Stanley Cavell: Skepticism, Subjectivity and the Ordinary*, Cambridge: Polity Press.

Hampson, D. (ed.) (1996) *Swallowing the Fishbone: Feminist Theologians Debate Christianity*, London: SPCK.

Hand, S. (ed.) (1989) *The Levinas Reader*, Oxford: Blackwell.

Hawkes, T. (2002) *Shakespeare in the Present*, London and New York: Routledge.

Hazlitt, W. (1930) *The Complete Works of William Hazlitt*, vol. 4, ed. P. P. Howe, London and Toronto: Dent.

Heelas, P. (1996) *The New Age Movement: The Celebration of Self and the Sacralization of Modernity*, Oxford: Blackwell.

—— (ed.) (1998) *Religion, Modernity, and Postmodernity*, Oxford: Blackwell.

Hegel, G. W. F. (1959) *Enzyklopädie der philosophischen Wissenschaften*, Hamburg: Felix Meiner Verlag.

Heidegger, M. (1966) *Discourse on Thinking*, trans. J. M. Anderson and E. H. Freud, New York: Harper & Row.

—— (1971) 'The Thing', in *Poetry, Language, Thought*, trans. A. Hofstadter, New York: Harper & Row.

Hill, C. (1968) *Puritanism and Revolution*, London: Panther.

Hoeniger, D. F. (1992) *Medicine and Shakespeare in the English Renaissance*, Newark: University of Delaware Press.

Horner, R. (2001) *Rethinking God as Gift: Marion, Derrida, and the Limits of Phenomenology*, New York: Fordham University Press.

Hunt, M. (1998) 'The Hybrid Reformations of Shakespeare's Second Henriad', *Comparative Drama* 32: 176–206.

Irigaray, L. (1993) *Sex and Genealogies*, trans. G. C. Gill, New York: Columbia University Press.

Jackson, K. (2001) '"One Wish" or the Possibility of the Impossible: Derrida, the Gift, and God in *Timon of Athens*', *Shakespeare Quarterly* 52: 34–66.

—— and A. F. Marotti (2004) 'The Turn to Religion in Early Modern English Studies', *Criticism* 46: 167–90.

Jameson, F. (1981a) *The Political Unconscious: Narrative as a Socially Symbolic Act*, London: Routledge.

—— (1981b) 'Religion and Ideology: A Political Reading of *Paradise Lost*', in *1642: Literature and Power in the Seventeenth Century*, Proceedings of the Essex Conference in the Sociology of Literature July 1980, eds F. Barker, J. Bernstein, J. Coombes, P. Hulme, J. Stone, J. Stratton, Colchester, Department of Literature: University of Essex.

Janicaud, D., J. F. Courtine, J. L. Chrétien *et al.* (2000) *Phenomenology and the 'Theological Turn'*, trans. B. G. Prusak and J. L. Kosky, New York: Fordham University Press.

Janik, A. A. (2003) 'Allan Janik Talks to Knut Olav Amas', www.eurozine.com/article/2003-10-06-janik-en.html.

Janowitz, H. D. (2000) 'Prince Hamlet and Prince Hal: The Trial of Crowns', *The Shakespeare Newsletter* 50: 21.

Johnson, S. (1968) *The Works of Samuel Johnson*, vol. 7: *Johnson on Shakespeare*, ed. A. Sherbo, New Haven: Yale University Press.

Joughin, J. J. (ed.) (2000a) *Philosophical Shakespeares*, London and New York: Routledge.

—— (2000b) 'Shakespeare, Modernity and the Aesthetic: Art, Truth and Judgement in *The Winter's Tale*', in *Shakespeare and Modernity*, ed. H. Grady, London and New York: Routledge.

—— (2002) '*Lear*'s Afterlife', *Shakespeare Survey* 55: 67–81.

—— and S. Malpas (eds) (2003) *The New Aestheticism*, Manchester: Manchester University Press.

Joy, M., K. O'Grady and J. L. Poxon (eds) (2002) *French Feminists on Religion: A Reader*, London and New York: Routledge.

Joyce, J. (1992) *Ulysses*, London: Penguin.

Kahn, C. (1987) '"Magic of Bounty": *Timon of Athens*, Jacobean Patronage, and Maternal Power', *Shakespeare Quarterly* 38: 34–57.

Kamps, I. (1996) *Historiography and Ideology in Stuart Drama*, Cambridge: Cambridge University Press.

Kant, I. (1997) *Groundwork of the Metaphysics of Morals*, trans. M. Gregor, Cambridge: Cambridge University Press.

Kastan, D. S. (1999) *Shakespeare after Theory*, New York and London: Routledge.

Kearney, J. (2002) 'The Book and the Fetish: The Materiality of Prospero's Text', *Journal of Medieval and Early Modern Studies* 32.3: 433–68.

Kearney, R. (moderator) (1999) 'On the Gift: A Discussion between Jacques Derrida and Jean-Luc Marion', in Caputo and Scanlon 1999.

—— (2001) *The God Who May Be: A Hermeneutics of Religion*, Bloomington, IN: Indiana University Press.

—— (2002) *Strangers, Gods and Monsters*, London and New York, Routledge.

—— (2003) 'Kierkegaard on Hamlet: Between Art and Religion' in *The New Kierkegaard*, ed. Elsbet Jepstrup, Bloomington, IN: Indiana University Press.

Keats, J. (1983) *The Complete Poems*, ed. John Barnard, 2nd edn, Harmondsworth: Penguin.

Kierkegaard, S. (1955) *Fear and Trembling* and *The Sickness unto Death*, trans. W. Lowrie, Garden City, NY: Doubleday.

—— (1959) *Either/Or*, vol. 1, trans. D. F. Swenson and L. M. Swenson, Princeton, NJ: Princeton University Press.

—— (1966) *On Authority and Revelation*, trans. W. Lowrie, New York: Harper Torchbook.

—— (1967) *Journals and Papers*, ed. and trans. H. V. Hong and E. H. Hong, Bloomington, IN: Indiana University Press.

—— (1983) *Fear and Trembling and Repetition*, ed. and trans. H. V. Hong and E. H. Hong, Princeton, NJ: Princeton University Press.

—— (1985) *Fear and Trembling*, trans. A. Hannay, London: Penguin.

—— (1988) *Stages on Life's Way*, ed. and trans. H. V. Hong and E. H. Hong, Princeton, NJ: Princeton University Press.

Knapp, J. (2002) *Shakespeare's Tribe: Church, Nation, and Theater in Renaissance England*, Chicago: University of Chicago Press.

Kohanski, A. S. (1982) *Martin Buber's Philosophy of Interhuman Relation: A Response to the Human Problematic of Our Time*, Rutherford, NJ: Farleigh Dickinson University Press.

Krips, H. (1999) *Fetish: An Erotics of Culture*, Ithaca, NY: Cornell University Press.

Lacan, J. (1982) 'Desire and the Interpretation of Desire in Hamlet', in *Literature and Psychoanalysis*, ed. S. Felman, Baltimore, MD and London: Johns Hopkins University Press.

Laclau, E. and C. Mouffe (1985) *Hegemony and Socialist Strategy: Towards a Radical Democratic Politics*, London: Verso.

Lake, P. (1989) 'Anti-Popery: The Structure of a Prejudice', in *Conflict in Early Stuart England: Studies in Religion and Politics 1603–1642*, ed. R. Cust and A. Hughes, London and New York: Longman.

—— with M. Questier (2002) *The Antichrist's Lewd Hat: Protestants, Papists & Players in Post-Reformation England*, New Haven, CT and London: Yale University Press.

Levin, H. (1981) 'Falstaff's Encore', *Shakespeare Quarterly* 32: 5–17.

Levinas, E. (1969) *Totality and Infinity: An Essay on Exteriority*, trans. A. Lingis, Pittsburgh, PA: Duquesne University Press.

—— (1976) *Noms Propres*, Montpellier: Fata Morgana.

—— (1981) *Otherwise than Being or Beyond Essence*, trans. A. Lingis, The Hague: Martinus Nijhoff.

—— (1985) *Ethics and Infinity: Conversations with Phillippe Nemo*, trans. R. A. Cohen, Pittsburgh, PA: Duquesne University Press.

—— (1989) *The Levinas Reader*, ed. S. Hand, Oxford and Malden, MA: Blackwell.

—— (1991) *Totality and Infinity: An Essay on Exteriority*, trans. A. Lingis, London: Kluwer Academic Publishers.

—— (1994) *In the Time of the Nations*, trans. M. B. Smith, Bloomington, IN: Indiana University Press.

—— (1998) *Entre nous: Thinking-of-the-Other*, trans. M. B. Smith and B. Harshaw, New York: Columbia University Press.

Levine, N. (2000) 'Extending Credit in the *Henry IV* Plays', *Shakespeare Quarterly* 51: 403–31.

Loomis, R. S. (1991) *The Grail: From Celtic Myth to Christian Symbol*, Princeton, NJ: Princeton University Press.

Lupton, J. Reinhard (1997) 'Othello Circumcised: Shakespeare and the Pauline Discourse of Nations', *Representations* 57: 73–89.

—— (2000a) 'Exegesis, Mimesis, and the Future of Humanism in *The Merchant of Venice*', *Religion and Literature* 32: 123–39.

—— (2000b) 'Creature Caliban', *Shakespeare Quarterly* 51: 1–23.

Lyotard, J.-F. (1984) *The Postmodern Condition: A Report on Knowledge*, trans. G. Bennington and B. Massumi, Minneapolis, MN: University of Minnesota Press.

McCoy, R. C. (2002) *Alterations of State: Sacred Kingship in the English Reformation*, New York: Columbia University Press.

McGee, C. E. (1984) '*2 Henry IV*: The Last Tudor Royal Entry', in *Mirror Up to Nature: Essays in Honour of G. R. Hibbard*, ed. J. C. Gray, Toronto: University of Toronto Press.

McLaverty, J. (1981) 'No Abuse: The Prince and Falstaff in the Tavern Scenes of *Henry IV*', *Shakespeare Survey* 34: 105–10.

MacLean, H. (1987) '"Looking Before and After": Hal and Hamlet Once More', *Papers on Language and Literature* 23: 273–89.

Manonni, O. (1969) 'Je sais bien, mais quand même', in *Clefs pour l'imaginaire, ou l'autre scène*, Paris: Éditions du Seuil.

Marion, J.-L. (2002) *Being Given: Toward a Phenomenology of Givenness*, trans. J. L. Kosky, Stanford, CA: Stanford University Press.

—— (2004) *The Crossing of the Visible*, trans. J. K. A. Smith, Stanford, CA: Stanford University Press.

Marlowe, C. (1999) *The Complete Plays*, ed. Mark Thornton Burnett, London: Dent.

Marotti, A. F. (ed.) (1999) *Catholicism and Anti-Catholicism in Early Modern English Texts*, Basingstoke: Macmillan.

Marsh, D. R. C. (1983) 'Hal and Hamlet: The Loneliness of Integrity', in *Jonson and Shakespeare*, ed. I. Donaldson, Atlantic Highlands, NJ: Humanities Press.

Marshall, D. (1982) 'Exchanging Visions: Reading *A Midsummer Night's Dream*', *English Literary History* 49: 543–75.

Mauss, M. (1990) *The Gift: The Form and Reason for Exchange in Archaic Societies*, trans. W. D. Halls, New York: W. W. Norton.

Mazzotta, G. (1978) 'The Canzoniere and the Language of the Self', *Studies in Philology* 75: 271–96.

Metzger, B. M. and R. E. Murphy (eds) (1994) *The New Oxford Annotated Bible* (NRSV), New York: Oxford University Press.

Milbank, J. (2003) *Being Reconciled: Ontology and Pardon*, New York: Routledge.

Milton, J. (1991) *Paradise Lost*, ed. A. Fowler, London: Longman.

Moore, H. (2003) 'Present and Correct', *Times Literary Supplement* 15 August: 22.

Mullaney, S. (1983) 'Strange Things, Gross Terms, Curious Customs: The Rehearsal of Cultures in the Late Renaissance', *Representations* 3: 40–67.

Mulvey, L. (1975) 'Visual Pleasure and Narrative Cinema', *Screen* 16: 6–18.

—— (1993) 'Some Thoughts on Theories of Fetishism in the Context of Contemporary Culture', *October* 65: 3–20.

Murphy, J. W. (1983) *The Social Philosophy of Martin Buber: The Social World as a Human Dimension*, Washington, DC: University Press of America.

Newell, P. (2003) *Shakespeare and the Human Mystery*, London: Azure.

Newman, F. B. (1966) 'The Rejection of Falstaff and the Rigorous Charity of the King', *Shakespeare Studies* 2: 153–61.

Newman, K. (1996) 'Reprise: Gender, Sexuality and Theories of Exchange', in *The Merchant of Venice*, ed. N. Wood, Buckingham: Open University Press.

Nietzsche, F. ([1889/1895] 1968) *Twilight of the Idols* and *The Anti-Christ*, trans. and intro. by R. J. Hollingdale, Harmondsworth: Penguin.

—— ([1881] 1982) *Daybreak: thoughts on the Prejudices of Morality*, trans. R. J. Hollingdale, intro. M. Tanner, Cambridge: Cambridge University Press.

—— ([1882/1887] 2001) *The Gay Science*, ed. B. Williams, trans. J. Nauckhoff, Cambridge: Cambridge University Press.

Otto, R. (1958) *The Idea of the Holy*, Oxford: Oxford University Press.

Ouditt, S. (1996) 'Explaining Woman's Frailty: Feminist Readings of Gertrude', in *Hamlet*, ed. Peter J. Smith and Nigel Wood, Buckingham: Open University Press.

Ovid (1965) *Ovid's Metamorphoses: The Arthur Golding Translation 1567*, ed. J. F. Nims, New York: Macmillan.

Parker, P. (1993) 'Preposterous Reversals: *Love's Labour's Lost*', *Modern Language Quarterly* 54: 435–82.

—— (1996) *Shakespeare from the Margins: Language, Culture, Context*, Chicago: University of Chicago Press.

Pechter, E. (2003) 'What's Wrong with Literature?', *Textual Practice* 17: 505–26.

Petrarch (1976) *Petrarch's Lyric Poems: The* Rime sparse *and Other Lyrics*, trans. and ed. R. M. Durling, Cambridge, MA: Harvard University Press.

Phan, C. (1991) 'La tornada et l'envoi: fonctions structurelles et pöiétiques', *Cahiers de Civilisation Medievale* XXXIV: 57–61.

Pietz, W. (1985) 'The Problem of the Fetish, I', *Res* 9: 5–17.

—— (1987) 'The Problem of the Fetish, II', *Res* 13: 23–45.

—— (1988) 'The Problem of the Fetish, IIIa', *Res* 16: 105–23.

Poole, K. (1995) 'Saints Alive! Falstaff, Martin Marprelate, and the Staging of Puritanism', *Shakespeare Quarterly* 46: 47–75.

Porter, J. (1979) *The Drama of Speech Acts: Shakespeare's Lancastrian Tetralogy*, Berkeley: University of California Press.

Potter, L. (1999) 'Humor Out of Breath: Francis Gentleman and the *Henry IV* Plays', in *Shakespeare Text and Theater: Essays in Honor of Jay Halio*, ed. L. Potter and A. F. Kinney, Newark: University of Delaware Press.

Puttenham, G. (1589) *The Arte of English Poesie*, London: Richard Field, Short Title Catalogue 20519.

Quintilian ([88] 1959) *Institutio Oratoria*, trans. H. E. Butler, Cambridge, MA: Harvard University Press.

Rheim's New Testament (1582) Rheim: John Fogny.

Rockas, L. (1973) '"A Dish of Doves": The Merchant of Venice', *English Literary History* 40: 339–51.

Rorty, R. (1996) 'The Inspirational Value of Great Works of Literature', *Raritan* 16: 8–17.

Rose, G. (1995) *Love's Work*, London: Chatto & Windus.

—— (1996) *Mourning Becomes the Law: Philosophy and Representation*, Cambridge: Cambridge University Press.

—— (1999) *Paradiso*, London: Menard Press.

Rubinstein, F. (1989) *A Dictionary of Shakespeare's Sexual Puns and their Significance*, 2nd edn, Basingstoke: Macmillan.

Rushdie, S. (1991) 'Is Nothing Sacred?', in *Imaginary Homelands*, London: Granta.

Ryan, K. (1995) 'The Future of History in Henry IV', in *Henry IV, Parts One and Two*, ed. N. Wood, Buckingham: Open University Press.

—— (2002) *Shakespeare*, 3rd edn, Basingstoke and New York: Palgrave.

Sardar, Z. (1979) *The Future of Muslim Civilisation*, London: Croom Helm.

Schalkwyk, D. (2002) 'Historicism in Purgatory', *Pretexts: Literary and Cultural Studies* 11: 75–92.

—— (2004) *Literature and the Touch of the Real*, Newark, DE: University of Delaware Press.

Schlegel, A. W. (1846) *A Course of Lectures on Dramatic Art and Literature*, revised by A. J. W. Morrison, in Bate 1997.

Shakespeare, W. (1982) *The Sonnets and A Lover's Complaint*, ed. J. Kerrigan, The New Penguin Shakespeare, Harmondsworth: Penguin.

—— (1987) *Hamlet*, ed. G. R. Hibbard, Oxford: Oxford University Press.

Sheldrake, P. (1992) *Spirituality and History: Questions of Interpretation and Method*, New York: Crossroad.

Shell, A. (1999) *Catholicism, Controversy and the English Literary Imagination, 1558–1660*, Cambridge: Cambridge University Press.

Shuchter, J. D. (1968) 'Prince Hal and Francis: The Imitation of An Action', *Shakespeare Studies* 3: 129–37.

Shuger, D. (1990) *Habits of Thought in the English Renaissance: Religion, Politics, and the Dominant Culture*, Berkeley, CA: University of California Press.

—— (1994) *The Renaissance Bible: Scholarship, Sacrifice and Subjectivity*, Berkeley, CA and London: University of California Press.

—— (2001) *Political Theologies in Shakespeare's England: The Sacred and the State in Measure for Measure*, Basingstoke and New York: Palgrave.

Silberstein, L. J. (1989) *Martin Buber's Social and Religious Thought: Alienation and the Quest for Meaning*, New York: New York University Press.

Sinfield, A. (1992) *Faultlines: Cultural Materialism and the Politics of Dissident Reading*, Oxford: Clarendon.

Smith, R. (1980) '"A Heart Cleft in Twain": The Dilemma of Shakespeare's Gertrude', in *The Woman's Part: Feminist Criticism of Shakespeare*, ed. C. R. S. Lenz, G. Greene and C. Thomas Neely, Urbana, IL: University of Illinois Press.

Spenser, E. (1977) '*The Faerie Queene*', in *Spenser: Poetical Works*, ed. J. C. Smith and E. de Selincourt, Oxford: Oxford University Press.

Stallybrass, P. (1999) 'Editing as Cultural Formation: The Sexing of Shakespeare's Sonnets', in *The Sonnets: Critical Essays*, ed. James Schiffer, New York and London: Garland Publishing.

—— (2002) 'The Value of Culture and the Disavowal of Things', in *The Culture of Capital: Property, Cities, and Knowledge in Early Modern England*, ed. H. S. Turner, New York and London: Routledge.

—— and A. R. Jones (2000), 'Fetishisms and Renaissances', in *Historicism, Psychoanalysis, and Early Modern Culture*, ed. C. Mazzio and D. Trevor, New York and London: Routledge.

——, M. de Grazia and M. Quilligan (eds) (1996) *Subject and Object in Renaissance Culture*, Cambridge: Cambridge University Press.

Starling, R. (1997/8) 'Shakespeare's Haunt: The Translations of *Hamlet* in Derrida's *Specters of Marx*', *Actes de langue française et de linguistine (ALFA)* 10/11: 193–213.

Swinburne, R. (1994) *The Christian God*, Oxford: Clarendon.

Taylor, G. (2001) 'Divine [ ]sences', *Shakespeare Survey* 54: 13–30.

Taylor, M. C. (2003) *The Moment of Complexity: Emerging Network Culture*, Chicago: University of Chicago Press.

—— (2004) *Confidence Games: Money and Markets in a World without Redemption*, Chicago; University of Chicago Press.

Tyacke, N. (1987) *Anti-Calvinists: the rise of English Arminianism c.1590–1640*, Oxford: Clarendon.

Vickers, N. (1981) 'Diana Described: Scattered Woman and Scattered Rhyme', *Critical Inquiry* 8.2: 265–79.

—— (1982) 'The Body Re-Membered: Petrarchan Lyric and the Strategies of Description', in *Mimesis: From Mirror to Method, Augustine to Descartes*, ed. S. G. Nichols Jr, Hanover, NH: University Presses of New England.

—— (1985) '"The Blazon of Sweet Beauty's Best": Shakespeare's Lucrece', in *Shakespeare and the Question of Theory*, ed. P. Parker and G. Hartman, New York and London: Methuen.

Ward, G. (1998) 'Kenosis and Naming: Beyond Analogy and Towards *Allegoria Amoris*', in Heelas 1998.

—— (1999) 'Kenosis: Death, Discourse and Resurrection', in L. Gardner, D. Moss, B. Quash and G. Ward 1999.

Wells, R. Headlam (2000a) 'Historicism and "Presentism" in Early Modern Studies', *The Cambridge Quarterly* 29: 37–60.

—— (2000b) *Shakespeare on Masculinity*, Cambridge: Cambridge University Press.

Wheeler, W. (1999) 'Melancholic Modernity and Contemporary Grief: The Novels of Graham Swift', in *Literature and the Contemporary: Fictions and Theories of the Present*, ed. R. Luckhurst and P. Marks, Harlow: Longman.

Whitney, C. (1999) '"Usually in the werking Daies": Playgoing Journeymen, Apprentices, and Servants in Guild Records, 1582–1592', *Shakespeare Quarterly* 50: 433–58.

Williams, G. (1997) *A Glossary of Shakespeare's Sexual Language*, London: Athlone.

Wilson, R. (2004) *Secret Shakespeare: Studies in Theatre, Religion and Resistance*, Manchester: Manchester University Press.

Witmore, M. (2001) *Culture of Accidents: Unexpected Knowledges in Early Modern England*, Stanford, CA: Stanford University Press.

Wright, E. P. (1975–6) 'Hal and Francis in *King Henry IV, Part I*: Another View', *McNeese Review* 22: 62–9.

Yan, Y. (1996) *The Flow of Gifts: Reciprocity and Social Networks in a Chinese Village*, Stanford, CA: Stanford University Press.

Young, D. P. (1966) *Something of Great Constancy: The Art of* A Midsummer Night's Dream, New Haven, CT: Yale University Press.

Žižek, S. (1989) *The Sublime Object of Ideology*, London: Verso.
—— (2000a) *The Ticklish Subject: The Absent Centre of Political Ontology*, London and New York: Verso.
—— (2000b) *The Fragile Absolute – Or, Why Is The Christian Legacy Worth Fighting For?*, London: Verso.
—— (2001) *On Belief*, London and New York: Routledge.
—— (2002) *Welcome to the Desert of the Real!: Five Essays on September 11 and Related Dates*, London and New York: Verso.
—— (2003) *The Puppet and the Dwarf: The Perverse Core of Christianity*, Cambridge, MA and London: MIT Press.

Index

Related titles from Routledge

Local Shakespeares:
Proximations and Power
Martin Orkin

'*Local Shakespeares* shows just how timid and predictable
most comparative criticism is. Timid and predictable,
Local Shakespeares is not.'

Bruce Smith, University of Southern California, USA

This remarkable volume challenges scholars and students to
look beyond a dominant European and North American
'metropolitan bank' of Shakespeare knowledge. As well as
revealing the potential for a new understanding of
Shakespeare's plays, Martin Orkin explores a fresh approach to
issues of power, where 'proximations' emerge from a process
of dialogue and challenge traditional notions of authority.

Since their first performances, Shakespeare's plays and their
audiences or readers have journeyed to one another across
time and space, to and from countless and always different
historical, geographical and ideological locations. Engagement
with a Shakespeare text always entails in part, then, cultural
encounter or clash, and readings are shaped by a reader's
particular location and knowledge. Part I of this book
challenges us to recognise the way in which 'local' or 'non-
metropolitan' knowledges and experiences might extend
understanding of Shakespeare's texts and their locations. Part
II demonstrates the use of local as well as metropolitan
knowledges in exploring the presentation of masculinity in
Shakespeare's late plays. These plays themselves dramatise
encounters with different cultures and, crucially, challenges to
established authority.

Challenging the authority of metropolitan scholarship, twenty-
first-century global capitalism and the masculinist imperatives
that drive it, Orkin's daring, powerful work will have
reverbations throughout but also well beyond the field of
Shakespeare studies.

Hb: 0-415-34878-1
Pb: 0-415-34879-X
E-book: 0-203-641078

Available at all good bookshops
For ordering and further information please visit:
www.routledge.com